Getting to Work

DIRECTIONS IN DEVELOPMENT
Countries and Regions

Getting to Work

Unlocking Women's Potential in Sri Lanka's Labor Force

Jennifer L. Solotaroff, George Joseph, Anne T. Kuriakose, and
Jayati Sethi

WORLD BANK GROUP

Contents

Figures

Acknowledgments

This report was prepared by a core team led by Jennifer L. Solotaroff, Senior Social Development Specialist of the World Bank's Gender Group (GTGDR) and formerly of the South Asia Social Development Unit, Social, Urban, Rural and Resilience Global Practice (GSU06). David Warren (Practice Manager, GSU06) provided managerial guidance and support.

Idah Z. Pswarayi-Riddihough (Country Director, Sri Lanka and Maldives), Françoise Clottes (Director, Strategy and Operations, and former Country Director, Sri Lanka and Maldives), Rolande Simone Pryce (Manager, World Bank Indonesia Program, and former Operations Advisor, Sri Lanka and Maldives), and Valerie Marie Helene Layrol (Senior Operations Officer, Sri Lanka and Maldives) provided overall guidance.

The core team members included Jennifer L. Solotaroff (GTGDR), George Joseph (Water Global Practice for the South and East Asia Region), Anne T. Kuriakose (Climate Investment Funds Group), Jayati Sethi (GSU06), and Mohamed Ghani Razaak (Social Development Unit in the Social, Urban, Rural and Resilience Global Practice for Europe and Central Asia). Maria Isabel Larenas Gonzalez (GSU06) provided quantitative data analysis and maps, and Yukari Shibuya (GSU06) provided support on select background research and logistics.

Dilinika Peiris, Smriti Daniel, Joe Qian, and Yann Doignon (South Asia Region, External Communications) offered guidance and written inputs on communications. Special thanks go to Kamani Jinadasa and Bandita Sijapati (GSU06) for serving as liaisons with client counterparts and for general coordination. For excellent editorial and publication support, thanks go to Aziz Gökdemir (Global Corporate Solutions, Creative Services), with assistance from Jewel McFadden (Development Economics, Knowledge and Strategy). Kerima Thilakasena and Niluka Nirmalie Karunaratne Sriskanthan (Sri Lanka Country Management Unit) provided administrative support. Thanks also are due to Rohanthi Perera and her staff at the Sri Lanka Business Development Centre for data collection.

The report also draws on a background paper, "Getting to Work Supplement: Inspiring Sri Lanka's Growing Economic Prosperity," written for this book by Siri Anderson. Dr. Anderson serves as an administrator and Associate Professor in the Education Department at the largest women's university in the United States, St. Catherine University. The team would like to thank key informants acknowledged in appendix E for sharing their valuable insights to inform the background paper.

The team extends heartfelt thanks for the care and attention that the Honorable Ms. K. D. M. Chandrani Bandara (Minister, Ministry of Women and Child Affairs, Government of Sri Lanka), Ms. Chandrani Senaratne (former Secretary, Ministry of Women and Child Affairs), and Mrs. Ashoka Alawatte (former Additional Secretary, Ministry of Women and Child Affairs) gave to the final report draft through written comments and constructive suggestions.

The report peer reviewers were Gladys Lopez Acevedo (Poverty Global Practice for the South Asia Region), Nistha Sinha (Poverty Global Practice for the Middle East and North Africa Region), Varun Singh (GSU06), Emcet Oktay Tas (GSU06), and Dileni Gunewardena (Professor of Economics, University of Peradeniya, Sri Lanka).

Discussions on framing the issues benefited greatly from the views of Harini Amrasekera (Open University), Luis Andres (World Bank Water Global Practice for the Africa Region), Nisha Arunatilake (Institute of Policy Studies of Sri Lanka), Harsha Aturupane (World Bank Education Global Practice for the South Asia Region), Juergen Depta and his colleagues at Deutsche Gesellschaft für Internationale Zusammenarbeit (GIZ), Halil Dundar (World Bank Education Global Practice for the Africa Region), Nilan Fernando (Asia Foundation), Priyanthi Fernando (Center for Poverty Analysis, Sri Lanka), Nelan Gunasekera (Asian Development Bank), Carmen Niethammer and Graeme Harris (International Finance Corporation), Subangi Herath (University of Colombo), Swarna Jayaweera (Centre for Women's Research—CENWOR), Seenithamby Manoharan (World Bank Agriculture Global Practice for the South Asia Region), Rosanna Nitti (World Bank Urban Development Unit in the Social, Urban, Rural and Resilience Global Practice for Europe and Central Asia), David Newhouse (World Bank Poverty Global Practice for the Africa Region), and Nihal Somaweera (former Additional Secretary [Regional Development], Government of Sri Lanka).

This report has been made possible by trust fund support—from a Department of Foreign Affairs and Trade, Government of Australia, grant through the Partnership for South Asia, South Asia Gender Initiative window; and by the South Asia Gender Innovation Lab, which received an allocation from the World Bank Group's Umbrella Facility for Gender Equality, a multidonor trust fund; and by the World Bank budget.

About the Authors

JENNIFER LYNN SOLOTAROFF is a Senior Social Development Specialist in the Gender Group of the World Bank. Her research interests include gender and labor markets, gender-based violence, and social stratification in East Asia and South Asia. She has a PhD in sociology, an MA in economics, and an MA in East Asian studies from Stanford University; and a BA in English literature and East Asian studies from Oberlin College.

GEORGE JOSEPH is a Senior Economist in the Water Global Practice of the World Bank, Washington, DC. His research interests center on development economics and behavioral and applied microeconomics. He received his PhD in economics from Rutgers, the State University of New Jersey; and an MA in economics from Jawaharlal Nehru University, New Delhi, India.

ANNE T. KURIAKOSE is a Senior Social Development Specialist in the Climate Investment Funds at the World Bank in Washington, DC. Her research interests include gender and labor, social protection, climate adaptation, and rural livelihoods. She holds a PhD in development studies from the University of Wisconsin–Madison, an MA in gender and development from the University of Sussex, and a BA in political science from McGill University.

JAYATI SETHI is a consultant in the Social, Urban, Rural and Resilience Global Practice at the World Bank in Washington, DC. She has an MPP in international development from Georgetown University, an MSc in population and development from the London School of Economics and Political Science, and a BA in political science from the University of Delhi.

Executive Summary

This book updates and expands upon research conducted in 2012–13 into increasing women's labor force participation in Sri Lanka (Solotaroff 2013). The current study is intended to provide a better understanding of the puzzle of women's persistently low labor force participation (LFP) rates and other poor labor market outcomes in the country. The earlier research focused on the years leading up to the end of the Sri Lankan Civil War (2006–09), whereas this book compares the earlier findings to data from the years following the civil war (2010–15). Using nationally representative secondary survey data, as well as primary qualitative and quantitative research, both studies test three hypotheses that would explain gender gaps in labor market outcomes: (1) *household roles and responsibilities*, which fall disproportionately on women and constrain their time and mobility; (2) a *human capital mismatch*, whereby women are not acquiring the proper skills demanded by job markets; and (3) *gender bias* in job search, hiring, and promotion processes.

This book finds that not only are all three hypotheses supported, but also that the social norms that govern women's responsibilities for childcare, elder care, and housework—and that inhibit women from joining labor markets, obtaining employment, and closing gender wage gaps—have become more entrenched since the end of the civil war. Having young children in the household is now associated with even lower odds of LFP, lower chances of becoming a paid employee, and lower earnings for women compared with those before 2010, and compared with men for all three outcomes. The disparity between marriage's association with men's versus women's odds of LFP is the only gender gap associated with household roles that appears to be shrinking over time; however, marriage still penalizes women in labor markets (lowering their odds of LFP by 4.4 percentage points), whereas for men it provides an 11 percentage-point premium on their odds of LFP.[1] Gender norms that restrict women's mobility more than men's—especially lack of social support for women commuting to work—and that prevent women from accessing safe and comfortable transportation to work, as well as parents' greater encouragement of sons' rather than daughters' pursuit of careers (especially in the private sector), are other supply-side factors undermining women in labor markets.

The analysis also suggests that since the end of the civil conflict, women find it even more challenging than men to translate their educational attainment into high-skill and higher-paying jobs. This is true even of women with university education or higher, who still queue for public sector jobs in spite of limited openings, pushing up their rates of unemployment among young women. Another worrying trend is that poorer and less educated women are falling further behind more educated and wealthier women in regard to chances of LFP and other employment and wage-related outcomes.

The good news for women is that raw gender wage gaps are shrinking every year; moreover, the explained portions of these wage gaps are increasing over time. In other words, gender bias appears to play less and less of a role in these gaps in earnings; bias also appears to determine gender gaps in LFP rates to a diminishing degree over time. The primary data bolster these findings: employers, on average, report that they look for the same skills and experience in men and women, actively discriminating by gender to a much smaller degree than employees suspect. Employers in some industries studied in the primary research—such as the garment industry and the tea estate sector—express a preference for hiring women workers because they believe them to be more reliable and harder working than men. Yet persistent occupational sex segregation across industries suggests that these preferences may not hold for promotions—especially into high-skill and management jobs, which men continue to dominate.

The book concludes with four priority areas (summarized in chapter 4) for addressing the multiple supply- and demand-side factors to improve women's LFP rates and reduce other gender gaps in labor market outcomes. It also offers specific recommendations for improving women's participation in the five private sector industries studied for the primary data collection: information and communication technology (ICT), tea estate work, tourism, garments, and commercial agriculture (see chapter 5). Common recommendations across the five industries include the provision of care services to ease women's time poverty; and improvements in providing safe, comfortable transportation to and from worksites or near-worksite accommodations for women so that they are at lower risk of the gender-based violence that is highly prevalent on public transportation and in public spaces. Together, these recommendations are intended to help the government, the private sector, and other stakeholders in Sri Lanka collaborate and harmonize efforts in getting women to work.

Note

1. A full discussion of the study's methodology, as well as tables of all results from the analyses of primary and secondary data (including results from multivariate analysis of nationally representative secondary data) can be found in appendixes B, C, and D of this book.

Reference

Solotaroff, Jennifer. 2013. "Getting In and Staying In: Improving Women's Labor Force Participation in Sri Lanka." Unpublished, World Bank, Washington, DC.

Abbreviations

A-level	General Certificate of Education Advanced Level
CEDAW	Convention on the Elimination of all Forms of Discrimination against Women
DCS	Department of Census and Statistics
EPZ	export processing zone
FGD	focus group discussion
FHH	female-headed household
FLFP	female labor force participation
GDP	gross domestic product
GoSL	government of Sri Lanka
HIES	Household Income and Expenditure Survey
ICT	information and communication technology
ISCO	International Standard Classification of Occupations
IT	information technology
KII	key informant interview
LFP	labor force participation
LFS	Labour Force Survey
LKR	Sri Lankan rupee
NVQ	National Vocational Qualification
O-level	General Certificate of Education Ordinary Level
SGBV	sexual and gender-based violence
SLBFE	Sri Lanka Bureau of Foreign Employment
STEM	science, technology, engineering, and mathematics
TVET	technical and vocational education and training

SRI LANKA

Legend:
- ○ SELECTED CITIES AND TOWNS
- ◉ PROVINCE CAPITALS
- ✹ NATIONAL CAPITAL
- RIVERS
- MAIN ROADS
- RAILROADS
- PROVINCE BOUNDARIES
- INTERNATIONAL BOUNDARIES

INDIA

Palk Strait
Point Pedro
Jaffna
Elephant Pass
Delft Island
Palk Bay
Killinochchi
Iranamadu Tank
Mullaittivu
Talaimannar
Ferry
Adam's Bridge
Mannar Island
Mannar
Manakulam
NORTHERN
Aruvi Aru
Vavuniya
Pulmoddai
Karaitivu Island
NORTH CENTRAL
Anuradhapura
Rambewa
Trincomalee
Mutur
Galkulama
Yan Oya
Kalpitiya
Kala Oya
Kaudulla Oya
Puttalan
Habarane
Bay of Bengal
NORTH WESTERN
Deduru Oya
Maho
Madura Oya
EASTERN
Batticaloa
Kattankudi
Chilaw
Kurunegala
Maha Oya
CENTRAL
Mahaweli Ganga
Madura Oya Reservoir
Kalmunai
Ampara
Gal Oya
Negombo
Kegalla
Kandy
Victoria Falls Reservoir
UVA
Senanayake Samudra
WESTERN
Kelani Ganga
Pidurutalagala (2,524 m)
Badulla
Moratuwa
COLOMBO
Sri Jayewardenepura Kotte
Monaragala
Pottuvil
Ratnapura
SABARAGAMUWA
Kalu Ganga
Wellawaya
Kirindi Oya
Kalutara
Walawe Ganga
Katagarama
Kumana
Laccadive Sea
SOUTHERN
Galle
Matara
Tangalla
Hambantota
INDIAN OCEAN
Dondra Head

Gulf of Mannar

SRI LANKA

0 20 40 60 Kilometers
0 10 20 30 40 Miles

CHAPTER 1

Study Background, Motivation, and Approach

Introduction

Sri Lanka has the 20th-largest gender gap in labor force participation (LFP) out of 149 countries (WEF 2018). This large gap is surprising given the country's long-standing achievements in human development outcomes, such as high levels of female education (including gender parity at most levels) and low total fertility rates, as well as its status as an upper-middle-income country with overall improvements in economic growth averaging about 6 percent annually over the past decade (World Bank 2015, 2019). (See appendix A for a detailed statistical profile of gender gaps in Sri Lanka.) LFP rates among Sri Lankan women age 15 years and older were 36–37 percent for 2015–17, but fell to 34 percent in 2018; LFP rates for same-age men were 75 percent in 2015–17, but fell to 73 percent in 2018 (DCS 2016, 2017, 2018). In contrast, the 2016 LFP rates for women age 15 and older in Thailand and Malaysia—which are upper-middle-income countries—were 60 percent (compared with 77 percent for same-age men) and 54 percent (compared with 80 percent for same-age men), respectively (World Bank 2019). Sri Lanka's LFP gender gap is even greater than that of several other South Asian countries (figure 1.1), despite Sri Lanka serving as a model for the region in many other gender outcomes.

Sri Lanka shows remarkable persistence in low LFP rates for women over the past three decades—with even a slight decline as the economy has expanded (figure 1.2). This presents significant challenges to the country's growth and equity goals, such as the current government of Sri Lanka's aim of creating 1 million jobs, fostering investment in the private sector, and enhancing social inclusion outcomes.[1] Recent economic policy statements have emphasized the need to create an enabling environment for women's participation in the economy to achieve the government's goal of inclusive and balanced development. The government envisages that 40 percent of the jobs created by 2020 will employ women, and it seeks to encourage women's greater involvement and leadership in small and medium enterprises. The most potent route to growing

Figure 1.1 Labor Force Participation, by Country

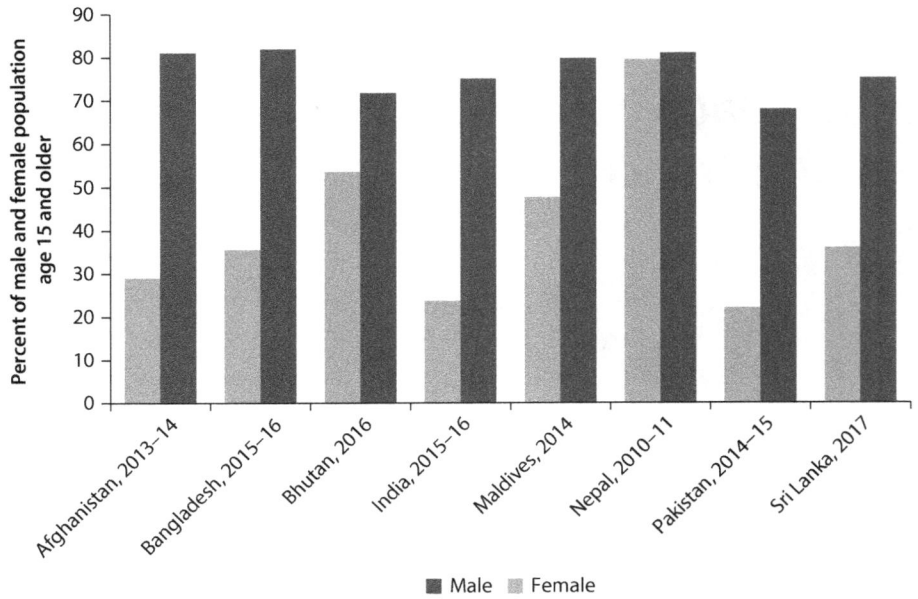

Source: National estimates, multiple years.

Figure 1.2 Female Labor Force Participation, by Select Country, Economic Status, and Region, 1993–2017

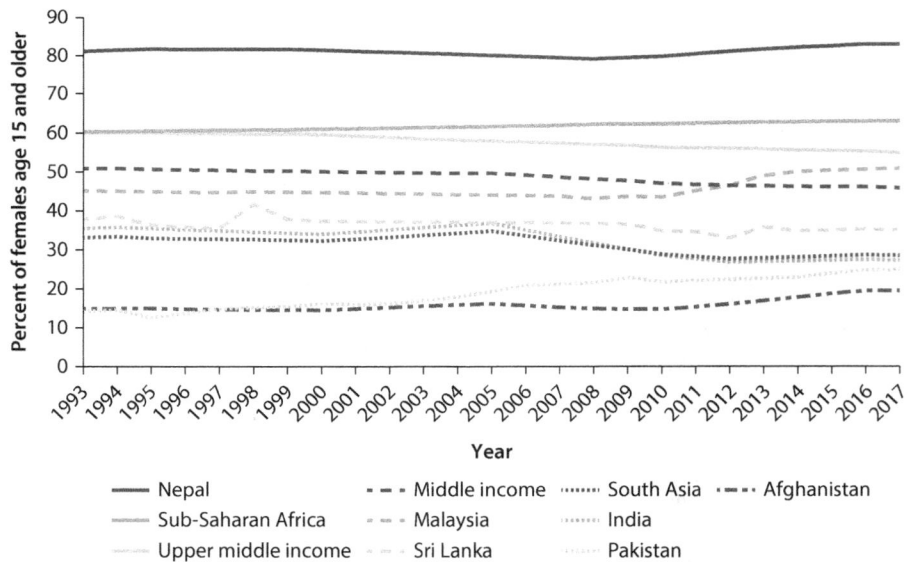

Source: World Bank datacenter, modeled ILO estimate.
Note: Some ILO data may predate the 2017 LFS data noted in the text. ILO = International Labour Organization; LFS = Labour Force Survey.

Sri Lanka's overall workforce will come from increased numbers of women working. Raising the rate of women's LFP by 15 percentage points will add more than 1 million workers to the labor market each year (Sinha 2012).

Nonetheless, women's experience in Sri Lanka's labor market remains characterized by low LFP; high unemployment, especially for women younger than age 30; and persistent, though shrinking, wage disparities between the sexes. As this study shows, determinants of these poor gender outcomes include household roles and responsibilities, a mismatch between skills acquired in school and those demanded in the labor market, and gender bias and discrimination in labor supply as well as labor demand dynamics.

This book is intended for policy makers and employment program practitioners in the Sri Lankan government, the private sector, and the donor and nongovernmental organization communities. It also targets academia and other research institutions, in part to call upon them to undertake additional studies that can continue to identify the most effective means of engaging and sustaining more women in the workforce—particularly in the private sector. Finally, this study is intended to reach any others who have a stake in helping Sri Lanka's economy grow by taking advantage of this relatively untapped population of potential labor, innovation, and productivity: women.

By examining gender norms about work as well as the typical economic factors in analyses of gender and labor dynamics, this study explores why, compared with men, women continue to be well educated but less commonly working for pay in Sri Lanka. It identifies means of promoting women's entry into and continued employment in the labor market, which will grow the economy. Improved female LFP (FLFP) will also be critical to helping the country cope with its now-rising inverse dependency ratio: the demographic transition now underway suggests that the population older than age 60 will double in the next quarter-century, whereas the younger working-age population will continue to decrease because of lower total fertility rates (World Bank 2016).

This book updates and expands upon research conducted in 2012–13 about increasing women's labor force participation in Sri Lanka (Solotaroff 2013). Both the previous research and this study are intended to provide a better understanding of the puzzle of women's persistently low LFP rates and other poor labor market outcomes in the country as a whole rather than in a particular city or province. Quantitative analyses are nationally representative. Most earlier economic analyses attribute gender gaps in these outcomes (that is, LFP, employment, and earnings) that were unexplained by household time constraints or human capital factors to the "black box" of social factors, including gender-based discrimination.

The 2012–13 analysis, which used primary data as well as existing national-level survey data from the Sri Lanka 2006–10 Labour Force Survey (LFS) and the 2009–10 Household Income Expenditure Survey (HIES), sought to unpack the social processes underlying these gender differences. It posed three hypotheses that would explain gender gaps in labor market outcomes: (1) *household roles and responsibilities*, which fall disproportionately on women;

(2) *human capital mismatch*, whereby women are not acquiring the proper skills demanded by job markets; and (3) *gender discrimination* in job search, hiring, and promotion processes. Multivariate analysis of the secondary data found support for all three hypotheses.

The earlier (2013) analysis of secondary data reflected gender-biased labor market dynamics in the final years of Sri Lanka's civil war, which ended in 2009. Although the analysis summarized these dynamics in Sri Lanka, national-level surveys tended to exclude the more conflict-affected areas[2] (for example, districts in the Northern Province and sometimes the Eastern Province) until 2011. Primary research for the earlier analysis was conducted in 2012 in select industry sectors in the Badulla, Gampaha, and Trincomalee districts in lower-central, western, and eastern Sri Lanka, respectively. The researchers used quantitative and qualitative methods in 2012 to ask questions of different groups of workers, household members, and employers about their labor market experiences and attitudes toward work. Industry sectors were selected to include a mix of "new" and traditional drivers of the economy: information and communication technology (ICT), tea estates, tourism, the garment sector, and commercial agriculture.

The primary research (particularly the qualitative data, which include a second phase of qualitative research conducted in 2018) helps explain employer preferences and incentives as well as gender differences in educational choices, job preferences, occupational aspirations, job search channels, household decision making, and time use patterns—among other labor-related factors—between men and women of different ages, education and income levels, ethnicities, and employment types. The analysis of secondary and primary data together adds value to existing labor studies of Sri Lanka by using the additional lenses of gender norms, identity, and agency (the ability to make decisions as well as take advantage of opportunities).[3] One of the more recent studies (Gunewardena 2015) analyzes the 2012 World Bank Skills toward Employability and Productivity (STEP) Skills Measurement Program survey data to explore why Sri Lankan women's educational gains are not translating into workforce advantages. The findings contribute an unprecedented, nuanced understanding of Sri Lankans' perceptions of their own skills and how they are linked to labor market advantages. The findings also provide sharper definition to the 2013 analysis' mixed-methods exploration of the mismatch between women's educational attainments, on the one hand, and skills sought by employers—especially those in the private sector—on the other.

This book adds to the previous analysis more recent national survey data (2011–15 LFS and 2012–13 HIES) to shed light on whether and how labor force patterns have changed for women over the past decade, with particular attention to the years since the end of the civil war. Any quantitative analysis using national survey data (that is, LFS and HIES) was conducted twice for each survey year—first using the full sample (all provinces) from that year and then using a sample that dropped the districts and provinces not included in surveys from the years before 2011 to allow for comparability across years.[4] The book presents findings from the qualitative and quantitative primary data more comprehensively than the previous study; it also presents findings from additional qualitative research conducted in 2018. (See appendix E for a list of key informants interviewed in 2018. Appendix B provides a detailed description of the book's data and methods.)

Finally, this book identifies ways to promote women's entry into and sustained employment in the labor market. The recommendations in chapters 4 and 5 are tailored to different stakeholders, and also provide special focus on certain industries in the private sector that have strong potential to absorb and sustain Sri Lankan women in decent paid work.

Conceptual Framework for Examining Women's Labor Market Outcomes in Sri Lanka

The conceptual framework of this study draws from the fields of behavioral economics, labor economics, and economic sociology to explain the persistence of low FLFP rates in Sri Lanka (see figure 1.3). Based on the work of Becker (1975), Bielby and Baron (1986), Carter and Katz (1997), Folbre (1994), and Goldin (2006), this analysis identifies three key drivers of gender differences in labor market participation: household roles and responsibilities, human capital and skills mismatch, and gender bias. The following analysis investigates the extent to which these drivers have a bearing on female labor market outcomes as measured by LFP, employment, and wages in the Sri Lankan context. The study takes a life-cycle approach, applying a gender lens to the decisions and investments workers

Figure 1.3 Conceptual Framework

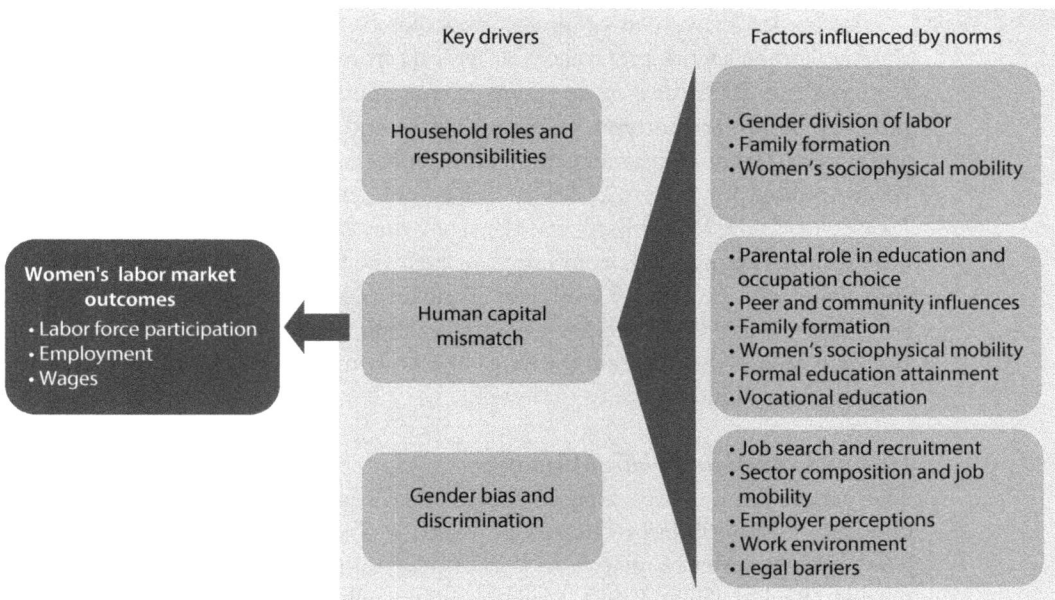

and potential workers make as they move through the key life stages of obtaining an education, making the transition from school to work, forming a family, entering the workforce, and advancing in the labor market. The study framework also follows Akerlof and Kranton (2010), Danziger and Ratner (2010), and Elder (1994) to examine the influence of social norms throughout the life course in shaping Sri Lankan men's and women's labor market behavior. This study asserts that *decision stages* (the life stage individuals are in) and *decision sites* (the arenas that contribute to individual decision making) should be key considerations in policy research and intervention design aimed at improving women's LFP.

Drivers of Women's Labor Force Participation
Household Roles and Responsibilities

Household roles and responsibilities—the *reproductive* tasks of bearing and raising children as well as caring for the home and other family members—impose labor burdens on women that are not shared by men in equal measure. These gendered responsibilities are shaped to a large extent by intrahousehold negotiation processes. Gender-biased bargaining outcomes in the household are attributed to women's weaker "fallback positions" determined by the opportunities and resources available to individual members independent of the household, such as personal assets, access to employment and income, and other earned characteristics such as education (Agarwal 1997), and by women's lower "perceived contribution response," whereby women's domestic work is not seen as a legitimate contribution to the economic prosperity of the household (Sen 1990). Malhotra and Mather (1997) argue that in Sri Lanka, women's influence in domestic decision making is not only a simple function of their personal achievements and economic power, but also of broader social structures such as class and ethnicity.

The burden of women's reproductive roles creates time poverty, thus conditioning women's work preferences differently from men's (Becker 1975; also see Cunningham 2008 for a more recent examination). Female workers, for example, tend to prefer the types of organizations and jobs that offer flexible hours and where returns to human capital do not depreciate if they spend time out of the workforce for maternity leave, childcare, or other domestic responsibilities (Solotaroff 2005; World Bank 2011b). They may hold particular locational preferences, prioritizing work from home, or near the home, to more easily combine paid work with household work (see Kuriakose and Kono 2008). These supply-side factors—together with social norms around gender identity, family formation, and mobility—constrain the range of employment choices and opportunities women are willing or able to undertake.

Human Capital and Skills Mismatch

The human capital theory posits that women's labor-intensive housework and childcare responsibilities contribute to their lower education, training, and on-the-job experience relative to that of men, disadvantaging them in the labor market (Becker 1975, 1985). Marriage is typically associated with a decline in

FLFP and the number of hours worked by women, which undergo further reductions after childbirth (World Bank 2011b). This may happen either directly—in terms of weeks or years of work experience forgone due to pregnancy, childbirth, and child-rearing (Polachek 1975, cited in Gunewardena 2010)—or indirectly as a result of employers' reluctance to hire female staff because they perceive married women to be less productive workers than men (Becker 1975, cited in Meyer 2003).

Constraints on women's human capital development can come into play fairly early in their lives, when norms prescribe educational trajectories and skills acquisition in areas that are more conducive to female roles within the household (Becker 1975; Goldin 2006; Halaby 2003). Women tend to get streamed into fields of work that are considered less demanding and less technical so that they do not have to compromise on their primary social role within the household as caregivers. Age at first marriage and age at first birth are important predictors of human capital accumulation for women, often determining their number of years of education, field of study, vocational training, and eventually job prospects and future earnings (Becker 1975; Willis 1973; World Bank 2011b). Such norms and practices can create a human capital mismatch, such that women acquire the education and skills considered gender appropriate rather than those needed or demanded by the labor market.

Gender Discrimination

Gender discrimination, or bias, in labor and employment can manifest through formal institutional barriers or active "statistical" discrimination in the form of employer biases or discriminatory workplaces (Bielby and Baron 1986; Goldin 2006). Formal institutional barriers established by law—as well as informal institutional barriers established by social norms—may prohibit female employment in certain industries or sectors, hinder women's safe travel to and from work and threaten their safety in the workplace, restrict the number of hours women can work relative to men, or make employment conditional on obtaining permission from a male member of the household. More than 100 economies globally continue to apply such gender-based job restrictions (World Bank 2018). Another measure of gender bias in the labor market is the *gender wage gap*, reflecting differences in male and female earnings in similar occupations after controlling for other employee characteristics such as educational attainment and work experience.

Employers' decisions based on unfavorable perceptions of women workers as a group are a form of statistical discrimination.[5] These biases result in fewer opportunities for women in hiring and promotion, lower wages, and occupational segregation—both by industry and skill (Akerlof and Kranton 2010). Occupations that become gender typed as more "feminine" tend to be perceived as "low skill" and—compared with jobs held mostly by men—become remunerated at a lower rate over time as greater shares of women occupy and "feminize" them. Such jobs also receive less on-the-job training and fewer opportunities for advancement compared with professions dominated by men (Meyer 2003).

Gender-discriminatory work settings, regulations, and processes hinder women's full participation in the labor market. Lack of gender-sensitive infrastructure and policies in the workplace (such as the absence of proper toilet facilities, inadequate safeguards against sexual harassment, and unsupportive attitudes toward maternity leave) indirectly discourage women's LFP. Limits on physical mobility can also hamper women's access to information by spatially constraining their access to networks (Hanson and Blake 2009; McDonald and Elder 2006). Such gender-biased distortions together work in direct and indirect ways to dampen women's participation in the labor market due to an expected lack of returns and support.

Labor Decision Sites during the Life Course

Reflecting a life course perspective, this study highlights stages of the life course at which men and women make decisions regarding educational attainment, career, and family formation. These decision sites range from the natal and marital homes to schools, the community, and finally to workplaces across a range of sectors, and eventually have an impact on labor force participation and other labor market outcomes.

The natal family is the first formative site for the transfer of norms and values related to educational attainment and occupational choice (Cooley 1902, cited in Hitlin 2006; Halaby 2003; Johnson 2002). Parental perceptions—influenced in part by their own occupational status—determine the allocation of resources to their children's education and skills development. Gender differences arise when material and nonmaterial resources—such as tuition fees for education, moral support, encouragement, and career guidance—are distributed differently between girls and boys based on what parents deem appropriate or desirable for their children. Additionally, household composition, educational attainment, and socioeconomic status play key roles in shaping the school-to-work transition and LFP processes. According to evidence from Sri Lanka, the presence of adult women in the household increases the odds of unmarried women's participation in the labor force, but the presence of employed adult men in the family is likely to have the opposite effect, given that it reduces the need for younger women of the household to supplement the family income. Single women with secondary education and beyond have higher rates of LFP compared with married women and female household heads, but could also be more likely to remain unemployed as a result of the mismatch between their career aspirations and the limited pool of available jobs. Whereas unmarried women from high-income households are less likely to enter the labor force than women from less affluent households—due to wealthy parents' low expectations for daughters' careers and lack of need for daughters to contribute financially to the household—these unmarried women are more likely to acquire jobs when they do participate because of their privileged status (Gunatilaka 2013; Gunewardena 2015; Malhotra and DeGraff 1997).

Educators, peers, social networks, and the wider community support the formation of occupational values, expectations, and aspirations. These external sites continue the socialization of individuals from adolescence into adulthood (Little and Sabates 2008). Young adults engage actively with societal influences to form their own values (as opposed to being passive recipients), yet prevailing cultural and social norms are often reproduced in some form or another (Eder and Nenga 2003). Community norms can also persist over generations and across spaces, such as among migrant groups.[6] Little and Sabates (2008) find evidence of widening inequalities in occupational expectations among youth belonging to middle- and lower-income groups in Sri Lanka, despite the new economic structures and opportunities ushered in by economic liberalization. Lynch (2007) shows that rural Sri Lankan women who migrate to urban export-processing zones for employment in garment factories continue to be subject to the traditional norms of their natal villages.[7]

Family formation norms and practices in the marital home underpin women's educational and career pursuits. Global experience suggests that young women's family formation goals and gender identity influence educational attainment, career choice, and job persistence (Eccles 2011; Cech et al. 2011; Schoon and Eccles 2014). Modernization theories trace shifts in family formation from arranged marriages to choice-based marriages and the growing preference for nuclear (rather than extended) family residence as factors that support the economic and social independence of women. This independence, in turn, could imply greater support for women's higher education, increases in the mean age of first marriage, and women's greater participation in the workforce. Nevertheless, the transition from traditional to modern family practices is neither homogeneous nor universally applicable. Evidence from several nonwestern countries, including Sri Lanka, suggests that traditional prescriptions and family influences continue to maintain a strong hold on individuals' preferences—even with the introduction of more modern ideas and norms (Desai and Andrist 2010; Malhotra and Tsui 1996; Nobles and Buttenheim 2008; Ting and Chiu 2002).

Class and gender norms, along with cognitive ability, influence the values around desired job characteristics. The criteria for judging good versus bad jobs are based on individuals' rational assessments of labor market success in the short and long runs. Halaby (2003) shows that the choice between "entrepreneurial" and "bureaucratic" positions largely aligns with individuals' own risk-reward matrices, with women and other disadvantaged groups showing a preference for safer, stable, and low-risk "bureaucratic" positions (Halaby 2003). In comparison, individuals from more privileged groups, such as young men from the ethnic majorities or higher-income tiers, are more oriented toward independent and high-risk "entrepreneurial" jobs that yield higher rewards (Halaby 2003). Commonly formed before the school-to-work transition, these job preferences can be persistent and determine career paths and socioeconomic achievement during an individual's lifetime (Halaby 2003).[8] There is a growing body of literature examining the ways in which gender identity shapes labor market preferences, particularly attitudes toward risk taking and competition in employment decisions (see Bertrand 2011, cited in Gunewardena 2015; Borghans et al. 2008; Borghans, ter Weel, and Weinberg 2008; Niederle and Vesterlund 2007).

In the workplace, women contend with glass ceilings and sticky floors, among other gender-biased attitudes. Explanations for gender-discriminatory attitudes in hiring, promotion, and retention at the firm level range from arguments about homophilic preferences—that is, the greater affinity for forming same-sex networks, which are more advantageous for men (see Ibarra 1992)—to long-standing evidence of sex-based occupational segregation that promotes single-gender composition of particular sectors and industries (Akerlof and Kranton 2000). The pervasiveness of glass ceilings is well documented across countries and industries, including Sri Lanka: despite holding the requisite skills and qualifications, female candidates are not promoted beyond a certain point (Fortin, Bell, and Böhm 2017; Pendakur and Pendakur 2007; Wickramasinghe and Jayatilaka 2005). Gunewardena et al. (2008) find that in Sri Lanka, gender wage gaps are particularly wide in low-skill and unskilled jobs at the bottom of the wage distribution, indicating that the problem is not so much one of glass ceilings as one of sticky floors. These labor market norms influence women's own decision making and assessment of whether to enter and how long to stay in the workforce.

Women's sociophysical mobility is another area in which gender norms can constrain their labor market participation. In gender-segregated societies or ethnic communities, women may be expected to limit their interactions outside the household. Even when such rules are not strictly enforced, other gender norms around household care responsibilities may make it difficult for women to stay away from the home for long periods, undertake long commutes, or migrate for work. Such limits on mobility hinder access to educational opportunities and workforce participation. Historically, in the United States and elsewhere, the availability of infrastructure services—including access to piped water, electricity, sanitation, safe transportation, and, later, the introduction of electric home appliances—reduces the time burden of women's domestic work, which has positive implications for FLFP (Goldin 2006; World Bank 2011b).

Dynamics between Social Norms and Labor Market Behavior

Social norms and labor market behavior interact and evolve in complex, nonlinear ways. As discussed previously, labor market actors do not make decisions about work in a vacuum, but rather in relation to the broader institutional context, social milieu, and organizational spaces they inhabit. Social change processes may be gradual, as seen in the expansion of women's paid employment in the United States over the span of a century (Akerlof and Kranton 2010; Goldin 2006),[9] but norms can also shift quite rapidly during periods of drastic social or economic transition. Gender identities that are otherwise taken for granted have been actively contested or negotiated in times of physical displacement through war or disaster, migration, and economic transformation. Areas affected by conflict or fragility, for example, tend to exhibit higher levels of FLFP than are customary because women are forced to support their families in the absence of male household members (World Bank 2011a).

Changes in the demand for female labor can create incentives for relaxing gendered social norms around work and family formation. In Bangladesh and China, the expansion of employment opportunities in the manufacturing sector precipitated the entry of women into the workforce in large numbers, thus shifting norms around the propriety of women's work (Chen, Liu, and Xie 2010; Judd 2010). The migration of young women from rural to peri-urban and urban areas for employment can also make way for greater female autonomy in choices relating to marriage, fertility, and mobility. These processes, however, do not follow a simple or linear progression; they often are a complex and messy clash between modern and traditional ideas (Lynch 2007; Malhotra and Tsui 2006).

Increases in female labor supply, on the other hand, are not necessarily accompanied by corresponding adjustments in labor demand. Greater access to schooling and education can positively influence the supply of female labor by raising women's aspirations for employment, but these expectations may not be adequately met with appropriate job opportunities. Changes in labor market behavior may also lag behind shifting values and norms because labor buyers' (that is, employers') beliefs regarding working women may not match those of labor sellers, who are often younger and more comfortable with modern ideas about women's participation in the labor force (see Hofmann and Buckley 2012). Malhotra and DeGraff (1997) thus emphasize the important distinction between women's labor market participation and employment. A small and limited pool of available jobs can create high levels of unemployment. Studies find this pattern in Sri Lanka, where the share of women who aspired to a university education increased from 34 percent in 1973 to 60 percent in 1998. Yet FLFP did not reflect these changes. Malhotra and Tsui (1996) find that 82 percent of the 341 women they interviewed considered a job before marriage to be important (for both dowry and income), but only 30 percent had ever worked, and more than half of those had worked for no more than two years because of a severe shortage of jobs for educated women. A more recent analysis of gender differences in Sri Lanka's labor market finds that even though women demonstrate higher cognitive skill levels than men, as measured by the World Bank STEP Skills Measurement survey, the labor market disadvantages women to a greater extent than men, exacerbating gender disparities in labor force and employment outcomes (Gunewardena 2015).

Notes

1. As articulated by the Honorable Prime Minister in his Economic Policy Statement of November 5, 2015 (http://www.news.lk/fetures/item/10674-economic-policy -statement-made-by-prime-minister-ranil-wickremesinghe-in-parliament). More recently, the Prime Minister has said of the government's new (2017) policy document, "Powerful Sri Lanka," that the government aims to "establish an economy providing equal opportunities to one and all...not an economy that will yield benefits to a few" (http://mnpea.gov.lk/web/index.php?option=com_content&view=article&id =170:our-aim-is-to-enhance-the-economic-condition-of-all-sri-lankans&catid =9&Itemid=112&lang=en).

2. Conflict-affected areas were excluded because of the absence of a sampling frame. It had not been possible to conduct a census in these areas from 1981 until after the end of the conflict.

3. The 2012 *World Development Report* on gender and development understands agency as "the process through which women and men use their endowments and take advantage of economic opportunities to achieve desired outcomes" (World Bank 2011b, 150).

4. For example, the same descriptive and multivariate analysis of 2015 LFS data has been conducted using the full 2015 LFS samples as well as the 2015 LFS without Northern and Eastern Provinces. Estimates from both samples are virtually identical, with the same directionality, same levels of statistical significance, and, except in a few cases, same magnitudes.

5. The economic theory of statistical discrimination, pioneered by Kenneth Arrow and Edmund Phelps, hypothesizes that a decision maker substitutes group averages in the absence of direct, factual information about a certain ability (Fang and Moro 2011).

6. Community norms can persist over time and space. Antecol (2000) finds that half of the overall variation in the gender gap in LFP rates of first-generation immigrants in the United States can be attributed to FLFP rates in the countries of origin. For second- and later-generation women born in the United States, ancestral country FLFP rates explain much less of women's participation in the US labor market; this suggests greater cultural assimilation among younger generations (Antecol 2000).

7. Female garment sector workers employed in Sri Lanka's urban export-processing zones are increasingly willing to question traditional village norms and practices such as restrictions on social mingling between upper and lower castes, but speak candidly about "performing" the role of "good girls" while visiting their natal villages, including adopting changes in their attire and demeanor (Lynch 2007).

8. Johnson (2002), however, finds that while job values (that is, preference criteria) are formed during adolescence, and vary by gender and race, they do change over the life course and reflect "growing realism with age" (Johnson 2002, 1347).

9. Married women's participation in the US workforce increased from just 8 percent of adult women in 1890 to 25 percent by 1930, and to 47 percent by 1950 (Goldin 2006). Generational differences in attitude can be observed, including among women. Fortin (2005) finds that 36 percent of women born before 1935 across 25 Organisation for Economic Co-operation and Development countries believed that "scarce jobs should go to men first" (Goldin 2006), compared with just 15 percent of women born after 1965.

References

Agarwal, Bina. 1997. "'Bargaining' and Gender Relations: Within and Beyond the Household." *Feminist Economics* 3 (1): 1–51.

Akerlof, George A., and Rachel E. Kranton. 2000. "Economics and Identity." *Quarterly Journal of Economics* 115 (3): 715–53.

———. 2010. *Identity Economics: How Our Identities Shape Our Work, Wages, and Well-Being.* Princeton, NJ: Princeton University Press.

Antecol, Heather. 2000. "An Examination of Cross-Country Differences in the Gender Gap in Labor Force Participation Rates." *Labor Economics* 7 (4): 409–26.

Becker, Gary. 1975. *Human Capital*, 2nd edition. New York: Columbia University Press.

———. 1985. "Human Capital, Effort, and the Sexual Division of Labor." *Journal of Labor Economics* 3 (1): S33–S58.

Bertrand, Marianne. 2011. "New Perspectives on Gender." In *Handbook of Labor Economics*, Vol. 4B, edited by Orley Ashenfelter and David, 1543–90. Amsterdam: Elsevier B.V.

Bielby, William T., and James N. Baron. 1986. "Men and Women at Work: Sex Segregation and Statistical Discrimination." *American Journal of Sociology* 91 (4): 759–99.

Borghans, Lex, Angela Lee Duckworth, James J. Heckman, and Bas ter Weel. 2008. "The Economics and Psychology of Personality Traits." *Journal of Human Resources* 43 (4): 972–1059.

Borghans, Lex, Bas ter Weel, and Bruce A. Weinberg. 2008. "Interpersonal Styles and Labor Market Outcomes." *Journal of Human Resources* 43 (4): 815–58.

Carter, Michael R., and Elizabeth Katz. 1997. "Separate Spheres and the Conjugal Contract: Understanding the Impact of Gender-Biased Development." In *Intra-Household Resource Allocation in Developing Countries: Methods, Models and Policy*, edited by L. Haddad, J. Hoddinott, and H. Alderman. Baltimore: Johns Hopkins University Press.

Cech, Erin, Brian Rubineau, Susan Silbey, and Caroll Seron. 2011. "Professional Role Confidence and Gendered Persistence in Engineering." *American Sociological Review* 76 (5): 641–66.

Chen, Jiajin, Hongyan Liu, and Zhenming Xie. 2010. "Effects of Rural-Urban Migration on Women's Family Planning and Reproductive Health Attitudes and Behavior in Rural China." *Studies in Family Planning* 41 (1): 31–44.

Cooley, Charles H. 1902. *Human Nature and the Social Order.* New York: Scribner.

Cunningham, Mick. 2008. "Influences of Gender Ideology and Housework Allocation on Women's Employment over the Life Course." *Social Science Research* 37 (1): 254–67.

Danziger, Sheldon, and David Ratner. 2010. "Labor Market Outcomes and Transitions to Adulthood." *Future of Children* 20 (1): 133–58.

DCS (Department of Census and Statistics). 2016. *Sri Lanka Labour Force Survey 2015 Annual Report.* Colombo: DCS. http://www.statistics.gov.lk/samplesurvey/LFS _Annual%20Report_2015.pdf.

———. 2017. *Sri Lanka Labour Force Survey 2016 Annual Report.* Colombo: DCS. http:// www.statistics.gov.lk/samplesurvey/LFS_Annual%20Report_2017.pdf.

———. 2019. *Sri Lanka Labour Force Survey 2018 Annual Bulletin.* Colombo: DCS. http://www.statistics.gov.lk/samplesurvey/LFS_Annual%20Bulletin_2018.pdf.

Desai, Sonalde, and Lester Andrist. 2010. "Gender Scripts and Age at Marriage in India." *Demography* 47 (3): 667–87.

Eccles, Jacquelynne S. 2011. "Gendered Educational and Occupational Choices: Applying the Eccles et al. Model of Achievement-Related Choices." *International Journal of Behavioral Development* 35 (3): 195-201.

Eder, Donna, and Sandi Kawecka Nenga. 2003. "Socialization in Adolescence." In *Handbook of Social Psychology*, edited by J. Delamater, 157–82. New York: Kluwer.

Elder, Glen H., Jr. 1994. "Time, Human Agency and Social Change: Perspectives on the Life Course." *Social Psychology Quarterly* 57: 4–15.

Fang, Hanming, and Andrea Moro. 2011. "Theories of Statistical Discrimination and Affirmative Action: A Survey." In *Handbook of Social Economics*, Vol. 1A, edited by Jess Benhabib, Matthew O. Jackson, and Alberto Bisin, 133–200. Amsterdam: Elsevier.

Folbre, Nancy. 1994. *Who Pays for the Kids? Gender and the Structures of Constraint*. New York: Routledge.

Fortin, Nicole M. 2005. "Gender Role Attitudes and the Labor Market Outcomes of Women across OECD Countries." *Oxford Review of Economic Policy* 21 (3): 416–38.

Fortin, Nicole M., Brian Bell, and Michael Böhm. 2017. "Top Earnings Inequality and the Gender Pay Gap: Canada, Sweden, and the United Kingdom." *Labour Economics* 47: 107–23.

Goldin, Claudia. 2006. "The Quiet Revolution That Transformed Women's Employment, Education, and Family." *American Economic Review* 96 (2): 1–21.

Gunatilaka, Ramani. 2013. "To Work or Not to Work? Factors Holding Women Back from Market Work in Sri Lanka." Working Paper, International Labour Organization, ILO DWT for South Asia and Country Office for India.

Gunewardena, Dileni. 2010. "An Analysis of Gender and Ethnic Wage Differentials among Youth in Sri Lanka." In *The Challenge of Youth Employment in Sri Lanka*, edited by Ramani Gunatilaka, Markus Mayer, and Milan Vodopivec. Washington, DC: World Bank.

———. 2015. "Why Aren't Sri Lankan Women Translating Their Educational Gains Into Workforce Advantages?" 2015 Echidna Global Scholars Working Paper, Center for Universal Education, Brookings Institution, Washington, DC.

Gunewardena, Dileni, Darshi Abeyrathna, Amalie Ellagala, Kamani Rajakaruna, and Shobana Rajedran. 2008. "Glass Ceilings, Sticky Floors or Sticky Doors? A Quantile Regression Approach to Exploring Gender Wage Gaps in Sri Lanka." Poverty and Economic Policy Research Network Working Paper 04-2008, Poverty and Economic Policy Research Network, Quebec, Canada.

Halaby, Charles N. 2003. "Where Job Values Come From: Family and Schooling Background, Cognitive Ability and Gender." *American Sociological Review* 68 (2): 251–78.

Hanson, Susan, and Megan Blake. 2009. "Gender and Entrepreneurial Networks." *Regional Studies* 43 (1): 135–49.

Hitlin, Steven. 2006. "Parental Influences on Children's Values and Aspirations: Bridging Two Theories of Social Class and Socialization." *Sociological Perspectives* 49 (1): 25–46.

Hofmann, Erin Trouth, and Cynthia J. Buckley. 2012. "Cultural Responses to Changing Gender Patterns of Migration in Georgia." *International Migration* 50 (5): 77–94.

Ibarra, H. 1992. "Homophily and Differential Returns: Sex Differences in Network Structure and Access in an Advertising Firm." *Administrative Science Quarterly* 37 (3): 422–47.

Johnson, Monica K. 2002. "Social Origins, Adolescent Experiences, and Work Value Trajectories during the Transition to Adulthood." *Social Forces* 80 (4): 1307–41.

Judd, Ellen R. 2010. "Family Strategies: Fluidities of Gender, Community, and Mobility in Rural West China." *China Quarterly* 204: 921–38.

Kuriakose, Anne T., and Satoko Kono. 2008. "Empowerment for the Poor in Siem Reap: Preliminary Participatory Poverty and Gender Assessment (PPGA)." Unpublished, World Bank, Washington, DC.

Little, Angela W., and Ricardo Sabates. 2008. "Economic Globalization, Youth Expectations and Social Class: The Case of Sri Lanka." *International Journal of Educational Development* 28 (6): 708–22.

Lynch, Caitrin. 2007. *Juki Girls, Good Girls: Gender and Cultural Politics in Sri Lanka's Global Garment Industry.* Ithaca, NY: Cornell University Press.

Malhotra, Anju, and Deborah DeGraff. 1997. "Entry versus Success in the Labor Force: Young Women's Employment in Sri Lanka." *World Development* 25 (3): 379–94.

Malhotra, Anju, and Mark Mather. 1997. "Do Schooling and Work Empower Women in Developing Countries? Gender and Domestic Decisions in Sri Lanka." *Sociological Forum* 12 (4): 599–630.

Malhotra, Anju, and Amy Ong Tsui. 1996. "Marriage Timing in Sri Lanka: The Role of Modern Norms and Ideas." *Journal of Marriage and Family* 58 (2): 476–90.

McDonald, Steve, and Glen H. Elder. 2006. "When Does Social Capital Matter? Non-Searching for Jobs across the Life Course." *Social Forces* 85 (1): 521–49.

Meyer, Lisa B. 2003. "Economic Globalization and Women's Status in the Labor Market: A Cross-National Investigation of Occupational Sex Segregation and Inequality." *Sociological Quarterly* 44 (3): 351–83.

Niederle, Muriel, and Lise Vesterlund. 2007. "Do Women Shy Away from Competition? Do Men Compete Too Much?" *Quarterly Journal of Economics* 122 (3): 1067–101.

Nobles, Jenna, and Alison Buttenheim. 2008. "Marriage and Socioeconomic Change in Contemporary Indonesia." *Journal of Marriage and Family* 70 (4): 904–18.

Pendakur, Krishna, and Ravi Pendakur. 2007. "Minority Earnings Disparity across the Distribution." *Canadian Public Policy* 33 (1): 41–61.

Polachek, Solomon William. 1975. "Differences in Expected Post-School Investment as a Determinant of Market Wage Differentials." *International Economic Review* 16 (2): 451–70.

Schoon, Ingrid, and Jacquelynne S. Eccles. 2014. *Gender Differences in Aspirations and Attainment: A Life Course Perspective.* Cambridge: Cambridge University Press.

Sen, Amartya K. 1990. "Gender and Cooperative Conflicts." In *Persistent Inequalities: Women and World Development*, edited by I. Tinker. Oxford: Oxford University Press.

Sinha, Nistha. 2012. "Demographic Transition and Female Labor Force Participation in Sri Lanka." South Asia Human Development Sector Discussion Paper 41, World Bank, Washington, DC.

Solotaroff, Jennifer. 2005. "The Entrenchment of Gender Inequalities in Urban China's Workplace Hierarchies." PhD dissertation, Stanford University, Palo Alto, CA.

———. 2013. "Getting In and Staying In: Improving Women's Labor Force Participation in Sri Lanka." Informal, World Bank, Washington, DC.

Ting, Kwok-fai, and Stephen W. K. Chiu. 2002. "Leaving the Parental Home: Chinese Culture in an Urban Context." *Journal of Marriage and Family* 64 (3): 614–26.

Wickramasinghe, Maithree, and Wijaya Jayatilaka. 2006. *Beyond Glass Ceilings and Brick Walls: Gender at the Workplace.* Colombo: International Labor Organization.

Willis, Robert. 1973. "A New Approach to the Economic Theory of Fertility Behavior." *Journal of Political Economy* 81 (2): S14–S64.

World Bank. 2011a. *More and Better Jobs in South Asia.* Washington, DC: World Bank.

———. 2011b. *World Development Report 2012: Gender Equality and Development.* Washington, DC: World Bank.

———. 2015. *Sri Lanka—Ending Poverty and Promoting Shared Prosperity: A Systematic Country Diagnostic.* Washington, DC: World Bank.

———. 2016. "International Bank for Reconstruction and Development, International Development Association, International Finance Corporation, Multilateral Investment Guarantee Agency Country Partnership Framework for the Democratic Socialist Republic of Sri Lanka for the Period FY17–FY20." Report 104606-LK, World Bank, Washington, DC.

———. 2018. *Women, Business and the Law.* Washington, DC: World Bank.

———. 2019. World Development Indicators Database. Washington, DC: World Bank.

WEF (World Economic Forum). 2018. *Global Gender Gap Report 2018.* Geneva: World Economic Forum. http://www3.weforum.org/docs/WEF_GGGR_2018.pdf.

CHAPTER 2

Summary of Descriptive Data on Labor Market Outcomes: Demographic Changes over Time

In recent years, broader macroeconomic changes in Sri Lanka have reflected an ongoing transition from agriculture to the industry and services sectors. Construction, transport, domestic trade and banking, and insurance and real estate have become important contributors to economic growth. Together, these sectors accounted for 50 percent of the total increase in gross domestic product (GDP) between 2009 and 2014 (World Bank 2015). Manufacturing and services constituted the second-largest share of GDP growth, at 44.7 percent. In comparison, the agriculture sector's contribution was only 5.3 percent. Understandably,

Figure 2.1 Labor Force Participation, by Age and Gender, 2009 and 2015

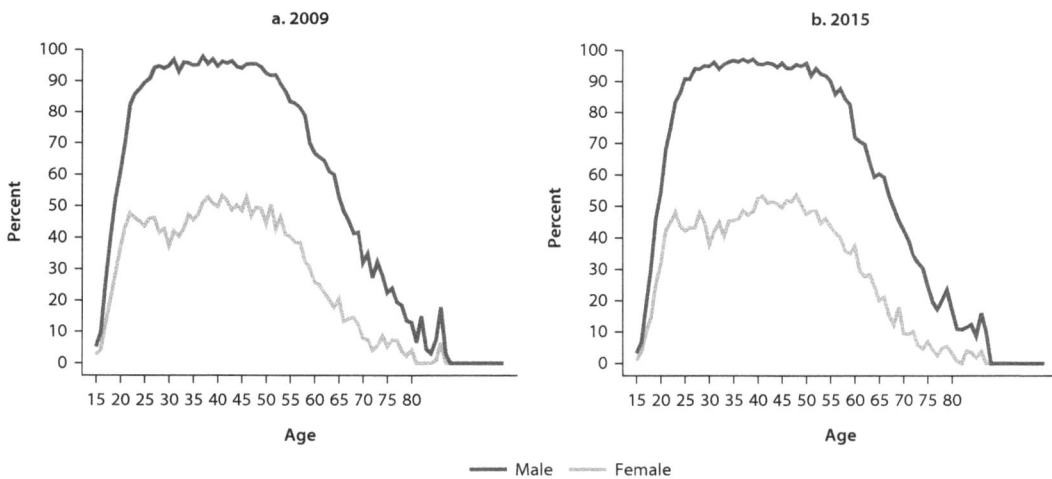

Source: World Bank calculation based on 2009 and 2015 Sri Lanka Labour Force Surveys, population age 15 and older.
Note: Data from Northern Province were excluded to maintain comparability over time. The 2009 weight factor was adjusted by the World Bank's projection of total population from the 2012 census.

overall employment trends are analogous. National Labour Force Survey (LFS) data from 2000 through 2015 show employment rates expanding for the industry and services sectors but contracting for agriculture.

Gender Gaps in Labor Force Participation by Residential Sector, Age, District, and Ethnicity

Throughout these macroeconomic transitions, the female labor force participation (FLFP) rate has been declining and remains lowest for urban women. The 36 percent FLFP rate for 2015 (and 2016) indicates a distinct decline since 2010, when it was 41 percent, versus a labor force participation (LFP) rate of 82 percent for men in the same age group (age 15 and older).[1] In 2006, the FLFP rate was even higher, at 46 percent. Over nearly a decade, therefore, FLFP rates have dropped by roughly 10 percentage points. Like the population at large, the Sri Lankan workforce is aging—particularly for women—because of the ongoing demographic transition (figure 2.1, panels a and b).

Although urban women continue to participate the least in labor markets (with their LFP hovering around 30 percent), LFP rates have fallen most among women who work in the estate sector (that is, tea plantation and other plantation estates on the island), by nearly 10 percentage points between 2006 and 2015 (figure 2.2). The LFP rate of women in estates still far surpasses that of rural and urban women, however. In all residential sectors, men's participation is considerably and consistently higher than women's participation, though the LFP rate for urban men has declined by about 5 percentage points since 2006.

Figure 2.2 Labor Force Participation, by Gender and Residential Sector, 2006–15

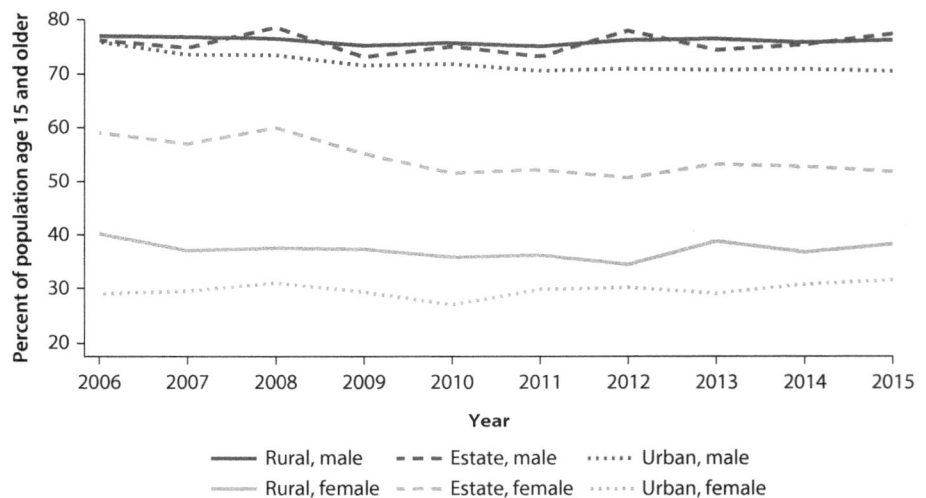

Source: World Bank calculation based on Labour Force Surveys for 2006 through 2015, population age 15 and older.
Note: The Northern and Eastern Provinces were excluded to keep comparability among years. The weight factor was adjusted by the World Bank's projection of total population from the 2012 census, except 2014 and 2015.

Map 2.1 geographically depicts the stark disparity between men's and women's LFP rates by district. Women's participation rates were lowest (less than 20 percent) in Kilinochchi District and peaked in the range of 40–60 percent in eight districts—all in the middle of the island (except Kandy) in 2015. Not surprisingly, many of these districts are in the estate sector, particularly those with heavy tea cultivation, such as Badulla and Nuwara Eliya, and rubber cultivation, such as Ratnapura. Men's participation rates, on the other hand, are consistently 60–80 percent.

FLFP rates also vary considerably by ethnicity[2] (figure 2.3), income level, and education: Indian Tamil women and women with the greatest wealth and educational attainment exhibit the highest participation rates in the most recent years. Despite falling FLFP rates in the estate sector, Indian Tamil women there continue to attain the highest FLFP rates (58 percent in 2009 and 50 percent in 2015) of all ethnic groups in Sri Lanka, including the Sinhala majority. Sri Lankan Moor women tend to have the lowest rates (17 percent in 2009 and 15 percent in 2015). Men's LFP rates are much more uniform—hovering between 65 and 77 percent for the six main ethnic groups in 2015—which suggests greater cultural constraints on women's participation than on men's in the same ethnic group. The lower comparative LFP rates for both men and women

Map 2.1 Labor Force Participation Rate, by District

a. Female

b. Male

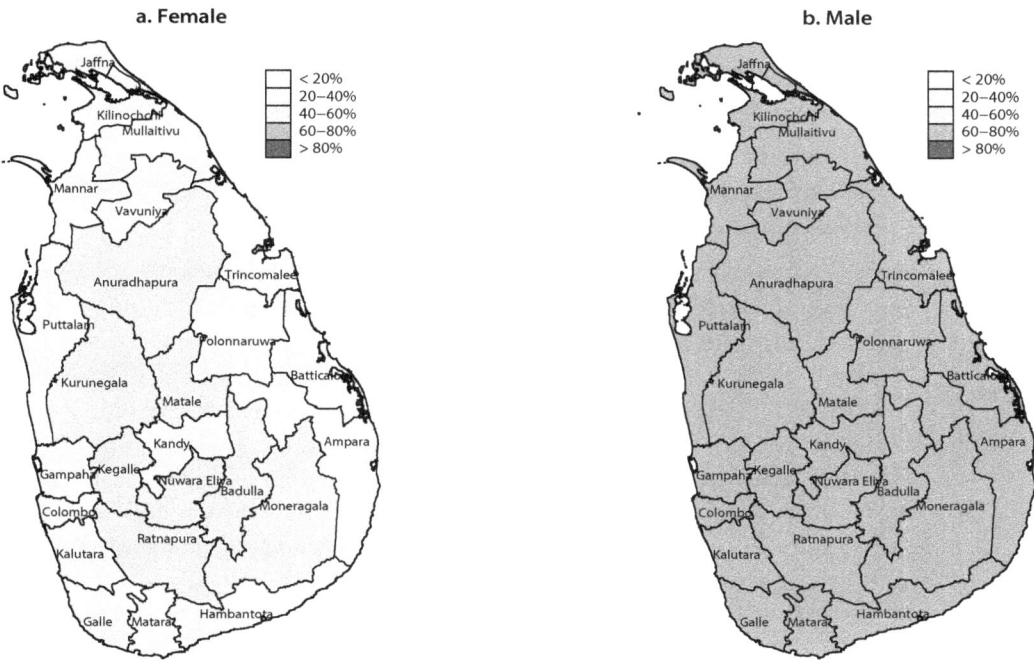

Source: World Bank calculation based on the 2015 Labour Force Survey.
Note: Population age 15 and older.

Getting to Work • http://dx.doi.org/10.1596/978-1-4648-1067-1

Figure 2.3 Labor Force Participation, by Gender and Ethnicity, 2009 and 2015

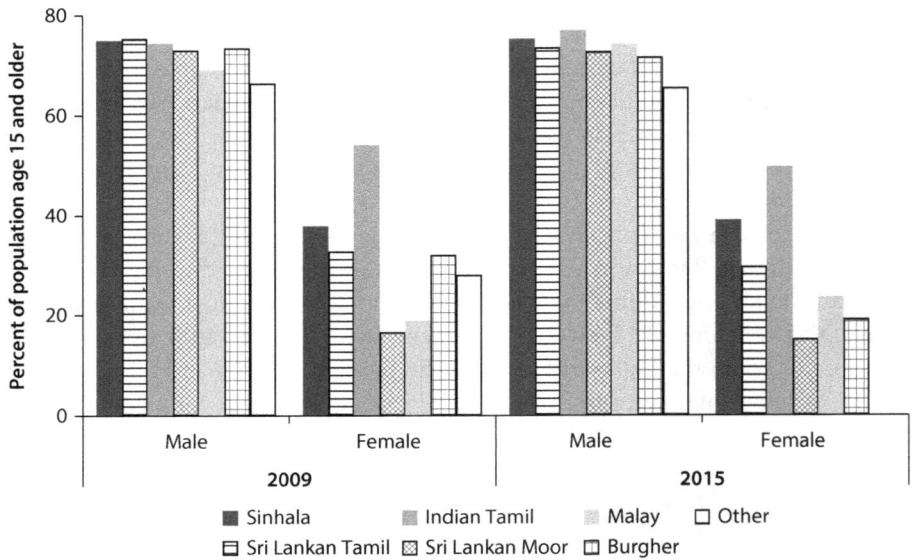

Source: World Bank calculation based on the 2009 and 2015 Labour Force Surveys, population age 15 and older.
Notes: Data from the Northern Province were excluded to maintain comparability over time. The 2009 weight factor was adjusted by the World Bank's projection of total population from the 2012 census.

in the Sri Lankan Tamil, Moor, Malay, and Burgher ethnic groups (in comparison with Sinhalese and Indian Tamils) suggest persistent socioeconomic exclusion of these four groups.

Gender Gaps in LFP by Household Income Level, Poverty, and Migration

The U-shaped curves that characterized women's LFP by income and schooling in 2009–10 no longer hold; the curves are "flatter" for those with lower levels of wealth and education, suggesting that perhaps the poorest and least-educated women in Sri Lanka may be bearing the brunt of deteriorating labor outcomes for women. Before the end of the civil war, women from households with the lowest incomes (consumption deciles 1–2) and the highest incomes (deciles 8–10) participated more in labor markets than women from middle-income households (table 2.1), according to 2009–10 Household Income and Expenditure Survey (HIES) data. This U-shaped pattern is evident for national averages of FLFP and is especially pronounced for women in the urban and rural sectors, whereas urban and rural men's LFP rates remain similar across income deciles, dipping only at the highest levels of wealth. The relatively high rates of estate sector women's LFP—compared with those of other women—are fairly consistent across all but the highest income decile.

Table 2.1 Labor Force Participation, by Consumption Decile, 2009–10
Percent

Consumption decile	All	National		Urban		Rural		Estate	
		Male	Female	Male	Female	Male	Female	Male	Female
1	60.2	83.1	39.3	80.4	38.2	83.6	37.9	80.5	60.1
2	60.1	83.3	39.6	78.3	35.4	83.5	38.3	87.3	59.0
3	59.3	84.0	37.4	80.6	29.4	84.3	36.2	85.8	61.3
4	58.7	83.4	36.6	80.0	35.0	83.9	34.9	83.4	61.7
5	58.8	83.0	37.8	80.8	30.1	82.9	37.2	88.7	58.7
6	58.2	84.5	34.8	83.9	28.9	84.3	34.0	89.3	59.5
7	58.2	83.0	36.8	77.0	34.9	83.6	35.9	91.5	59.9
8	58.7	81.4	39.1	79.1	39.2	81.9	38.5	82.2	56.8
9	58.8	81.0	39.6	79.8	36.8	81.3	39.7	81.4	65.0
10	59.2	78.4	42.5	76.4	40.5	79.0	43.2	85.2	47.0

Source: Data from Household Income and Expenditure Survey 2009–10.
Note: Population age 15 and older.

Table 2.2 Labor Force Participation, by Consumption Decile, 2012–13
Percent

Consumption decile	All	National		Urban		Rural		Estate	
		Male	Female	Male	Female	Male	Female	Male	Female
1	51.3	76.0	30.2	72.9	25.1	76.6	29.8	71.8	40.5
2	51.8	75.9	30.6	74.2	24.1	76.4	29.5	73.2	51.5
3	53.6	78.8	31.1	75.1	22.9	79.6	30.9	76.5	50.3
4	54.5	78.2	33.9	75.0	25.7	78.7	33.6	78.7	56.0
5	53.8	78.7	32.0	77.6	23.1	78.8	32.3	79.8	52.4
6	53.0	77.4	32.7	73.2	21.1	78.4	34.5	77.8	52.2
7	53.5	77.7	33.8	72.9	27.0	78.8	34.6	80.6	54.2
8	52.9	77.2	32.9	69.8	27.2	79.5	34.2	82.1	51.2
9	53.3	74.8	35.6	68.4	30.2	76.9	37.3	90.1	47.3
10	55.2	74.5	39.3	69.1	34.8	77.0	41.4	84.4	48.6

Source: Data from Household Income and Expenditure Survey 2012–13.
Note: Population age 15 and older.

According to the more recent 2012–13 HIES data for the country as a whole, however, women from the poorest households participate the least (30–31 percent) and the wealthiest the most (36–39 percent), with rates for middle-income women at 32–34 percent (table 2.2). This monotonically increasing pattern is strongest in the rural sector, where FLFP rates are less than 30 percent for the two lowest income deciles and more than 37 percent for the highest two deciles. Also important to note is the overall decline in the estate sector's LFP rates—for men and women alike—between 2009 and 2013.[3] The relative disadvantage of poor women in the rural and estate sectors appears to be more pronounced than before, as is, by extension, the need to prioritize these groups with interventions to improve access to labor markets.

If poverty were the sole driver of women's labor market participation in Sri Lanka, women's participation rates would be highest in the most impoverished districts and lower in districts with lower poverty rates. The data do not bear out this pattern, however. Using the district-level poverty head count ratio[4] from HIES 2012–13, map 2.2 displays each district's poverty head count ratio by FLFP rates in that district. The map shows many areas where women's participation is low but poverty is high (all the eastern and northern coastal districts—Trincomalee, Batticaloa, Mullaitivu, Mannar,

Map 2.2 Poverty Head Count Ratio (HCR) and FLFP, by District

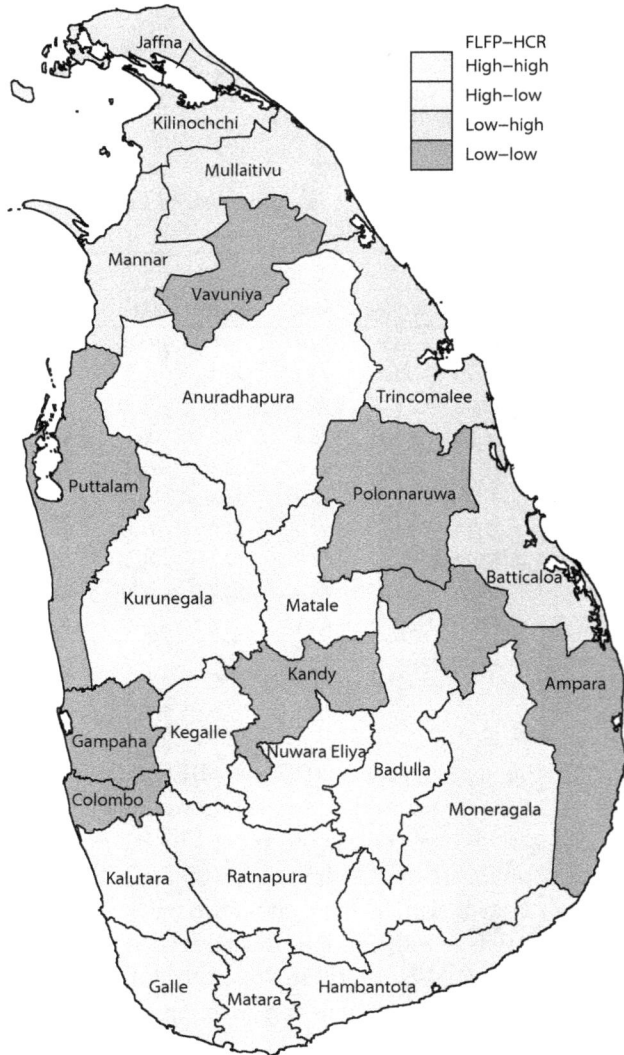

Source: World Bank calculation based on Household Income and Expenditure Survey 2012–13.
Note: FLFP = female labor force participation. Population age 15 and older.

Jaffna, and Kilinochchi) and in which women's participation is high but poverty is low (Kurunegala, Matale, Kegalle, Kalutara, Nuwara Eliya, and Hambantota).

Women continue to make up a significant proportion of the overseas Sri Lankan labor force, though their share—relative to men's—has decreased since 1997 and since 2012 has dropped to less than 50 percent. In 2003, women made up 53 percent of the total overseas workforce (World Bank 2007) and as much as 62 percent in the later years of that decade (Arunatilake et al. 2010).

Map 2.3 FLFP and Domestic

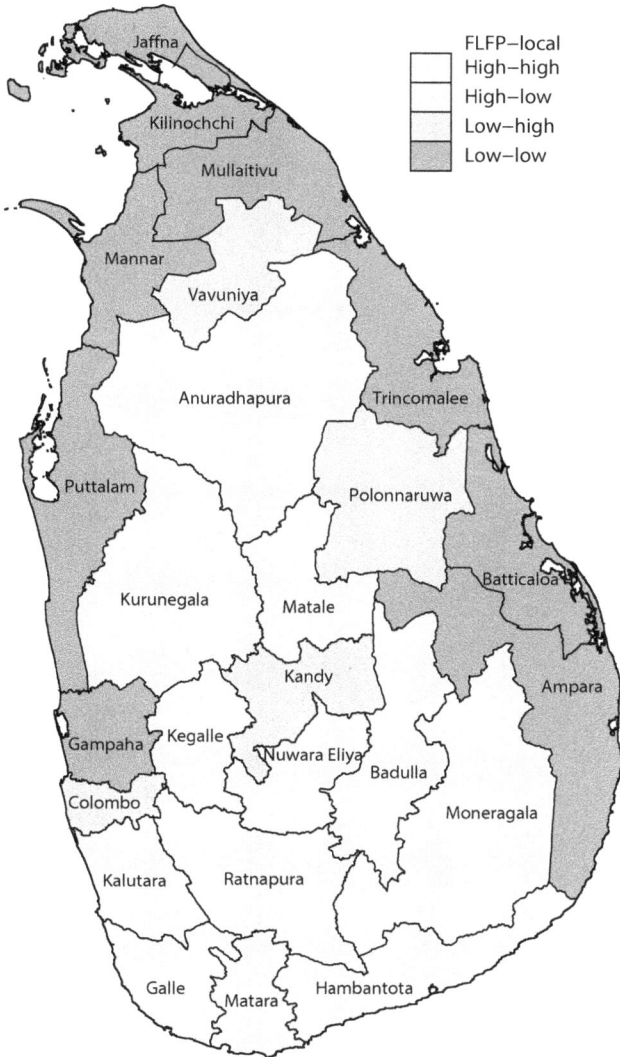

Source: World Bank calculation based on Household Income and Expenditure Survey 2012–13.
Note: FLFP = female labor force participation. Population age 15 and older.

Map 2.4 FLFP and International

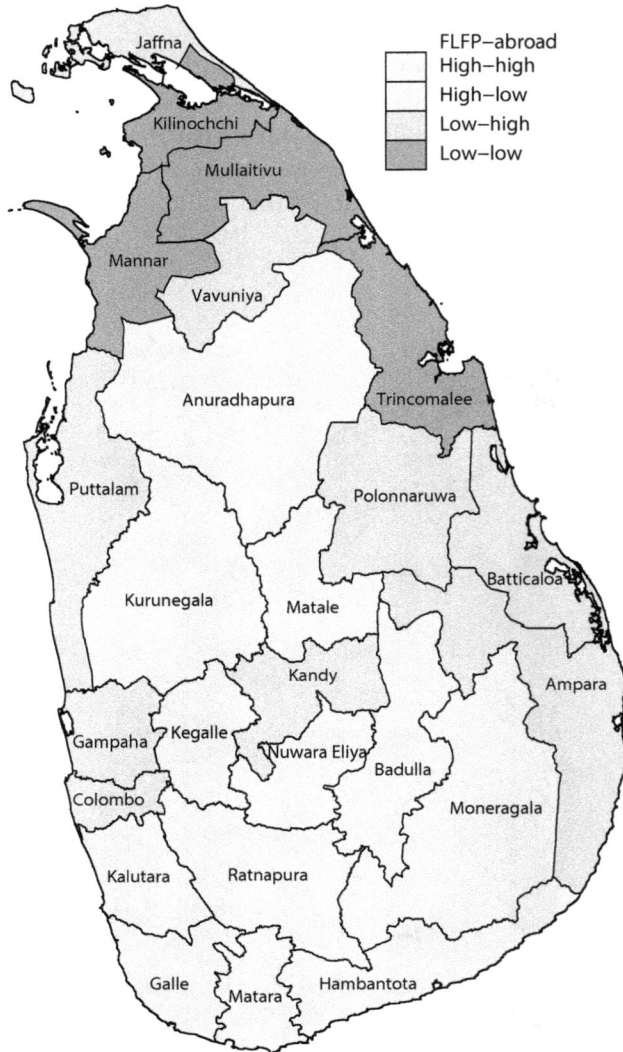

Source: World Bank calculation based on Household Income and Expenditure Survey 2012–13.
Note: FLFP = female labor force participation. Population age 15 and older.

Of the 282,331 Sri Lankans working abroad in 2012, 138,547 (49 percent) were women, and 86 percent of these women were housemaids in domestic service (Jayasura and Opeskin 2015).

Using the number of departures for foreign employment, disaggregated by sex, to investigate changes over time in shares of men and women migrating overseas, the Sri Lanka Bureau of Foreign Employment (SLBFE) reports that, even though the total number of departures has increased over the past 30 years (from 14,456 in 1986 to 263,443 in 2015), the share of women has fluctuated widely. This share was 24 percent in 1986, peaked at slightly more than 75 percent in 1997, and declined thereafter to 52 percent in 2009 and 34 percent in 2015. SLBFE (2016) attributes the sharp decline of women among overseas workers to the rapid increase in men's out-migration along with several SLBFE policy changes occurring in late 2013, including raising the minimum age for women who emigrate for domestic work.

Female overseas workers employed in domestic service and in the health sector contribute greatly to national and household incomes. Remittances from migrating household members may partly explain some of the spatial variation in FLFP rates.[5] HIES data limitations do not allow identification of who in the household—especially whether male or female—is migrating for work and sending remittances. Still, it is worth noting that districts in northern, eastern, and western Sri Lanka have both low FLFP rates and low receipts of domestic household remittances (map 2.3); both FLFP and domestic (local) remittances are high throughout most of the center of the country and in the southeastern districts of Matara and Hambantota. Only Kurunegala, Matale, and Kalutara have both high international household remittances and high FLFP rates; most districts with high international receipts tend to have low FLFP rates—Kandy; Jaffna in the far north; Ampara, Polonnaruwa, and Batticoloa in the east; and the west coast districts except for Galle and Kalutara (map 2.4). The low levels of both domestic and international migration from the conflict-affected Northern and Eastern Provinces are surprising. Given that these areas have among the highest poverty rates in the country, the relative lack of out-migrating women suggests that mobility and other sociocultural constraints may be acting on women in the largely Tamil Muslim local population. Other explanations could be that these women lack the social networks that facilitate migration, or that they simply lack the funds required for travel to the destination.

Gender Gaps in LFP Are Rising at All but the Highest Education Levels

Women's LFP rates with respect to education also resembled a U-shaped curve before the end of the conflict (panel a of figure 2.4), with LFP at its lowest for those who stopped schooling right after completing exams for grade 10 (General Certificate of Education Ordinary Levels, or O-levels). However, the slope on the right side of the U-shaped curve was much steeper than on the left (that is, education beyond O-levels was associated with much higher FLFP rates than education completed at or before O-levels).

More recent data (panel b of figure 2.4) show a similar skewed-U-shaped curve for FLFP with respect to education; however, the lowest levels of education (education below grade 6, or no education) are associated with slightly lower FLFP than before, whereas the middle-upper range of educational attainment is associated with higher FLFP rates than before. Although O-level education is still associated with the lowest FLFP rates, the 2015 rate is about 35 percent—a few percentage points higher than in 2009. In 2015, women's

Figure 2.4 Labor Force Participation, by Education and Gender, 2009 and 2015

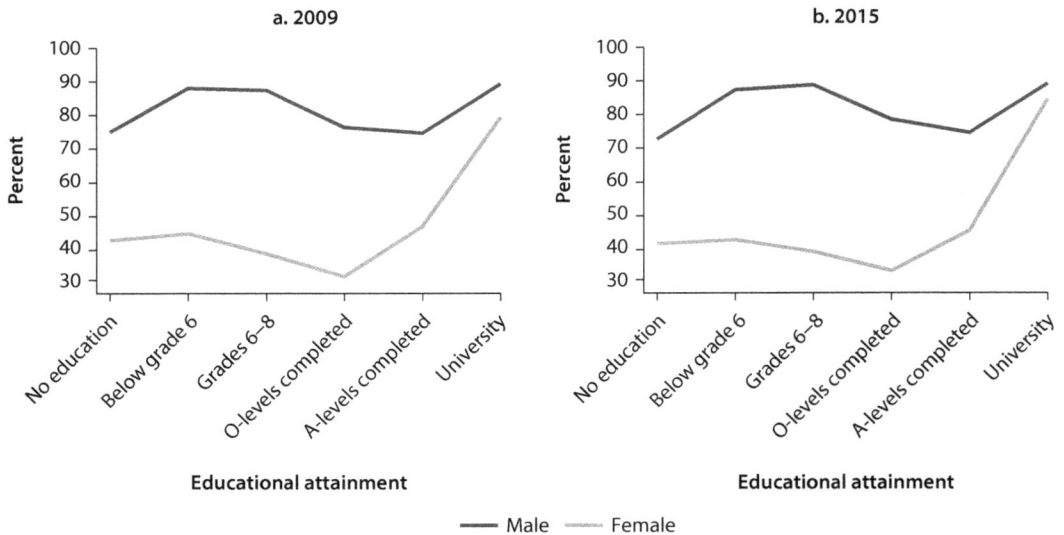

Source: World Bank calculation based on 2009 and 2015 Labour Force Surveys.
Note: Population age 15 and over. Data from the Northern Provinces were excluded to maintain comparability over time. The 2009 weight factor was adjusted by the World Bank's projection of total population from the 2012 census.

participation rates also were higher for those who continued beyond O-levels and A-levels (General Certificate of Education Advanced Levels) to university education, where the FLFP rate increased sharply to more than 85 percent for women with a university education, as opposed to less than 80 percent in 2009.

FLFP rates for those with less than a grade 6 education fell from roughly 46 percent to about 42 percent. For women with no education, LFP rates have dropped slightly, to about 41 percent in 2015. LFP rates have also declined for men with no schooling through a grade 6 education, risen for those completing education between grade 6 and O-levels, and held steady for those with A-levels and above.

The gender gap in the LFP "payoff" to men's and women's investments in education has narrowed, but only at higher levels of education. One large factor is the rising returns to schooling for women with more advanced educational attainment. The gender differential in participation rates is shrinking for those who attend university (from a 10 percentage-point gap in 2009 to a 2015 gap of less than 5 percentage points). The new trend showing LFP rates falling more in 2015 for men who continue on to complete their A-levels is of some concern. It is likely reflecting the higher numbers of boys dropping out of secondary education compared with girls—in part because boys, as well as their parents and teachers, have more confidence in boys' than in girls' ability to secure jobs and earnings regardless of educational attainment (Aturupane, Shojo, and Ebenezer 2018).

Gender Gaps in Unemployment, Wages, and Employment Type

The gender gap in unemployment appears to be shrinking slightly as well, especially in the rural sector. This gap has dropped steadily each year, from 5 percentage points in 2006 (when the unemployment rate for women was 9.7 percent, compared with 4.7 percent for men) to 2.9 percentage points in 2015 (DCS 2016). Rural women continue to have the highest unemployment rates of all, though these rates have declined from nearly 11 percent in 2006 to 8 percent in 2015—thus the shrinking gender gap in rural unemployment (rural men's unemployment rates range from 2.9 percent to 5 percent over the same period). Estate sector women tend to have the lowest unemployment rates among all women; since 2008, their rates also have stayed within 2 percentage points of those of estate sector men. Men's unemployment is highest in urban areas, at 3.5 percent, while urban women's unemployment is nearly twice that, at 6.7 percent (DCS 2016).

Young women still have the highest rates of unemployment in Sri Lanka (figure 2.5), and the gender gap in youth unemployment rates is expanding. In 2015, unemployment appeared to be most entrenched for women age 20–37 or so. Female unemployment rates are consistently higher than those for same-age males—except around age 18, at which point they converged in 2015. Unlike in previous years, when female unemployment peaked at higher ages, more recently its apex occurs for girls age 15–16, drops to about 22 percent around age 18, and shoots up again to 35 percent for 20-year-old women. Female unemployment rates do not fall below 5 percent until age 37. Male unemployment peaks at age 17, falls below 7 percent by age 25, and

Figure 2.5 Unemployment, by Age and Gender, 2015

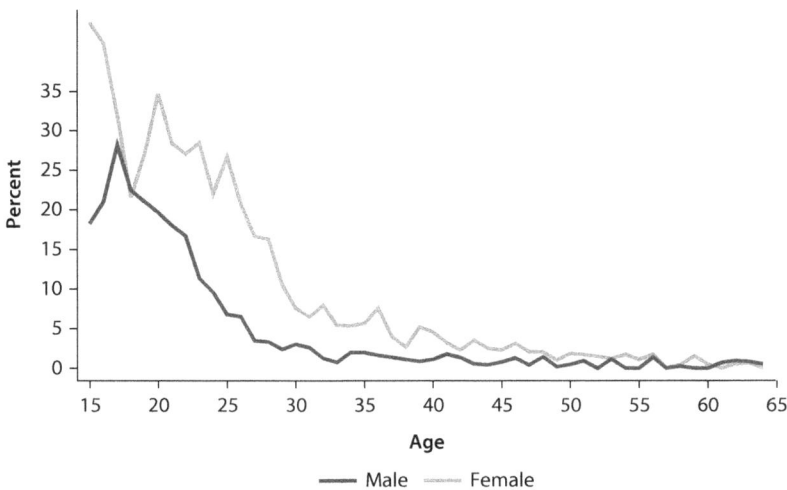

Source: World Bank calculation based on 2015 Labour Force Survey.
Note: Population age 15 and older.

remains under 5 percent for men age 27 and older. Even if this shift primarily reflects the addition of the many poor in the conflict-affected Northern Province—who have no choice but to seek work, even though job opportunities are scarce compared with most other parts of the country—young women are generally facing increasing barriers to employment, compared with young men, in Sri Lanka as a whole. The new trend of high female unemployment rates at the young ages of 15 and 16 may signal an uptick in dropout rates among girls around O-levels (grade 10), perhaps because of an increasing need among the poorest households for as many family members as possible to generate income.

Unemployment by education level also differs for men and women: whereas unemployment tends to rise with education for both groups, it rises at an increasing rate for women who complete their educations between grade 6 and grade 12 (A-levels) (figure 2.6). As of 2015, the gender gap in unemployment rates is largest for those who stop education after A-levels. It shrinks only slightly for university attendance, remaining above 10 percent for women but dropping to about 3 percent for men. If Sri Lanka is to improve its unemployment as well as its LFP rates, it will need to ensure that (1) more girls and boys complete their educations at least through grade 12, and (2) skills acquired at higher levels of education are better aligned with jobs—in particular, for women who graduate from high school but do not continue to university.

Figure 2.6 Unemployment, by Education Level and Gender, 2015

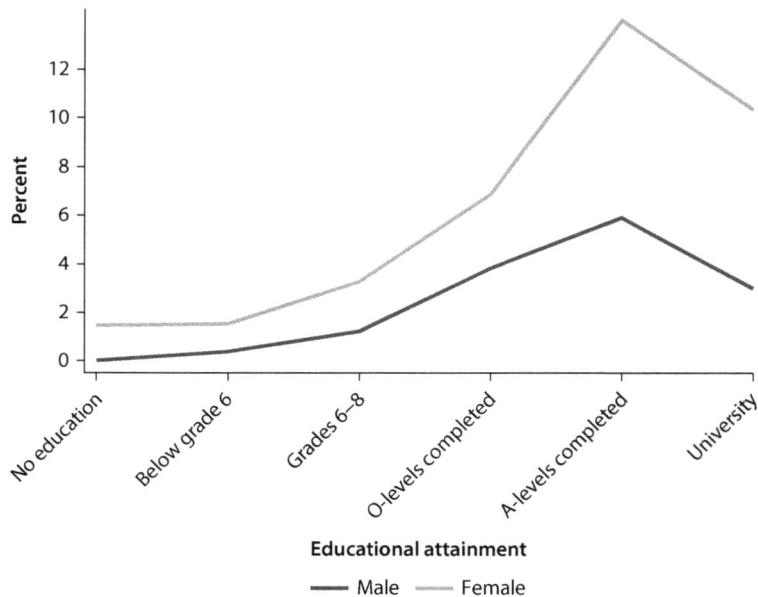

Source: World Bank calculation based on 2015 Labour Force Survey.
Note: All provinces. Population age 15 and over.

Women also remain on the losing end of gender wage gaps, although the average raw earnings gap has narrowed over time. According to the 2015 data, the raw earnings gap (calculated by multiplying the hourly wage by hours worked in the month before the survey, plus all other earnings including benefits) averaged across all provinces was 15.9 percent, with women's average monthly wage being 17,729.5 Sri Lankan rupees (LKR) and men's being 20,839.6 LKR. This is smaller than the 2011 gap of 18.7 percent. In fact, the raw earnings gap has been steadily shrinking, even since before the end of the civil war. Dropping the Northern Province from the samples to allow for comparison across years, the gender gap was 19.9 percent in 2009 compared with 15.8 percent in 2015. Women may thus be benefiting from the higher labor earnings that helped drive the country's impressive poverty reduction between 2002 and 2012–13.[6] The gender wage gap is highest in the estate sector and lowest in the urban sector. Although women earn less than men in all sectors, urban women on average earn more than both men and women in the rural and estate sectors.

As for changes over time in the type of work women are doing, this investigation finds only small improvements in their employment status. The share of women among own-account workers increased slightly during the past decade— from 26 percent in 2006 to 27 percent in 2015—as did the share of women among employers (from 9.4 percent in 2006 to 12.8 percent in 2015), with the shares of men decreasing by the same margin on both counts. However, the share of women among those with contributing-family-worker status, which is unpaid, rose from 72 percent to 78 percent over the same period. To provide a better sense of scale, with the denominator being all employed individuals, in 2015, contributing family workers accounted for 18.8 percent of all employed females (DCS 2016), though this share is low compared with other countries in South Asia. Still, it is far higher than for employed males, among whom only 2.8 percent engage in unpaid work. More than 36 percent of working men are engaged in own-account work and 57 percent of men work as paid employees—compared with 25 percent and 55 percent of working women, respectively (DCS 2016). Only 1.1 percent of working women are employers, compared with 4.2 percent of working men. These numbers have not changed much over the years, although the increase in female employers (from 0.8 percent of employed women in 2006, as opposed to the decrease in male employers, from 4.4 in 2006) and in women own-account workers is promising (DCS 2007, 2016). Women clearly continue to be vastly overrepresented among unpaid workers, however. They also are overrepresented among public sector employees (19 percent of all employed women versus 13 percent of employed men) and are underrepresented among private sector employees (36 percent of employed women versus 44 percent of employed men).

Women have indeed shifted from private to public sector employment more than men since 2006, when 15.6 percent of employed women worked in the public sector (compared with 12 percent of all employed men) and 39 percent worked in the private sector (compared with 44 percent of employed men, the same as in 2015). Among paid employees in Sri Lanka's private sector, slightly more than 50 percent are formal workers; the remaining persons are informal workers in informal (19 percent) or formal (31 percent) enterprises (DCS 2016). More than half of working women are employed in the informal sector, which is characterized by low wages, lack of social protection, and the failure to reward workers' skills at levels comparable to those in the formal sector (ADB and GIZ 2015; DCS 2016). Men are more likely to be employed in informal jobs than are women—56 percent of men versus 37 percent of women (DCS 2016; World Bank 2012). More than one-third (36 percent) of all informal workers are employed in microenterprises. Private sector formal employment accounts for just one-fourth of those who are working (DCS 2016).

Although women are moving out of agriculture at a pace similar to that of men, compared with men they are moving more into the services sector and less into the manufacturing sector. Among women participating in the labor force in 2011, 37.5 percent were in agriculture, 24.2 percent in manufacturing, and 38.3 percent in services (compared with 30.6 percent, 23.4 percent, and 45.9 percent of men distributed across agriculture, manufacturing, and services in 2011). As of 2015, the share of working men in agriculture dropped by 4 percentage points (to 26.5 percent) and increased by 2 percentage points in manufacturing (to 25.4 percent) and by more than 2 percentage points in services (to 48.1 percent). Women, on the other hand, saw a 5 percentage-point drop in agriculture (to 32.5 percent of working women), but a 4 percentage-point increase in services and only a 0.5 percentage-point increase in manufacturing (to 24.7 percent). Occupational segregation has grown within the services sector as well: between 2011 and 2015, the share of working men in traditional services dropped by 9 percentage points, but by less than 0.5 percentage point for women; in intermediate services, the share among working women also fell, whereas the share rose for men by nearly 9 percentage points. The good news is that women are moving more into modern services than men are.[7]

Notes

1. In this study, LFP rates for all years and both sexes are measured as the percentage of that population group, age 15 and older, that is employed or actively seeking employment.

2. Sri Lanka's Department of Census and Statistics (DCS) identifies the presence of the following ethnic groups in its Labour Force Survey and other relevant surveys, including the 2012 Census of Population and Housing: Sinhalese, Sri Lankan Tamil, Indian Tamil, Sri Lankan Moor, Burgher, Malay, and Other (the 2012 census also identifies the Sri Lanka Chetty and Bharatha ethnicities, but their share of Sri Lanka's population is reported to be 0 percent). According to the 2012 census, the shares of population among ethnic groups, in declining order, are 74.9 percent Sinhalese, 11.2 percent Sri Lankan Tamil, 9.3 percent Sri Lankan Moor, 4.1 percent Indian Tamil, 0.2 percent Burgher, 0.2 percent Malay, and 0.1 percent Other (DCS 2015a).

3. To ensure that the changes in LFP rates by income level over time are not simply a function of different samples (some districts in the Northern Province were omitted from the 2009–10 HIES survey, while all districts in all provinces were included in the 2012–13 survey), the authors also calculated LFP estimates using a sample of the 2012–13 HIES data that excluded the same Northern Province districts as in 2009–10. The results show no statistically meaningful difference. There is absolutely no change in the sign of the coefficients, and any differentials in magnitude are minimal—ranging between 0 and 1 percent. This outcome is also true for all descriptive and regression results calculated using data from Sri Lanka's Labour Force Surveys. Tables of the quantitative analysis results using different samples of these secondary data sources can be found in appendix C.

4. The poverty head count ratio is calculated as the share of the population living below the national poverty line. The national poverty head count ratio for Sri Lanka, including the Northern and Eastern Provinces, was 6.7 percent in 2013; excluding the northern province, it was 8.9 percent in 2010 (https://data.worldbank.org/indicator /SI.POV.NAHC?locations=LK).

5. Remittances may lead to low FLFP for several reasons. Remittances may lead to labor substitution within the household to compensate for the migrant household member's absence, could have positive education effects by increasing enrollment of female children in school, and can lead to labor market inactivity because of the work-leisure tradeoff as incomes rise from remittances.

6. It is important to note that the estimated decline in head count poverty from 22.7 percent to 6.1 percent between 2002 and 2012/13 does not include data from districts in the Northern and Eastern Provinces (World Bank 2016).

7. Based on World Bank calculations from data in the LFS 2011, LFS 2013, and LFS 2015 for population age 15 and older. Traditional services include retail and wholesale trade, transport and storage, public administration, and defense (Eichengreen and Gupta 2011). Intermediate services are a hybrid of traditional and modern services, consumed mainly by households—education, health and social work, hotels and restaurants, and other community, social, and personal services. Modern services include financial intermediation, computer services, business services, communications, and legal and technical services.

References

ADB (Asian Development Bank) and GIZ (Deutsche Gesellschaft für Internationale Zusammenarbeit GmbH). 2015. *Country Gender Assessment, Sri Lanka: An Update.* Manila: Asian Development Bank.

Arunatilake, Nisha, Suwendrani Jayaratne, Priyanka Jayawardena, Roshini Jayaweera, and Dushni Weerakoon. 2010. "Impact of Remittances on the Household of the Emigrant and on the Economy of the Migrant's Country: Sri Lanka." In *Social Mobility: Experiences and Lessons from Asia*, edited by Taejong Kim and Anthea Mulakala. Sejong City: Korea Development Institute.

Aturupane, Harsha, Mari Shojo, and Roshini Ebenezer. 2018. "Gender Dimensions of Education Access and Achievement in Sri Lanka." South Asia Region Education Global Practice Discussion Paper No. 90, World Bank, Washington, DC.

DCS (Department of Census and Statistics). 2007. *Sri Lanka Labour Force Survey, Final Report 2006.* Colombo: DCS.

————. 2010. *Sri Lanka Labour Force Survey, Annual Report 2009.* Colombo: DCS.

————. 2011. "Sri Lanka Household Income and Expenditure Survey, 2009/10." DCS, Colombo.

————. 2012. *Sri Lanka Labour Force Survey, Annual Report 2011.* Colombo: DCS.

————. 2014. *Sri Lanka Labour Force Survey, Annual Report 2013.* Colombo: DCS.

————. 2015a. *Sri Lanka Census of Population and Housing 2011.* Colombo: DCS and Ministry of Policy Planning and Economic Affairs. http://www.statistics.gov.lk /PopHouSat/CPH2011/index.php?fileName=FinalReportE&gp=Activities&tpl=3.

————. 2015b. "Sri Lanka Household Income and Expenditure Survey, 2012/13." DCS, Colombo.

————. 2016. *Sri Lanka Labour Force Survey, Annual Report 2015.* Colombo: DCS.

Eichengreen, B., and P. Gupta. 2011. "The Service Sector as India's Road to Economic Growth." NBER Working Paper 16757, National Bureau of Economic Research, Cambridge, MA.

Jayasura, R., and B. Opeskin. 2015. "The Migration of Women Domestic Workers from Sri Lanka: Protecting the Rights of Children Left Behind." *Cornell International Law Journal* 48 (3): 579–638.

SLBFE (Sri Lanka Bureau of Foreign Employment). 2016. "Annual Statistical Report of Foreign Employment—2016." SLBFE, Colombo (http://migrantinfo.lk/wp-content /uploads/2018/01/SLBFE-2016-stats.pdf).

World Bank. 2007. *Sri Lanka Poverty Assessment: Engendering Growth with Equity— Opportunities and Challenges.* Washington, DC: World Bank.

————. 2012. "Sri Lanka: Gender and Economic Opportunities—Securing Jobs for Women and Men." Unpublished, World Bank, Washington, DC.

————. 2015. *Sri Lanka: Ending Poverty and Promoting Shared Prosperity—A Systematic Country Diagnostic.* Washington, DC: World Bank.

————. 2016. "International Bank for Reconstruction and Development, International Development Association, International Finance Corporation, Multilateral Investment Guarantee Agency Country Partnership Framework for the Democratic Socialist Republic of Sri Lanka for the Period FY17–FY20." Report 104606-LK, World Bank, Washington, DC.

CHAPTER 3

Hypothesis Testing: All Explanations for Women's Poor Outcomes Are Still Supported

All three explanations for low female labor force participation (FLFP) in Sri Lanka—traditional household roles and related mobility constraints, human capital mismatch, and gender discrimination—continue to play significant roles in labor outcome gender gaps, though to different degrees than before the end of the civil conflict. The multivariate analysis of more recent data suggests that women's roles in the marital household still are associated with significantly lower odds of women joining the labor force—and even more so than before the end of the civil war. Qualitative research confirms the increasingly powerful influence that gender norms have on family roles and on women's safety and mobility. These gender norms obstruct women from getting to work, diminishing both labor supply and labor demand for women workers: employers as well as families and communities expect women either to not enter or to leave the workforce if they are married and have children. Traveling to work becomes even less acceptable once women move into these family roles.

Household and Family Roles and Mobility Constraints Still Penalize Women in Labor Markets, Especially Women with Young Children

As found in the earlier analysis (Solotaroff 2013) and in Gunewardena (2015), gender norms around household roles—such that housework, elder care, and childcare responsibilities typically fall to women—continue to create time poverty and reduce social support for women's labor force participation (LFP) and employment. The negative effects of some household roles have been dampened in recent years, whereas for other roles the negative effects have intensified. As always, these roles and responsibilities create significant hurdles for women in entering the labor market and continuing employment, especially after marriage and childbirth.

Marriage penalizes women's participation in labor markets, but the penalty has shrunk over the past decade. In 2015, odds of participation were 4.4 percentage points lower for married women than for unmarried women—whereas marriage provides an 11 percentage-point premium for men nationwide (see appendix C, table C.1, for full regression results). Compared with the years before the conflict's end, the penalty on married women appears to have shrunk (from 8 percentage points in 2006 and 6 percentage points in 2009), as has the premium for married men (14 percentage points in both 2006 and 2009). In other words, the gender gap in marriage's effect on LFP appears to have narrowed over the past decade, when considering residential areas in the aggregate (see appendix C, tables C.4 and C.5, for full regression results).

When looking at the urban population alone, the gender gap continues to be more pronounced than in other residential sectors: in 2015, marriage was associated with 11 percentage points lower LFP odds for urban women (compared with those of unmarried urban women), but with 10.3 percentage points higher odds for urban men. This is an improvement since 2006, however, when marriage was associated with a 17 percentage-point penalty for urban women (and a 15 percentage-point boost for urban men).

Marriage now is associated with even lower odds—26 percentage points lower—of a woman becoming a paid employee, whereas for men it is associated with slightly increased odds of 2.5 percentage points. In 2009, marriage was associated with 18 percentage points lower odds for women (see appendix C, tables C.6–C.10, for full LFP regression results).

Similarly, the presence of children younger than age five in the household now has the greatest-ever association with lower chances of LFP for Sri Lankan women, whereas it has never had any significant relationship for men—at least over the decade covered in this book. Considering all residential areas together, having at least one child under age five in the household is significantly associated with 7.4 percentage points lower odds of joining the labor force for women—compared with women without young children—but has no significant association for men. This negative association for women in 2015 is larger than it was in 2009, 2011, and 2013, when child-rearing was associated with lower LFP odds for women of 7.0, 5.2, and 6.1 percentage points, respectively. In 2006 this negative association was more pronounced for women in the rural and estate sectors (8.4 percentage points) than for urban women (3.6 percentage points), but as of 2015 it is about the same for urban women and non-urban women (see appendix C, tables C.1–C.5, for full LFP regression results). For women with young children in the household, living in an estate or rural area is associated with 7.7 percentage points lower odds of LFP (compared with those of women without children) and with 6.2 percentage points lower odds for women living in an urban area. There was no significant relationship between having young children and men's LFP prospects in 2015, regardless of where men live. The need for childcare services may be rising for women in urban areas, and it remains high for women in the rural and estate sectors. This rising need is likely coupled with slight improvements in attitudes about the acceptability of women's paid work, which would encourage more women to enter the labor force.

On the other hand, being married and having young children was associated with lower odds of unemployment for most women and men in 2015, who have 2–3 percentage points lower odds of unemployment than those who are unmarried (see appendix C, table C.11, for full unemployment regression results). The only group for whom marriage and young children have no significant association with unemployment odds is urban women, possibly reflecting their relatively lower odds of LFP; those who do not join the labor market have no chance of being unemployed. The significance and magnitude of marriage and children's negative effects on unemployment in 2015 were virtually identical to those of earlier years.

The primary research further substantiates the hypothesis that being a wife and mother of small children restricts women's workforce participation. Among surveyed women from households with children, 40 percent indicated that housework and childcare led to their nonparticipation. Among women without children in the household, 29 percent stated that burdens surrounding the household gender division of labor kept them out of the labor force (figure 3.1). Key informant interviews conducted in 2018 corroborate this finding, with almost every respondent raising the issue of women having to take care of children—and parents—as the primary constraint on their LFP (Anderson 2018). Key informant interviews also reveal the structure of the school day and school year to be an additional barrier that compels mothers to prioritize their own provision of childcare over employment opportunities for the entirety of children's school years (Anderson 2018).

Figure 3.1 Reasons for Not Working Last Week

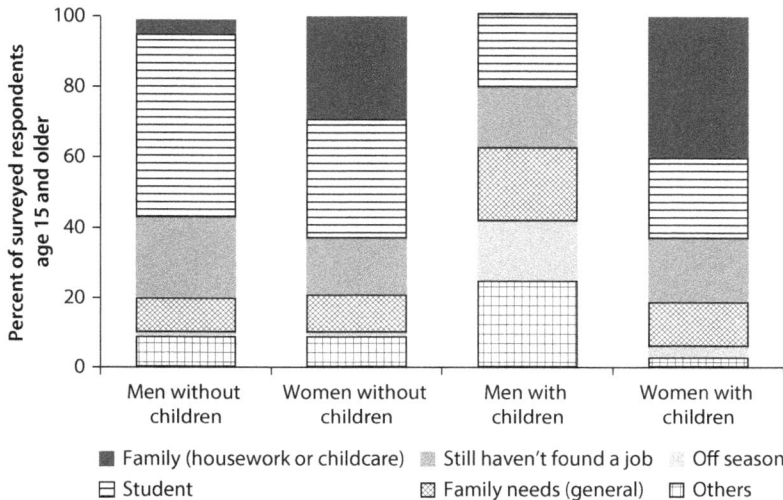

Source: World Bank calculations based on primary data collected in 2012.
Note: The data were collected in Gampaha, Badulla, and Trincomalee districts. Sampie size: 556 households and 157 employers.

Despite the dampening effect of child-rearing on women's LFP, the primary data reveal low awareness and acceptability of professional childcare facilities among survey respondents. As shown in figure 3.2, more than two-thirds of respondents had never used daycare or were not aware of any friends or relatives who had engaged such services. Furthermore, 70 percent believed that professional daycare support could not provide adequate care for their infants or children. In keeping with the prevalent social norm that mothers—as opposed to fathers—should be the main caretakers for their children, the low confidence in child support services also was reflected in respondents' lack of willingness to contribute to childcare costs. Less than 7 percent of workers in the sample said they would be willing to contribute to the cost of such services. Notably, those who had themselves used or knew of friends or relatives using childcare centers were 26 percent more likely to agree that childcare services could provide adequate care for their children. These findings underscore the need to expand the availability of well-regulated and affordable childcare centers and to promote their acceptability.

The presence of elderly household members has the potential to offset some of young mothers' childcare responsibilities; however, it could also add to their overall care burden. In 2009, the presence of those over age 64 had a positive, significant association with odds of LFP for both men and women in urban and non-urban areas, with the greatest positive association with LFP of urban women. This positive association appears to have shrunk in 2015 and shifted entirely to the rural and estate sectors: both men and women in these sectors who live with elderly household members have just 1 percentage point higher odds of joining the labor force compared with people in households without elderly members. These results suggest that the help elderly in the home provide

Figure 3.2 Perceptions and Knowledge of Childcare Facilities
Percent of surveyed respondents

a. Have you or any of your relatives or neighbors used a professional daycare facility?

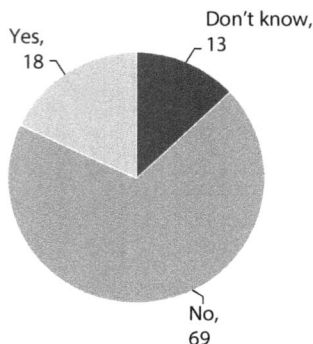

b. Do you believe professional daycare support can provide care for infants or children?

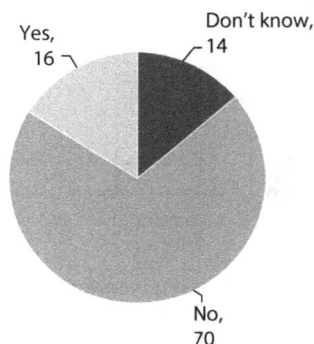

Source: Primary data collected in 2012.
Note: The data were collected In Gampaha, Badulla, and Trincomalee districts. Sample size: 556 households and 157 employers.

to offset women's home care responsibilities—to the extent that they can participate in the labor force—is declining and has vanished entirely for urban women. The loss of a positive association between LFP and the presence of elderly household support is likely another explanation for young women's declining LFP rates, signaling an even more urgent need for childcare support from outside the household.

As in the existing literature, the primary research points to substantial gender constraints on social and physical mobility, particularly after marriage, that restrict Sri Lankan women's employment. These constraints exist on a continuum from, for example, the most conservative preferences that women's paid work (if any) be limited to the physical homestead environs (such as through petty trade or small enterprise work), to preferences for shorter commutes, to restrictions on or lack of support for women's long-distance commuting and domestic or overseas migration. Figures 3.3 and 3.4 present responses from the household survey, disaggregated by gender. Respondents were asked about both married and unmarried men and women commuting long distances for work or migrating. Three valuable insights emerged to illuminate levels of support for these practices. First, regardless of marital status, men held more social leeway in commuting long distances for work and migrating away from the household among both male and female respondents. Second, according to the focus group discussions (FGDs), married women's mobility was to be more restricted than that of unmarried women.

Figure 3.3 Social Acceptability of Long-Distance Commuting and Migration for Unmarried Men and Women

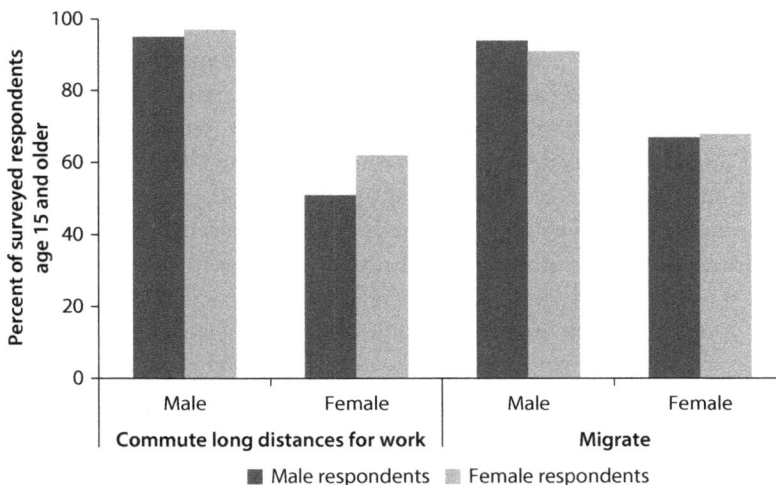

Source: Primary data collected in 2012.
Note: The data were collected in Gampaha, Badulla, and Trincomalee districts. Sample size: 556 households and 157 employers.

Figure 3.4 Social Acceptability of Long-Distance Commuting and Migration for Married Men and Women

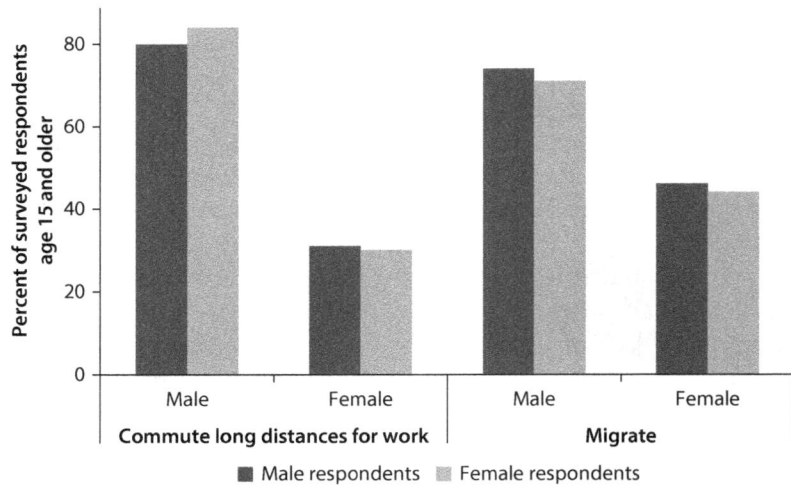

Source: Primary data collected in 2012.
Note: The data were collected in Gampaha, Badulla, and Trincomalee districts. Sample size: 556 households.

Qualitative research results regarding the social desirability of women's LFP and employment tend to vary by location, which may have some relationship to women's presence (or lack thereof) in the dominant local industry. In Badulla district, a young man employed in commercial agriculture (where men comprise the vast majority of workers) remarked, "[Culturally,] women being employed cannot be approved. The term 'housewife' means that the woman of the household should attend to all the household chores and be responsible for the upbringing of the children and not be someone who should go out and earn money."[1] His views reflected those of many men and women in this conservative rural Tamil village. In Gampaha district, where information and communication technology (ICT) and garments are prominent industries, a man said, "Local customs demand that women bring up their children and look after the home. The man of the house should work and provide for the family. Although these customs are changing now, generally parents consider that their male children should be employed full time."[2] Women in the tea estate FGDs provided more nuanced views, saying that, because men on the estate cannot be relied upon to earn income for the household, estate women must enter the workforce. This finding implies that the social norm that women should not work unless as secondary income earners in cases of household necessity has been overcome in the estate sector, primarily because of economic need.

Finally, for all women, migration is more acceptable than long-distance commuting. Other women, such as grandmothers, may be relied upon to carry out household care roles and act as substitutes for migrating mothers, which is more acceptable than for commuting mothers. This substitution appears to be less common for long-distance commuting, where women are still expected to fulfill household roles of preparing meals and caring for children (for example, "dinner on the table and school homework"). As one male FGD member stated, "It is better for a woman to carry on with a business or enterprise from her home, rather than being employed away from home. Then she can [fulfill her] dual roles of housewife and income-earner."[3] Another man said, "For women, proximity to home is the most important criterion in selecting a job, because they will spend less time on the road [and have] more time to attend to household chores. Apart from saving on transportation to and from work, there will be fewer worries about their security."[4]

Any man or woman who lives in a household that is headed by a woman has a significantly lower chance of participating in the labor force than someone living in a male-headed household, except for the female household head herself.[5] This may seem paradoxical, except when considering the intense pressure to earn income that female heads of household may experience: in 2015, their odds of working or seeking work were 12 percentage points higher than for women who were not household heads—and 13 percentage points higher for women in the rural and estate sectors, but 10 percentage points higher for urban women. For rural and estate women, the positive association between LFP and being a female household head was slightly higher in 2013 than in 2015 (15 percentage points compared with 13 percentage points, respectively), but was greater in 2015 than for these female household heads in earlier years. The positive association was smallest in 2006 (about 8 percent across all residential sectors); it grew slightly for non-urban women in 2009 (9 percentage points) and then again in 2011 for all women (9 and 11 percentage points for urban and non-urban women, respectively). The more recent years of LFS data (2011–15), which include the Eastern and Northern Provinces, evidently are picking up the large numbers of female-headed households (FHH) that were created during the conflict and in which the female heads have little choice but to enter the labor force to provide for their vulnerable households. About 58,000 of the country's 1.2 million FHHs lie in the Northern Province, with 20,000 in Jaffna district alone; this is in large part because of the high prevalence of war widows in the conflict-affected North and East, where an estimated 90,000 women were widowed after the war (United Nations, Sri Lanka 2015).

Unfortunately, greater odds of LFP do not translate into an enhanced likelihood of paid employment or increased earnings for these women. As of 2015, being a female household head was associated with lower odds of becoming a paid employee and with lower earnings than for all other groups in Sri Lanka. These findings suggest a deterioration in labor market conditions for female household heads.

On a more positive note, the extreme economic pressure on women heads of household is easing slightly, at least based on the size of the penalty on securing work as a paid employee. Being a female head was associated with about 10 percentage points lower chances of becoming a paid employee in 2015—which was less than the 12 percentage-point penalty in 2013 and the 17 percentage-point penalty in 2011. Analysis of 2006 data suggests a 12 percentage-point penalty, although the 2006 data do not cover the Eastern and Northern Provinces (see appendix C, tables C.6–C.10, for full Mincer earnings regression results).

Multivariate analysis results suggest that those who belong to an FHH are as vulnerable as the female heads themselves, with their vulnerabilities appearing to increase over time. For LFP, this is true for both men and women, though more so for urban women than for any other group; belonging to an FHH lowers urban women's chances of joining the labor market by more than 8 percentage points in 2015. More than any other household or individual characteristic (except for being married), being a female member of an FHH was also associated with substantially lower odds of becoming a paid employee—by 12 percentage points in 2015, 30 percentage points in 2011, and 29 percentage points in 2009. This negative relationship between becoming a paid employee and belonging to an FHH is true for men as well, though to a lesser degree, and it does not become statistically significant until 2011 and later. Finally, urban men who live in FHHs have lower rates of unemployment than men who do not; this is a reversal from 2009, when urban men in FHHs had slightly higher rates of unemployment (see appendix C, tables C.11 and C.12, for full unemployment regression results). The relationship between unemployment and estate and rural men in FHHs—as well as between unemployment and all women in FHHs—is not statistically significant in either year.

Labor dynamics in the Northern and Eastern Provinces have been severely affected by more than two decades of recurrent war. With the large-scale devastation of infrastructure, services, and links to markets, job opportunities in the predominant agriculture and fisheries sectors have declined, and employment is increasingly characterized by informal daily wage and unskilled labor (World Bank 2018). Income-earning opportunities continue to be relatively scarce in this region, which is still being rehabilitated. Because of the region's high incidence of extreme poverty (World Bank 2015a, 2015b), however, men in FHHs must at least try to obtain work. The high numbers of job seekers relative to available jobs elevates their rates of unemployment (see appendix C, table C.11, for full regression results). Poor urban men in this region might be especially prone to unemployment because the infrastructure and markets for nonagricultural work have developed in only a few pockets, while agricultural production remains sluggish. The finding that women in FHHs are not prone to unemployment may be capturing the relatively strong sociocultural constraints on women's job seeking among the ethnic groups that make up majority populations in the northern (Sri Lankan Tamil) and eastern (Sri Lankan Moor) parts of the island. LFP among these women is considerably lower (22 percent in Northern Province and 19 percent in Eastern Province) compared with the national FLFP rate of 36 percent. Women who do work in these areas encounter gender wage differentials as high as 50 percent (World Bank 2018). Together, these results provide a rough sketch of labor-related opportunities and behaviors of those who live in FHHs. The World Bank's strategic social assessment of the conflict-affected

Northern and Eastern Provinces provides a more comprehensive analysis of the demographic, social, and economic dynamics in these provinces in the aftermath of the conflict (World Bank 2018).

Skills Mismatch and Occupational Segregation

Gender Skills Gaps

Educational and occupational streaming continue to create a skills mismatch between women's human capital attainment and market demand for their paid labor. Men have retained their advantage in obtaining high-skill jobs, even though more women are now attending university compared with earlier years (and more women are attending than men). The gender gap for those with any university-level education who secure highly skilled employment (for example, as managers, professionals, or legislators) favors men by more than 2 percentage points. University-educated women who beat the relatively high odds of unemployment tended to work in medium-skill jobs instead—over 5 percentage points more than men who attend university, as of 2015 (figure 3.5).

These "gender skills gaps"—that is, the gender differences in the way education levels translate into jobs of various skill levels—have not changed much over time. In 2009 (figure 3.6), university-educated men had a slightly greater advantage (about 3 percentage points) over university-educated women in

Figure 3.5 Gender Differences in Skill Level, by Education, 2015

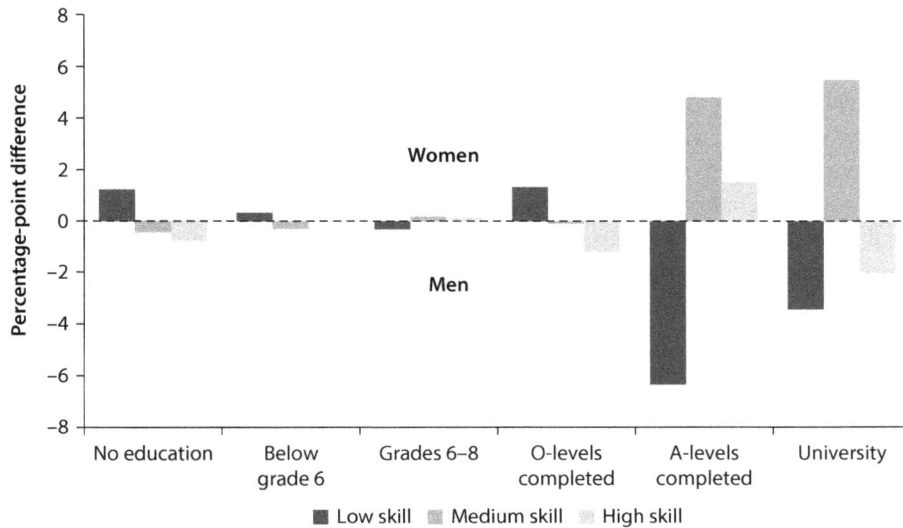

Source: World Bank calculation based on 2009 Labour Force Survey.
Note: All provinces; data from the Northern Province were not collected this year. Employed age 15–64. Occupation was classified according to International Standard Classification of Occupation 2008 (ISCO-88) definition. Occupations are definied as High Skill (managers, legislators professionals); Medium Skill (armed forces, technicians, clerk, service workers, skilled agricultural and fishery workers); and Low Skill (craft and related trade workers); plant and machine operators, elementary occupations).

Getting to Work • http://dx.doi.org/10.1596/978-1-4648-1067-1

Figure 3.6 Gender Differences in Skill Level, by Education, 2009

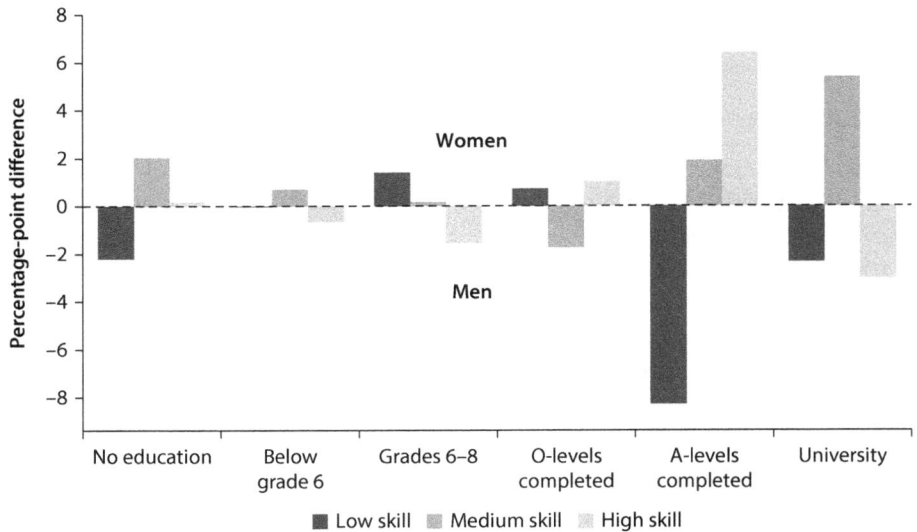

Source: World Bank calculation based on 2009 Labour Force Survey.
Note: All provinces; data from the Northern Province were not collected this year. Employed age 15–64. Occupation was classified according to International Standard Classification of Occupation 2008 (ISCO-88) definition. Occupations are defined as High Skill (managers, legislators, professionals); Medium Skill (armed forces, technicians, clerks, service workers, skilled agricultural and fishery workers); and Low Skill (craft and related trade workers, plant and machine oparation, elementary occupations).

landing high-skill jobs than in 2015 (about 2 percentage points). In 2009, university-educated women had about the same 5 percentage-point advantage over men as they did in 2015 in obtaining medium-skill jobs. Men with university education also were more likely than same-educated women to work in low-skill employment, and slightly more so in 2015 than in 2009. The only education level at which women had an advantage over men in obtaining high-skill jobs in 2015 was the completion of A-level exams (leaving school after grade 12), which may reflect the relative practicality of these women. University education is not necessarily required for high-skill jobs in the private sector; moreover, university-educated women prefer jobs in the public sector even though they tend not to occupy the highest-level positions there. Unfortunately, even female A-level graduates' advantage over men in obtaining high-skill employment has dissipated by about 5 percentage points (down to less than 2 percentage points) since 2009. In 2015, female A-level completers' advantage appeared to have shifted to obtaining medium-skill jobs; these women obtained medium-skill jobs at a rate of nearly 5 percentage points higher than male A-level completers, more than doubling their advantage over their male counterparts since 2009. The only reversal in gender gaps regarding high-skill employment has occurred among O-level completers: in 2009, women leaving school at this point had about a 1 percentage-point edge over men with the same educational attainment, whereas these men had a slightly greater edge over comparably schooled women as of 2015. Female O-level completers secured more low-skill jobs than males—even more so in 2015 than before. The gender skills gaps at lower levels of education that existed in 2009 have all but disappeared. Among those with no education, however, small gender disparities that resulted in more women than men in medium- and high-skill jobs in 2009 flipped to men's advantage by 2015. More unedu- cated women than uneducated men had low-skill jobs as of 2015, whereas the reverse was true in 2009.

In sum, women at all levels of educational attainment have lost ground to men in securing high-skill jobs. Women with A-level and higher education have shifted instead to medium-skill jobs, while women with O-level and lower schooling are increasingly concentrated in low-skill jobs. Even though the odds of university-educated women joining labor markets have improved over time, these women have seen a concomitant loss in their ability (or will- ingness) to obtain low-skill jobs—compared with university-educated men. The findings suggest a strong aversion to "settling" for low-skill jobs among women who attend university or complete their schooling after A-levels—as opposed to higher-educated men and women with less education, who are more amenable to low-skill employment. Gender skills gaps among those who complete their schooling at O-levels or less seem to be disappearing— except for those with no schooling at all, among whom we see women shift- ing over time toward low-skill jobs and men toward high- and especially medium-skill jobs.

Gender Gaps in LFP, Earnings, and Employment, by Education Level

University-educated women have much higher LFP probabilities than other women; however, when university-educated women secure jobs at any level, they still receive lower pay and lower returns to higher education than men do. Compared with having no education, university education is significantly associ- ated with women's much higher odds of LFP (by 22 and 26 percentage points in 2009 and 2015, respectively), but with only slightly higher odds for men— especially in more recent years. Women from the rural and estate sectors who attend university appear to enjoy the greatest boost in LFP odds for all years in the analysis (27 percentage points in 2015, and ranging from 22 to 33 percentage points in earlier years after 2009). University education is also associated with higher odds of unemployment for women than for men, however, although the unemployment gender gap is not nearly as pronounced as it is for those who stop schooling right after A-levels (Gunatilaka 2013).

Compared with lower levels of education, university education is associated with the greatest increase in earnings and greater odds of obtaining a job as a paid employee for both men and women, with gender disparities in both shrinking between 2009 and 2015 (see appendix C, tables C.6–C.9, for full Mincer earnings regression results). Still, a gap remains: men with a university education have 66 percent higher earnings and 70 percent higher odds of becoming a paid employee than men with no education, whereas university-educated women have 52 percent higher earnings and 45 percent higher odds of becoming a paid employee compared with women with no education. Men also receive higher returns than women do from completing their educations at A-levels: their earnings are 32 percent higher than men with no education, whereas women who leave school after A-levels have 25 percent higher earnings than uneducated women. A-level-educated women, moreover, are significantly less likely than uneducated women—by 27 percent—to become paid employees, whereas there is no significant relationship for A-level educated men. For both men and women, lower levels of education are associated with neither higher earnings nor greater odds of being a paid employee compared with no education at all. In fact, completing education at O-levels or below is associated with significantly lower odds of paid employment than never attending school; the negative effect is simply greater for women than for men. Controlling for all levels of educational attainment, women had 31 percent lower earnings than men as of 2015.

All below-university levels of educational attainment in 2015—even completion of A-levels—are associated with significantly lower FLFP rates than those for women with no schooling at all. Among all education levels for men that are below the university level, LFP odds are significantly higher (compared with the reference group of no education)—by 5 percentage points—only for those with education below grade 6. For men, only a few years of education (below grade 6) and a university education are significantly (and positively) associated with LFP probabilities that are an improvement over those associated with no schooling at all. These results underscore the need for secondary education to better prepare Sri Lankan youth—male and female alike—to participate in labor markets and, once there, to boost earnings and chances to become paid employees.

Sex Segregation in Educational Fields and Occupations

The primary research delves into what might underpin gender gaps in labor market outcomes related to education, skills, and experience. Highly educated women's losses over time in obtaining high-skill jobs (as opposed to highly educated men's gains) are very likely related to educational and occupational specialization among women. According to FGDs, women exhibit a preference for humanities and arts in their education, rather than science and mathematics-based technical skills that are better suited to jobs in industry. This trend also captures the vast numbers of female university graduates who seek jobs in the public sector, especially government jobs. The final chapters of this book suggest policy and other interventions to reverse this trend.

Young women are encouraged by parents to study humanities, arts, and biological sciences, even though parents are less invested in the career choices of daughters than sons. They are encouraged to aspire to jobs as doctors and especially as teachers and government workers, given that public sector jobs tend to have regular work hours, maternity leave, and decent benefits packages.

The reality of the labor market for public sector jobs, however, is that there are far fewer openings than women seeking them, such that high proportions of female university graduates queue for years awaiting such jobs—thus contributing to the very high rates of unemployment among young (especially educated) women. Young men, on the other hand, are encouraged to pursue majors and careers in engineering, computer science, and medicine, as well as in government.

Girls' and women's preferences about the level and type of education they acquire are one way in which their aspirations are not aligned with employers' needs for skilled workers. Another point of misalignment is the difference between the behaviors and "soft" skills that women seek to cultivate, on the one hand, and what employers value in new hires, on the other.

Female workers (34 percent) are more likely to believe that work ethics and honesty are valued by employers in new hires, whereas male workers (37 percent) cite industry experience as the most important characteristic that they believe employers seek (figure 3.7). What employers, in fact, value most is the educational qualifications (45 percent) of new hires (figure 3.8). This mismatch between what employers seek in new hires and what workers think is valued by employers could lead to reduced educational investment on the part of workers if they believe that the market will not reward such investment. Surveys from the primary fieldwork also reveal that there is no gender difference in the characteristics (such as education, experience, technical skills, and soft skills) that employers reportedly seek in new hires. In other words, employers report that they expect female workers to have the same educational qualifications for the job that male workers have.

Figure 3.7 Workers' Perceptions: Most Important Characteristics Employers Seek in New Hires

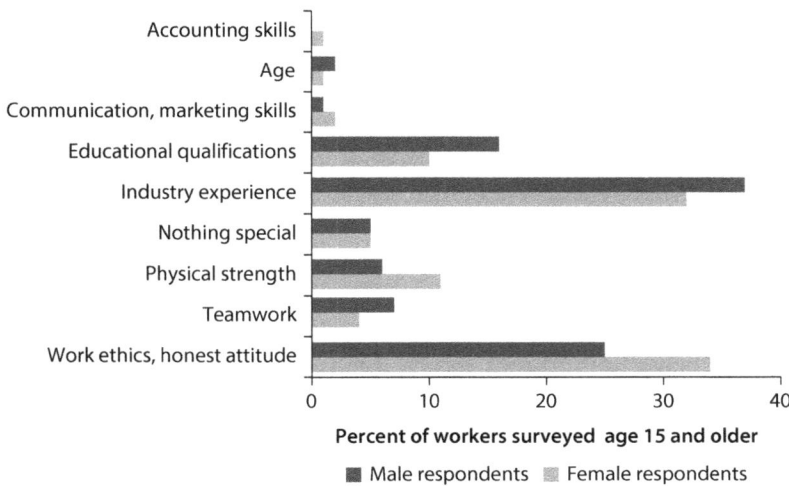

Source: Primary data collected in 2012.
Note: The data were collected in Gampaha, Badulla, and Trincomalee districts. Sample size: 556 households and 157 employers.

Figure 3.8 Employers' Expectations: Most Important Characteristics of Male and Female Workers

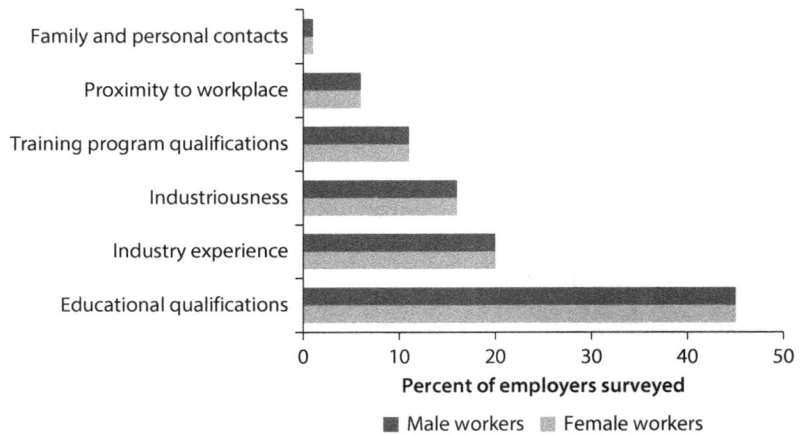

Source: Primary data collected in 2012.
Note: The data were collected in Gampaha, Badulla, and Trincomalee disiricts. Sample size: 556 households and 157 employers.

Overall, young women receive less "moral support" and career guidance (including parental expectations that they will work and choose a career) from information providers such as parents, compared with young men. Parents participating in the qualitative research were more willing to leave daughters' career decisions up to the girls themselves (20 percent and 12 percent for fathers and mothers, respectively). Conversely, for sons, only 8 percent of fathers and 9 percent of mothers were willing to leave the decision to the boys, reflecting the heavier importance that is placed on sons' career success in the Sri Lankan context. The strength of parental roles in occupational choice does vary by sector and industry: workers in the estate sector and in commercial agriculture did not consider the parental role in occupational choice to be as prominent as did workers in the tourism sector (96 percent of male and 94 percent of female tourism workers).

It is not surprising, then, that women also are vastly underrepresented in technical and vocational education and training (TVET), including apprenticeships, despite Sri Lanka having achieved gender parity in formal education years ago. The sample from the primary survey confirms relative parity in formal schooling, but a significant disparity in vocational education and apprenticeship among men and women (figure 3.9). Among surveyed households, attainment of vocational education for women was much lower than that for men in the same age cohort (24 percent vs. 15 percent). Among workers surveyed, 33 percent of men had apprenticeships, compared with just 20 percent of women.

The entrenched occupational segregation in Sri Lanka encourages girls to aspire to occupations that do not require a firm technical grounding; thus, they do not enroll in vocational training or in more technical engineering- and

Figure 3.9 Vocational Education and Apprenticeship

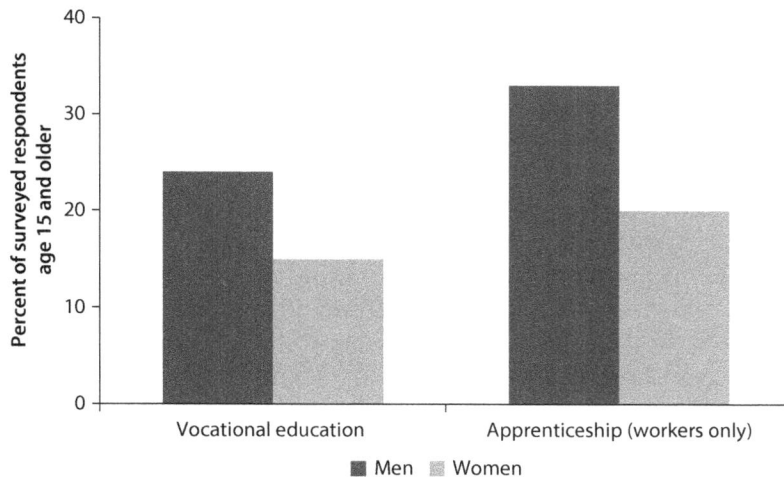

Source: Primary data collected in 2012.
Note: The data were collected in Gampaha, Badulla, and Trincomalee districts. Sample size: 556 households and 157 employers.

mathematics-based fields of education. This decision later places women at a greater disadvantage compared with men if they aim to advance to higher-skilled and more technical jobs, away from unskilled or clerical positions. The eschewing of vocational training may be more characteristic of urban women, however, given that rural participants in FGDs—both male and female—complained of poor access to market-oriented TVET facilities and job guidance centers, which are scarce in rural areas.

The advantage that TVET provides in improving women's and men's employment chances as well as earnings, however, will be negligible unless that training directly provides the skills that employers need in their workers. The finding in Gunewardena (2015) that TVET, training, and apprenticeships provide no advantage beyond that of general schooling suggests that such programs are not sufficiently aligned with employer demands. This lack of alignment— along with the lack of availability of TVET programs—is addressed in the next chapter.

Gender Bias and Discrimination

Analysis of the primary data does not provide any indication that parental perceptions are biased against female children with regard to scholastic ability, aptitude, and interest in the fields of science and engineering. In fact, a large majority of parents believe that children of both genders perform equally well in school and have similar aptitudes in science, technology, engineering, and mathematics. However, nearly half of the respondents surveyed believe that girls with education levels similar to those of boys are not offered the same job opportunities, confirming strong perceptions about gender-based labor market discrimination (figure 3.10). It is plausible, then, that occupational streaming could be emanating, at least partly, from parental perceptions of labor market discrimination. Parental expectations about the job market may be transferred to children, resulting in corresponding educational and career choices by boys and girls.

The primary research provides insight into differences in men's and women's job-seeking behavior. A higher proportion of women than men expressed low confidence in their labor market prospects. Half of working women surveyed felt discouraged about searching for new opportunities because they did not believe they would find suitable jobs, and 40 percent of these women did not believe they had the skills required to find new jobs. The shares of men with the same responses to these two questions were considerably lower, at 15 percent and 23 percent, respectively (figure 3.11).

A range of factors could be contributing to negative perceptions among women about the odds of improving their job prospects and mobility in the occupational structure. Women may not have the skills required to find another job; or, due to poor information networks or perceptions of gender discrimination in hiring, they may be discouraged about the likelihood of finding suitable jobs. These factors, together with the lack of female role models and social

Figure 3.10 Perceptions of Gender Discrimination in the Job Market Despite Similar Levels of Education

The respondents were asked the following question: "Do you think that girls with education levels similar to those of boys are offered the same job?"

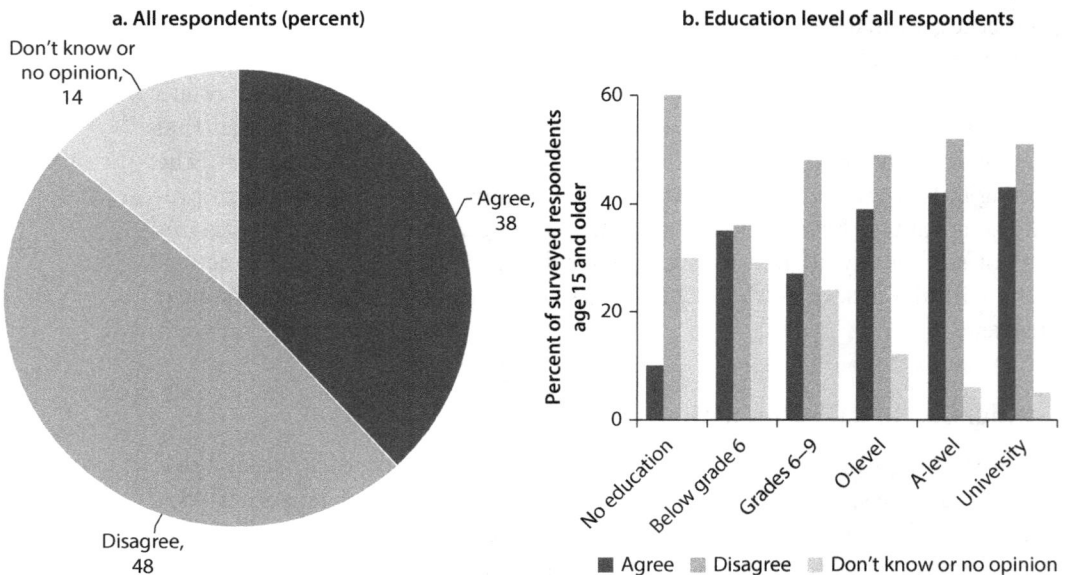

a. All respondents (percent)

Don't know or no opinion, 14

Agree, 38

Disagree, 48

b. Education level of all respondents

■ Agree ▨ Disagree ▫ Don't know or no opinion

Source: Primary data collected in 2012.
Note: The data were collected in Gampaha, Badulla, and Trincomalee districts. Sample size: 556 households and 157 employers.

Figure 3.11 Worker Perceptions of Industry Prospects

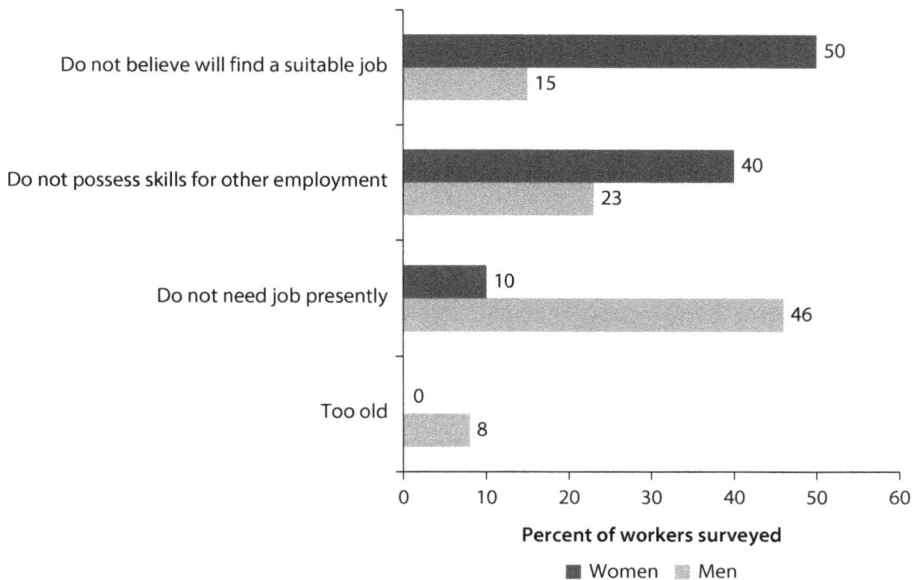

Source: Primary data collected in 2012.

Note: The data were Collected in Gampaha, Badulla, and Trincomalee districts. Sample Size: 556 households and 157 employers.

support for women in higher positions, may condition female job seekers to hold themselves back from the risk taking required to seek a new job. Gender bias in the labor market may also be internalized, limiting expectations and goals among women for their employment and career prospects. According to a female FGD participant from Gampaha district, men are promoted more often in their jobs "because men are more committed, prepared to take up more responsibilities, and more willing to advance themselves in their careers. Women on the other hand are more prone to merely safeguard their jobs and look after their households." Women in FGDs agreed that women are not generally interested in taking up higher responsibilities at work. The following section explores gender bias in labor markets through a sharper lens; it uses nationally representative labor survey data to move the analysis beyond qualitative findings on education- and skills-related perceptions.

Use of Oaxaca-Blinder decomposition models to further explore select labor market outcomes—which consider the influence of individual, household, and other characteristics on gender inequities in these outcomes—confirms the strong presence of gender bias that impedes women's entry into the labor force and reduces their wages relative to men's. Both active and institutional forms of gender bias—which manifest in gender wage gaps, discriminatory workplaces, and weaker job networks for women than for men—are associated with reduced FLFP and higher female unemployment.

Given such a poor forecast for their performance in the labor market, some women choose never to participate or are induced to withdraw from the market entirely (see appendix C, tables C.13–C.21, for full results from the Oaxaca-Blinder decomposition).

Labor Force Participation

Although the overall gender gap in LFP was 39 percent in 2015 (see appendix C, table C.13), just 6.8 percent of this gap is explained by differences in endowments (for example, education, ethnicity, family characteristics, age and experience, and so forth), while more than 93 percent of the gap remains unexplained.[6] It is the unexplained share that can be attributed to gender bias in labor markets—that is, the difference in how markets value men's versus women's endowments. Family characteristics and the presence of children younger than age five in the household tend to increase the explained portion of the gap in 2015. The presence of those older than age 64 in the household, educational attainment, ethnicity, and location tend to reduce it.

The explained portion of the LFP gender gap appears to be shrinking over time—with the unexplained portion increasing—which suggests progressive entrenchment of gender bias in labor markets' determination of the LFP gender gap. The explained portions range from 9.0 percent in 2006 and 7.8 percent in 2009 to 7.4 percent in 2011, 7.7 percent in 2013, and just 6.8 percent in 2015.[7] The unexplained portion thus increased from 91 percent in 2006 to 93.2 percent in 2015 (see appendix C, tables C.13 and C.14, for full regression results). Family characteristics and the presence of children younger than age five in the household consistently increase the explained portion, both before the end of the civil conflict (the 2006 and 2009 LFS samples) and after it (the 2011, 2013, and 2015 samples). The finding that education significantly reduces the explained part of LFP gender gaps only in 2013 and 2015 is indicative of the recent, though growing, influence of gender bias in how labor markets translate education of men and women into LFP. It also may provide further support to the skills mismatch hypothesis: overall, women's educational attainments are increasing, but the type of education they acquire is not being rewarded in labor markets.

The presence of elderly in the household and geographic location of the household—but not ethnicity—tend to reduce the explained portion over time. It is not until 2011 that ethnicity becomes significantly and negatively associated with LFP gender gaps (lowering the explained portion). This negative association with ethnicity continues in 2015, suggesting that ethnicity-related discrimination has emerged in these gaps in the years following the civil conflict. Another explanation for this emergence could be the inclusion of the Northern and Eastern Provinces in the 2011, 2013, and 2015 LFS samples; both provinces were excluded in 2006, and the Northern was excluded in 2009. These two explanations are not mutually exclusive.

Earnings

The Oaxaca-Blinder decomposition of log earnings suggests that, controlling for type of employment, women in the labor market are better endowed than men with characteristics that employers reward, such as education and experience, but still face lower wages because of gender bias. The decomposition, however, finds the 2015 gender gap in earnings to be about 26 percent; of this, 18 percent is explained by endowments (characteristics), while the remaining 82 percent is unexplained. Although having young children has no statistically significant association with the gender wage gap in 2015, other family characteristics, ethnicity, and location significantly increase the explained portion of the gap. For example, in conflict-affected northeastern Sri Lanka—where fewer jobs are available, on average, than in other parts of the country—women who do earn money may have to settle for the lowest-paying jobs. Education, age and experience, and employment category (that is, public sector, private formal sector, or private informal sector) appear to significantly reduce the explained portion of the gap in 2015. In other words, labor markets are rewarding men and women with different earnings for the same experience, levels of education, and employment categories.

Considering changes in the gender earnings gap over time, the good news for women is that the gap itself is shrinking; moreover, the gap is increasingly attributable to endowments. That is, gender bias in determining wage gaps is diminishing over time. Not only is the raw wage gap consistently narrowing, as discussed earlier, but the gap estimated when controlling for men's and women's characteristics is narrowing as well—from 33 percent in 2006 and 30 percent in 2009, to 28 percent in 2013 and 26 percent in 2015. Family characteristics, location, and ethnicity tend to expand the explained portion of the gap over time, whereas education, employment category, and age and experience shrink it. The explained portion was only 2 percent in 2009, and jumped to 4 percent, then 8 percent, and finally 18 percent in 2011, 2013, and 2015, respectively.

The types of industries and occupations that women choose tend to increase the explained portion of the wage gap, implying that these choices are contributing to the increase in the wage gap. Further decomposition of 2015 log earnings by employment category finds gender wage disparities to be greatest in the private informal sector (a 61 percent gap) and least in the public sector (7 percent), with the private formal sector gap (40 percent) in between. In 2011 and 2013, the earnings gap itself was again largest in the private informal sector (58 percent and 56 percent in 2011 and 2013, respectively) and smallest in the public sector (14.5 percent and 15 percent, respectively), with the size of the private formal sector gap (37.5 percent and 38 percent) falling in between. In 2006 and 2009, the gaps across employment categories followed the same pattern, although the greatest range occurred in 2006, which shows an 11 percent gap in the public sector and a 62 percent gap in the private informal sector.

Despite smaller gender wage gaps in the public sector than in the formal and informal private sectors, the explained portions of these gaps are consistently smallest in public sector employment. Its explained portion was as small as 3 percent in 2011 and 14 percent in 2009, though it increased to 22 percent in 2013. The private formal sector consistently had the largest explained portions of gender wage gaps, from a high of 52 percent in 2006 to its lowest share yet (41 percent) in 2015.

Gender wage gaps thus appear to be more attributable to gender bias in the public sector than in the private sector, even though the raw gaps are smaller in the public sector. Despite greater bias in the public sector, women are more attracted to public sector jobs, as shown by the primary research and existing literature. Even though women are increasing their educational attainments over time—and are thus becoming better qualified than men for public sector jobs—women's wages in the public sector are not reflecting their higher attainments and qualifications. If they were, the gender wage gap would most likely disappear in the public sector, or even reverse itself to favor women. If Sri Lankan women were to look more to the private sector—especially the formal private sector—for employment, the chances that their endowments, rather than gender bias, would determine their earnings would improve. Endowments such as family characteristics, location, age, and years of experience tend to significantly increase the explained portion of the gender wage gap in the private sector. In the public sector, however, age and experience tend to reduce the explained portion of the wage gap, whereas ethnicity tends to increase it.

These findings shed further light on the causes of women's preference for public sector jobs, in spite of the drawbacks associated with seeking to acquire these jobs. Although the educated women who queue for public sector jobs risk unemployment, they are making rational calculations in prioritizing these jobs—not only because of the women-friendly benefits provided by the public sector, but also because raw gender wage gaps there are technically smaller than in the private sector. However, ultimately they would fare better by seeking jobs in the private sector—especially the formal private sector—in both earnings potential and chances of employment when joining the labor market. If they were to acquire the "right" kinds of education and skills (that is, those that employers value and those that tend to be acquired by men), these endowments would be rewarded with higher earnings for women, reducing the gender wage gap in the private sector. The formal private sector is also more regulated than the informal private sector; it thus is more likely to provide benefits of particular interest to women, such as maternity leave, flexible working hours, and transportation services. Multifaceted interventions are needed to redirect them toward private sector jobs and, hopefully, to break through the boundaries of occupational segregation in the economy.

Role of Employers

Occupational segregation results not only from "push factors" in labor supply, such as social norms that value women's roles as wives and mothers over their role in the workplace, parents' higher career aspirations for sons than for daughters, preferences for jobs that provide maternity leave but relatively low pay, and perceptions that employers discriminate between men and women with the same educational attainments (figure 3.10). It is also driven by "pull factors" of labor demand. The FGD findings uncover gender-biased values and norms held by employers that affect women's and men's experience of paid employment. Key informants interviewed in 2018 also consistently identified, as significant obstacles to FLFP, work policies that inadvertently discriminate against women by not accommodating their typical responsibilities as family caregivers (Anderson 2018).

Employer preferences for hiring men were not perceived universally by employees at any tier. In fact, the majority of workers at all levels believed that their employers do not prefer one sex over the other in hiring, promotion, or salary increases (figure 3.12). As worker skill level increases, the prevalence of workers holding the belief that employers are biased in favor of men also increases for the most part, especially among men. One explanation for this might be that women are generally clustered at lower tiers of employment and are not observed to face as much discrimination (or norms-transgressing) at that level, whereas both male and female workers competing for positions, promotions, and salary increases at the more male-dominated senior levels would have more repeated opportunities to encounter instances of biased workplace norms that favor men. More than one-third of managers (men and women combined)

Figure 3.12 Percentage of Workers Who Believe That Employers Prefer Men, by Skill Level and Sex

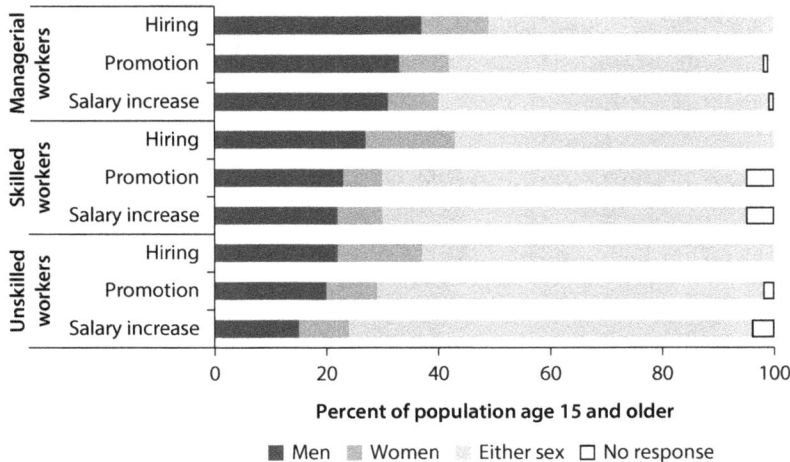

Percent of population age 15 and older

■ Men ■ Women ▨ Either sex □ No response

Source: Primary data collected in 2012.
Note: The data were collected in Gampaha, Badulla, and Trincomalee districts. Sample size: 556 households and 157 employers.

believed that employers prefer men in salary increase, promotion, and hiring decisions; roughly half believed this about hiring decisions in particular.

Gender discrimination may also be detectable from labor market tightness. About 60 percent of employers reported difficulty in finding new workers, reflecting excess demand for labor (figure 3.13, panel a). In situations of labor market tightness, economic theory predicts that employers will hire new workers from the reserve of unemployed or inactive workers—if employers believe that potential workers have the necessary skills for the job—to avoid rising wage costs. As the employer responses demonstrate, even in the context of labor market tightness, a substantial proportion of surveyed employers (53 percent) were not planning to hire women (figure 3.13, panel b).

Employers' perceptions about whether women or men are better workers differed by sector. Employers in the tea and tourism sectors deemed women to be better workers than men, whereas the reverse was true in the ICT and commercial agriculture sectors. Employers' views on the performance of workers by gender generally mirrored whether they planned to hire more women. For example, tea sector employers reported planning to increase the number of female workers, whereas those in the ICT and commercial agriculture sectors did not. Employers in the latter two sectors, which are two of Sri Lanka's most promising economic drivers and also have the potential for high earnings, appeared to be biased against the hiring of women.

Figure 3.13 Labor Market Tightness and the Hiring of Female Workers
Percent of employers surveyed

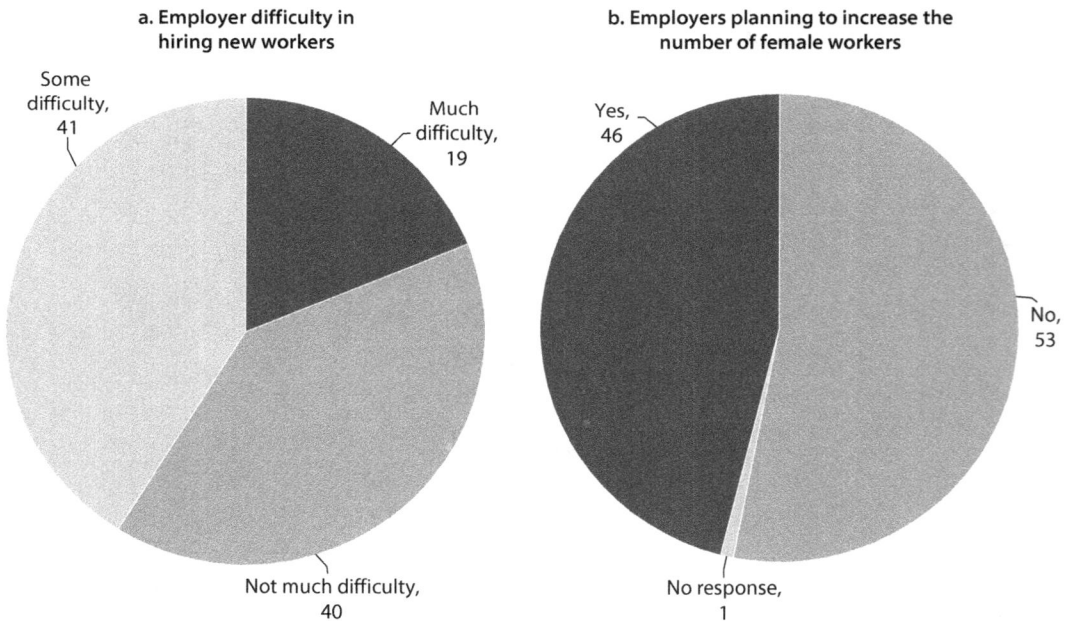

a. Employer difficulty in hiring new workers — Some difficulty, 41; Much difficulty, 19; Not much difficulty, 40

b. Employers planning to increase the number of female workers — Yes, 46; No, 53; No response, 1

Source: Primary data collection in 2012.
Note: The data were collected in Gampaha, Badulla, and Trincomalee districts. Sample size: 556 households and 157 employers.

Ethnicity

As with any discussion of discrimination—and, more broadly, social inclusion—the analysis must consider the intersection of gender with multiple axes of exclusion. In previous sections, the discussion centers on how gender intersects with age, education, marriage, and other individual as well as household-level characteristics. Another important consideration is the relationship between gender and ethnicity, and how it plays out in labor markets. The Oaxaca-Blinder decomposition models suggest that ethnicity[8] has had a statistically significant—though small—association with the LFP gender gap, in that it has tended to reduce the explained part of the gap since 2011, though not before then. As for earnings gaps, however, ethnicity tends to increase the explained part of the gap (with a significant association in 2009, 2011, and 2015). In other words, after the civil conflict ended, more ethnic minorities in conflict-affected areas (for example, Sri Lankan Tamils) entered the workforce—or already had been in the workforce but were included from national survey rounds only after the conflict. Because of the scarcity of well-paying jobs in these areas, however, the (mostly impoverished) ethnic minorities inhabiting them must accept low-paying jobs. Women in the labor market there thus face the double burden of being female and belonging to an ethnic minority.

Among the different ethnic groups of women in Sri Lanka, Indian Tamil women tend to fare best in labor market outcomes, except for earnings. Across years (2006–15)[9] and compared with women from all other ethnic groups (including the Sinhalese majority), Indian Tamil women have the greatest odds of participating in the labor force and the best chances of securing a job as a paid employee, according to the multivariate analysis. For securing a job as a paid employee, however, in more recent years Indian Tamil women have not retained the great advantage they had in 2006 and especially 2009, when they were 72 percent more likely than Sinhala women to become a paid employee, and more than twice as likely if they lived in the urban sector. (As of 2015, they were 37 percent more likely than Sinhala women to become a paid employee). Indian Tamil women also are less likely to be unemployed than other women. By contrast, women in Sri Lanka's Moor ethnic group fare the worst in labor markets. They are the least likely to participate, with 23 percentage points lower odds of participation than Sinhala women and nearly 30 percentage points lower odds than Indian Tamil women. (It is interesting to note that Malay women tended to fare almost as badly in LFP as Moor women up until 2013, after which Malay women pulled ahead.) Since 2011, Moor women have been the least likely to find work as paid employees; moreover, they have tended to have the highest rates of unemployment, except in 2015 when Burgher women's unemployment rates surpassed those of all other women (see appendix C, tables C.1–C.12, for full regression results).

Indian Tamil women's high rates of LFP and working as paid employees are not surprising, given that Indian Tamils are predominant in tea and other estates. Unfortunately, their extreme disadvantage in earnings—relative to women from other ethnic groups—also is not surprising, given the poor working conditions in the estate sector. Indian Tamil women earn significantly lower wages than any other group of women, even when considering only those women who live in the estate and rural sectors. This suggests that Indian Tamil women's relative wages have deteriorated in recent years; in 2006 and 2009 their wages were not significantly different from those of other women. That Tamil men also tend to have significantly lower earnings and lower LFP odds than other men (though not the case in 2006 for LFP) underscores the dire situation for estate sector residents in general. These findings are in line with the estate sector's identification as one of Sri Lanka's remaining pockets of poverty (World Bank 2016).

Notes

1. Unemployed male, 28 years old, O-level pass, unmarried—Konthahela village, Badulla district.
2. Unemployed male, 24 years old, unmarried—Henegama village, Gampaha district.
3. Unemployed male, 26 years old, grade 10 pass, married—Henegama village, Gampaha district.
4. Unemployed male, 26 years old, grade 10 pass, married—Henegama village, Gampaha district.
5. The only exception is for urban men in 2015, whose LFP odds had no significant association with being in a female-headed household. For all previous years of LFS data analyzed, urban men's LFP odds were significantly and negatively associated with being in a female-headed household.
6. According to results from the Oaxaca-Blinder decomposition of labor force participation, the overall gap in 2015 is 39 percentage points (that is, the coefficient is 0.390 with $p < 0.01$). The coefficient for the explained portion of the gap is 0.0267 ($p < 0.01$), or 2.67 percentage points. The gender differences in endowments (all variables) thus explain 6.8 percent of the gap, since $(2.67/39) \times 100 = 6.8$.
7. Samples from the three rounds include population age 15 years and older in all districts except those in the Northern and Eastern Provinces, which are excluded to allow for comparability across years.
8. The Oaxaca-Blinder analysis uses LFS data and thus defines ethnicity according to LFS and other surveys used by Sri Lanka's Department of Census and Statistics (see chapter 2, endnote 6, for a discussion of ethnicities in Sri Lanka and their relative shares among the national population).
9. This holds even when omitting from the 2009 and 2015 samples both the Eastern and Northern Provinces, which were the two provinces not represented in the 2006 LFS.

References

Anderson, Siri S. 2018. "Getting to Work Supplement: Inspiring Sri Lanka's Growing Economic Prosperity." Unpublished background paper for this publication. World Bank, Washington, DC.

DCS (Department of Census and Statistics). 2007. *Sri Lanka Labour Force Survey, Final Report 2006.* Colombo: DCS.

———. 2010. *Sri Lanka Labour Force Survey, Annual Report 2009.* Colombo: DCS.

————. 2012. *Sri Lanka Labour Force Survey, Annual Report 2011*. Colombo: DCS.

————. 2014. *Sri Lanka Labour Force Survey, Annual Report 2013*. Colombo: DCS.

————. 2016. *Sri Lanka Labour Force Survey, Annual Report 2015*. Colombo, DCS.

Gunatilaka, Ramani. 2013. "To Work or Not to Work: Factors Holding Women Back from Market Work in Sri Lanka." Working Paper, International Labour Office, ILO DWT for South Asia and Country Office for India, New Delhi.

Gunewardena, Dileni. 2015. "Why Aren't Sri Lankan Women Translating Their Educational Gains into Workforce Advantages?" The 2015 Echidna Global Scholars Working Paper, Center for Universal Education, Brookings Institution, Washington, DC.

Solotaroff, Jennifer. 2013. "Getting in and Staying in: Increasing Women's Labor Force Participation in Sri Lanka." Unpublished, World Bank, Washington, DC.

United Nations, Sri Lanka. 2015. *Mapping of Socio-Economic Support Services to Female Headed Households in the Northern Province of Sri Lanka*. Colombo: United Nations, Sri Lanka.

World Bank. 2015a. *Sri Lanka—Ending Poverty and Promoting Shared Prosperity: A Systematic Country Diagnostic*. Washington, DC: World Bank.

————. 2015b. *Sri Lanka—Poverty and Welfare: Recent Progress and Remaining Challenges*. Washington, DC: World Bank.

————. 2016. "International Bank for Reconstruction and Development, International Development Association, International Finance Corporation, Multilateral Investment Guarantee Agency Country Partnership Framework for the Democratic Socialist Republic of Sri Lanka for the Period FY17–FY20." Report 104606-LK, World Bank, Washington, DC.

————. 2018. *Sri Lanka—Socio-Economic Assessment of the Conflict Affected Northern and Eastern Provinces*. Washington, DC: World Bank.

CHAPTER 4

Conclusion and Way Forward: General Recommendations

This chapter first summarizes findings from the previous chapters, with special attention to groups among Sri Lanka's population that are on the losing end of gender gaps in labor market outcomes. It then draws from primary and secondary sources to present general, cross-cutting recommendations for addressing obstacles to women's labor force participation (LFP), acquisition of higher-skill jobs, and securing higher earnings in Sri Lanka. The primary research—both qualitative and quantitative—involves surveys as well as focus group discussions (FGDs) and other qualitative methods to gather information from household members, employers, and workers in Gampaha, Badulla, and Trincomalee districts. In addition, key informant interviews with more than two dozen Sri Lankan and international experts support suggestions on practical actions that can provide incentives to key industries to employ more women.[1] Women could thus be inclined to choose work aligned with their potential. The primary research is supplemented with a secondary review of the literature on facilitating women's improved participation and employment outcomes in the Sri Lankan economy. General recommendations derived from this research are presented in this chapter. Sector-specific recommendations are presented in chapter 5.

Summary

Gender Differences in Labor Market Outcomes: Aggregate Patterns

Several key factors contribute to women's low LFP and persistent gender wage gaps in Sri Lanka. Among them are prevailing gender roles developed from early childhood that steer girls and women toward primarily domestic identities within the household rather than toward well-remunerated jobs. Social prohibitions against women working after marriage—and especially after the birth of children—remain strong. The lack of childcare services outside the home, together with the structure of the school day and school year in Sri Lanka, reinforces social constraints on mothers' ability to work outside of the home. Commuting to jobs, as well as employment in certain sectors (such as the garment industry), retains a stigma, especially for married women.

As is common elsewhere in the world, Sri Lanka exhibits considerable educational and occupational streaming by gender, resulting in women's low rates of acquiring the skills valued in labor markets and intensifying occupational sex segregation. The human capital mismatch between women's education and training, on the one hand, and skills that employers seek in growth sectors of the economy, on the other, disadvantages women even more now than before the end of the civil war. Although higher education is even more strongly associated with increased chances of female labor force participation (FLFP) than it was a decade ago, it also is associated with a decline in women's acquisition of medium-skill and especially high-skill jobs. In other words, the gender gap in education as an avenue to obtaining higher-skill jobs expanded between 2009 and 2015 to increasingly favor men. Women face the added disadvantage that their perceptions of what employers seek—in soft skills and behavioral characteristics, as well as in technical skills—are quite different from employers' reported expectations.

Men appear to be gaining on the earnings front as well. Although more highly educated women in 2009 enjoyed greater earnings returns to education (compared with men who completed A-levels or attended a university), in 2015 men with university schooling had pulled ahead of university-educated women in their earnings potential. Women's university attendance is associated with a boost in earnings potential of about 50 percent (compared with women with no education), whereas men's university attendance is associated with a 65 percent boost in earnings. This gender gap has flipped in favor of men since 2011, when university education improved earnings for women by more than 65 percent and for men by 50 percent.

Finally, gender bias in labor markets as well as active (statistical) discrimination continues to lower women's odds of LFP as well as their earnings relative to men's. The role of bias in LFP gender gaps is increasing over time, but for gender wage gaps it is slightly declining, especially in the private sector. Primary data confirm the persistent influence of gender-based social norms, beliefs, and behaviors on labor market dynamics, which expands LFP gaps. These norms—which permeate the attitudes and beliefs of employers as well as workers, their families, and their communities—play out in various forms of statistical and institutional discrimination. They constrain employers' views as to who makes a good employee and manager, with the prevailing image of a manager being a man from the ethnic majority. Statistical discrimination on the part of employers not only remains a barrier to the hiring of women; it also combines with institutional bias to undermine women's safety and security in the workplace and on the forms of transportation that get them to work.

Overcoming gender gaps in labor market outcomes will require attention to the following: (1) reducing tradeoffs between women's household and market roles; (2) addressing occupational segregation, particularly through investment in human capital and skills valued by labor markets; and (3) establishing an enabling environment for gender equality in the workplace—particularly in the formal private sector—to help draw women into private sector jobs and away from public sector positions that are increasingly scarce relative to the number of women seeking them.

Gender Differences Disaggregated: Which Groups Are Losing Ground?

Considering changes over time, which particular groups are gaining and which are losing ground in Sri Lanka's labor markets? The study's findings underscore the need to differentiate between women from diverse age, educational, ethnic, regional, and family backgrounds. Disaggregated analysis is imperative so that program and policy responses can be customized to effectively address the different needs of different groups. Men have gained or maintained their advantage over women in all labor market outcomes since the civil war's end—and although most gender gaps in returns to education have narrowed, higher education's continuously increasing boost each year to men's earnings and acquisition of high-skill jobs is the exception.

Urban Women, Poor Women, and Youth Leaving School before A-Levels

Although urban women have seen a slight bump (1 to 2 percentage points) in LFP rates in the past decade, the LFP gender gap remains the greatest in urban areas when considering the polarizing effect of marriage: Getting married is associated with 11 percentage points lower odds of LFP for urban women and 10.3 percentage points higher odds for urban men—a gap of more than 21 percentage points. Urban women also have lost their relative advantage over rural and estate women with regard to household variables: Having young children now is negatively associated with their chances of LFP by the same degree as it is for other women. Moreover, the boost to urban women's LFP chances, which used to be associated with having elderly in the household, has disappeared.

The poorest and least-educated women, regardless of residential status, are falling further behind higher-educated and wealthier women in LFP chances and access to higher-skill, higher-wage jobs, according to the quantitative analysis. School dropouts—including women who have completed only O-levels—need special attention. They require the concerted efforts of general education and technical and vocational education and training (TVET) programs, employers, and their own families to help them succeed in the school-to-work transition. The fact that girls age 15–16 years have the highest unemployment rates in Sri Lanka (according to 2015 Labour Force Survey data) is unprecedented and is cause for great concern—primarily because it signals climbing dropout rates among girls around O-levels (and, it follows, declining rates of high school completion among girls). This worrisome trend may reflect an increasing need among the poorest households for as many family members as possible to generate income, even at the expense of their education, and with the unfortunate outcome that income-generating opportunities are not forthcoming to adolescent girls, despite their participation in the labor force. Another cause for concern is the stubborn, decade-old trend that women who leave school after completing O-levels have significantly lower LFP odds than women of all other levels of education, including women with no schooling at all. O-level-educated women also are significantly less likely than all other women to secure jobs as paid employees. Young men just a couple years older (age 18) who complete their education around grade 12 consistently have the highest unemployment rates and the lowest LFP rates of all men, although as of 2015 uneducated men had the lowest participation rates. These young men, too, need enhanced support in the school-to-work transition.

The need to target women from already-vulnerable groups appears to be increasingly urgent. Women who live in the estate sector, in the most conflict-affected areas in the Northern and Eastern Provinces, and in other "pockets of poverty"[2] in Sri Lanka should be prioritized in decisions about intervention locations, because their positions in labor markets continue to deteriorate. Not only do these locations need a greater presence of financial institutions (ideally, formal financial institutions, as opposed to just microfinance institutions) and TVET providers; the TVET programs themselves also need to be much better aligned with employers' needs regarding skills training, especially in local job markets. TVET programs also need to provide—or be linked to providers of—business development training and English language instruction. On the demand side of labor, these job markets could be developed to better tap into local comparative advantages, such as the availability of arable land and water sources for agriculture and livestock production or nonfarm rural enterprises; proximity to coastal hubs for the creation or expansion of trade routes and connectivity to trade partners in other South Asian countries and beyond; and, in the case of the estate sector, a large pool of women with experience in agricultural production. The economic opportunities for women in rural or otherwise remote regions of Sri Lanka would improve vastly if their virtual or actual mobility were enhanced. The easing of mobility constraints is a key factor in "getting to work" for Sri Lankan women. Providing them with safe, comfortable, and affordable transportation (see chapter 5) to jobs or job training programs would help increase social acceptance of their travel outside the household to access job opportunities. Alternatively, ensuring that women can utilize online tools to sell their products from a distance would facilitate improved livelihoods. A more robust Internet infrastructure across the country, coupled with improved educational outcomes, would advance women's access to tools to move their labor products in a global market.

Women in the Estate Sector

Women in the estate sector, despite having lower unemployment rates and higher LFP rates than other women, have been losing ground in labor force participation: Their LFP rates have declined by nearly 10 percentage points since 2006. They face not only the greatest gender wage gaps across residential areas, but significant hurdles in upward job mobility as well—both toward higher-skill and managerial jobs in estate work, and even more important, in making the transition to more remunerative employment outside the estates. Their growing disadvantage in earnings, compared with other women (and with men in the estate sector), is reflected in the deteriorating state of relative wages for women of the Indian Tamil ethnic group, the majority population in the estates. Some estates have been experimenting with middle-management models that place women in team leader positions over groups of workers, granting these women higher wages and greater decision-making responsibility. Given the ground that tea estates are losing in Sri Lanka's economy, however, interventions will need to offer alternative, sustainable livelihoods to these women. Such interventions could take the form of program responses—for example, expansion of already-successful rural livelihoods projects that organize women into savings groups, producer groups, and trader groups and provide them with skills and business development training—and policy responses, such as the reform of laws and practices around inheritance and ownership of land and other assets. Ownership of land is valuable to women for growing and selling crops and livestock and to use as collateral for loans to create and grow enterprises.

Sri Lankan Moor Women

The strikingly poor labor market outcomes of Sri Lankan Moor women—even when compared with women of other ethnic minorities—can be explained only up to a point by Moors' predominance in the eastern provinces (some of which were sites of armed conflict and thus are places where labor markets may still be recovering). Moor women's low LFP rates and poor odds of working as paid employees might indicate their own preferences (or family and community pressure) to opt out of labor markets—if it were not for their high unemployment rates in rural and estate sectors. Those who actively seek work are hard pressed to obtain it. That this is also the case for Moor men, who have high LFP but high unemployment rates and low odds of wage work, suggests a pattern of Moors' exclusion from labor markets. Oaxaca-Blinder decomposition (see discussion in chapter 3) confirms the increasing degree—in the years since the conflict—to which discrimination explains variations in LFP rates across ethnic groups, along with the obvious determinants related to endowments (or lack thereof), such as poverty and associated low levels of education. To the extent that sociocultural norms restrict Moor women from working outside the homestead, interventions to increase their income-earning possibilities should concentrate on opportunities within the homestead. Such opportunities could include providing microloans and skills training for farming high-value crops on family land, aquaculture in backyard pools, or (in the case of very small loans) the purchase and fattening of livestock for future sale. Information and communication technology (ICT) is another sector that could offer myriad possibilities for in-house paid work (see chapter 5 for details).

Female Household Heads

War widows and female heads of households, many of whom reside in the con-flict-affected Northeast, appear to have become increasingly vulnerable in labor markets since the civil war ended. Their high LFP rates are not translating into sustainable economic opportunities: Although it was not the case in 2009, since 2011 they have become significantly less likely than other women to become paid employees. Moreover, as of 2015, they had significantly lower earnings than all other women, which was not the case in previous years. Targeted, multifac-eted efforts are needed to improve labor market opportunities for women house-hold heads and their family members, who also face growing insecurity in their chances of LFP and obtaining wage employment; men from female-headed households have been experiencing significant drops in both since 2011. Land resettlement policies and practices should ensure that the names of female household heads are on land and other property titles. Livelihood programs should complement women's enhanced land inheritance and ownership with microcredit—or, in the most destitute circumstances, cash grants—and training in financial literacy and business development so that women can use their land for productive, remunerative purposes.

Female Migrant Returnees

Female overseas migrant returnees, like war widows and women heads of house-holds, are members of another target group who would greatly benefit from efforts to enhance the use of microfinance, complementary business develop-ment training, and land-titling reforms to help build women's assets for use as collateral or other economic leverage. A potential employment sector for return-ees—many of whom have worked as domestic servants providing childcare in households abroad—could be the sorely needed, high-quality care economy that has yet to develop in Sri Lanka, as in many South Asian countries: Fewer than one-quarter of children in South Asia benefit from preschool provision (Niethammer 2017). The Sri Lanka Bureau of Foreign Employment's institution of more stringent requirements for women seeking overseas employment in 2013 was meant to protect migrating women by endowing them with advanced skills that would preclude their need to settle for low-skill jobs, such as house-keeping work; however, these policy changes leave a growing population of poor Sri Lankan women in need of in-country alternative livelihoods. It should be noted that many overseas female migrant returnees come from estate back-grounds, meaning that there may be some overlap in these two target groups.

Public Sector Employees

Finally, women working or aiming to work in the public sector also constitute a vulnerable group. Although their earnings tend to be higher than those of women working in the informal private sector—and their maternity leave and other benefits are more assured than those for women in the informal and formal private sectors—women seeking public sector jobs far outnumber the jobs themselves, which contributes to high unemployment rates among well-educated women. Moreover, it is in the public sector that gender wage gaps are most attributable to bias rather than to worker endowments. For the benefit of women and Sri Lanka's macroeconomic growth, policy makers need to improve incentives for women to seek employment in the private formal sector (see the priority areas in the "General Recommendations" section, later in this chapter, for a more detailed discussion of these incentives) and for employers there to hire them. The informal private sector—with its lack of regulation, lack of benefits, and lowest wages among all employment types—is a precarious work environment for women and men alike. Still, until more workers can make their way into formal private sector jobs, the informal private sector will need to be held more accountable for adopting the recommendations discussed below and creating safer work environments for more decent work.

This report gives detail and direction to several policy areas that the government of Sri Lanka is already considering to expand female LFP, such as enhanced skills attainment, greater participation in the private sector, parity between the public and private sectors for maternity leave coverage, provision of childcare through early childhood education programs, and transportation and housing services for female workers. Primary research conducted in Badulla, Gampaha, and Trincomalee districts reveals intervention areas through which constraining factors on women's LFP, acquisition of market-valued skills, and wage gaps can be strategically addressed. Recommended interventions to improve women's labor market outcomes in general can be found below. Detailed recommendations regarding each private sector industry studied in the three districts can be found in chapter 5.

General Recommendations (Cross-Sectoral)

Based on the book's research, this section captures broad interventions to support the expansion of economic opportunities and to improve labor market outcomes for Sri Lankan women. Policy suggestions and other recommended interventions are applicable across industries and sectors. They are categorized thematically under four priority areas below and are summarized in table 4.1 under the three main hypotheses tested for women's poor labor market outcomes: household responsibilities and associated mobility constraints, skills mismatch and occupational segregation, and gender bias in workplaces and labor market dynamics.

PRIORITY AREA ONE: Reduce barriers to women's participation in paid work, particularly the lack of childcare services and the sociophysical constraints on women's mobility

Removing the obstacles that prevent women's participation—most notably their cultural, social, economic, and practical needs to take care of children—is an accessible target. Support in this area requires shifting a portion of childcare and elder care responsibilities away from women who seek outside work, ensuring women's safe travel to and from places of work, promoting more

Table 4.1 Summary of Recommended Interventions (Cross-Sectoral)

Key constraints	Range of interventions
Reduce tradeoffs between women's household and labor market roles	Childcare burden	*Childcare*
		• Ensure provision of accessible, high-quality, and affordable childcare (at the workplace; in community)
		• Improve social acceptance of paid childcare, for example, through media campaigns and awareness raising about the benefits of childcare
		• Promote part-time work to encourage workforce participation of mothers with young children
		• Reconsider the school day and school year schedule to better enable women with school-age children the opportunity to work
	Social constraints on female mobility and financial inclusion	*Transportation, housing, and finance (with a focus on the private sector)*
		• Offer safe and affordable transportation for women
		• Provide housing for female workers at or near their workplaces
		• Offer business development and financial services for self-employment and small enterprises run by women, especially in rural areas
		• Provide tax benefits to families with both parents employed at least half time
	Parents' and educators' roles in girls' educational and occupational choices	*Life planning and identity formation campaigns*
		• Conduct community campaigns and outreach in schools that target parents and teachers with TVET information about career benefits and salary ranges for particular careers; customize approaches to communities with lower female labor force participation rates (such as certain ethnic minority groups)
		• Continue improving the efficacy of public school teachers and make remuneration sufficient to draw talented educators to public education

table continues next page

Table 4.1 Summary of Recommended Interventions (Cross-Sectoral) *(continued)*

	Key constraints	Range of interventions
Invest in human capital and skills to address occupational segregation	Educational and occupational streaming by gender	*Improved jobs orientation in school and community settings* • Provide mentoring and peer group support for female students, particularly in STEM and business-related subjects, and compulsory computer science education for all secondary school students • Expand industry-linked internships and school-based business incubator programs • Support career counseling and placement function of high schools and universities, using trained counselors
	Low participation by women in employer-informed vocational training	*Technical and vocational education and training (TVET)* • Provide scholarships for girls to attend TVET in nontraditional fields • Coordinate with the private sector on training and job placement • Expand NVQ-accredited TVET providers in lagging regions, especially private sector providers • Ensure public-private coordination with industry in designing new TVET courses and outreach policy, focused on women's employment
	Information barriers in matching jobs and workers	*Job matching* • Offer job information services through local government, one-stop job centers, and a national communication channel offering information and resources in support of women's labor force participation, networking, and understanding of their rights and opportunities in the workforce

table continues next page

Table 4.1 Summary of Recommended Interventions (Cross-Sectoral) *(continued)*

	Key constraints	Range of interventions
Establish an enabling environment for gender equality in workplaces	Legal discrimination	*Antidiscrimination legislation* • Amend legislation that restricts women's rights to work[a] • Implement a zero-tolerance policy toward sexual harassment in the workplace and involve men in advocacy campaigns • Support maternity leave and parity for public and private sector guarantees
	Employer bias against hiring and promoting female workers	*Affirmative action in hiring and procurement* • Encourage colleges and TVET institutes to conduct outreach to employers about skilled female graduates • Ensure preferential government procurement from female-owned firms • Encourage firms' diversity goals (e.g., through tax incentives) to remedy the underrepresentation of women and ethnic minorities in the workplace
	Poor workplace facilities and conditions	*Labor monitoring* • Enforce safety regulations, including measures to mitigate sexual harassment, and workplace monitoring by the Labor Department • Encourage gender certification and ethical branding for firms

Note: NVQ = National Vocational Qualification; TVET = technical and vocational education and training.

a. As examples, "protective" legislation currently limits the number of night shifts per month and puts constraints on overseas work by mothers of small children.

home-based income-generating opportunities for women, and in the longer term, helping change attitudes toward women working outside the household, especially after marriage. Creating a more consistent school year and lengthening the school day (or at least linking schools to after-school childcare services) would provide women of school-age children much more opportunity to seek at least part-time employment and could be used to benefit children in areas identified as particularly relevant for the evolving needs of the Sri Lankan workforce. This should be complemented with continuing efforts to improve the public education system and teacher efficacy. Priority Area One might comprise the following interventions:

- Legislate or enforce policies that support family-friendly workforce practices, including opportunities for women to access part-time work, maternity leave, and tax incentives for full-time work.
- Expand opportunities for women to generate income in their homes—especially in rural areas—by providing some combination of technical and vocational training, financial literacy and business development training, access to credit or other financial assistance, and links to markets.
- Expand the care economy through (1) public-private partnerships that support a quality-focused accredited childcare system; (2) on-site day care at workplaces (some ICT companies based in Colombo already have incorporated day-care centers for workers' young children, with promising results; moreover, two recent reports [IFC 2017, 2018] present a compelling business case, supported by extensive cross-country research and case studies from Sri Lanka, for childcare that is supported by employers); and (3) more localized provision of care services that absorb women returning from employment abroad as domestic workers.
- Improve access to childcare services through short-term measures (for example, using Sri Lanka's expanding program of early childhood development centers, which can provide childcare without the stigma associated with pure childcare facilities) and long-term campaigns to remove the stigma (that is, expanding the market for, and acceptability of, childcare services through, for example, media tie-ins to promote images of working women and children in day care).
- If it is not possible to provide widespread access to childcare facilities, consider educational policy changes to extend the school day or change the structure of the school year so that women are not compelled to prioritize their own provision of childcare before employment opportunities for the entire time their children are in school; and make schools appropriate and consistent spaces for high-quality care (perhaps through public-private partnerships) and education of Sri Lankan children throughout the year.
- Improve public transportation safety for women, including through partnerships with private sector employers, to encourage firm- or industry-specific transportation for female workers.

- Expand the housing stock for firms' female workers (through the provision of firm incentives), as well as housing that is leased at affordable rates in the vicinity of worksites for female internal migrant workers and other working women.

PRIORITY AREA TWO: Strengthen girls' early orientation to career development and to acquiring the types of education and skills that prepare them for labor markets

One of the most effective ways to improve the social acceptance of women's employment (especially outside the home) and better align student outcomes with workforce needs is to start early in the life cycle and reinforce messages at each stage of girls' education and development. Related interventions could include the following:

- Provide support for girls' career identification and development—in the early years at home and in the community—through community campaigns and outreach to parents and teachers regarding girls' skills acquisition and employ-ment; tailor campaigns for communities with especially low FLFP rates, such as among certain ethnic minority groups.
- Incorporate in campaigns an emphasis on nontraditional fields for girls and women—with particular attention to science, technology, engineering, and mathematics (STEM) courses and a special emphasis on digital literacy and computer science—in the general education system; raise awareness about the benefits of TVET courses that build skills valued in the growth sectors of Sri Lanka's economy; and include information about career benefits and salary ranges for STEM-based careers in growth sectors.
- Provide in-school mentoring of girls and young women in general education (well before O-levels, to help mitigate dropout rates at around grade 10), higher education, and TVET programs to help them identify and refine their knowl-edge of career paths in the private sector. An affordable intervention could include creating and mandating the use of career information pamphlets each year across grades 6–10 showing existing employment opportunities as well as related pay, benefits, typical hours, and growth potential (Anderson 2018).
- Link adolescent girls and young women to successful adult women role mod-els in desired careers (particularly in the private sector) who can provide examples of balancing work with marriage and raising children—either in per-son or virtually.

PRIORITY AREA THREE: (1) Improve the jobs orientation of education and skills providers, and (2) expand the provision of job-matching services and TVET that target women and respond to employers' needs

Improving the jobs focus and the provision of vocational training and employment services in educational and community settings would help reduce educational and occupational streaming by gender. Such efforts would also bolster the general rec-ommendation to expand active labor market policies in Sri Lanka that focus on women through skills development as well as the enhancement of job information services and job matching. For both male and female job seekers—and for Sri Lanka's economy as a whole—it is critical to improve communication and coordination among (i) private sector employers, (ii) government ministries that oversee education and employment, and (iii) TVET providers and general education institutions regarding which skills are most needed and valued by labor markets. Specific interventions to support women in labor markets could include the following:

- Provide mentoring and peer group support for female students, particularly in STEM and business-related subjects.
- Expand industry-linked internships and scholarships and school-based business incubator and exposure programs for female students at the secondary level.
- Improve the jobs orientation of educational institutions and curricula, including improving teacher efficacy in key areas needed for economic growth, such as English language fluency and STEM content knowledge and skills. The government may make computational literacy education mandatory for girls and boys beginning in middle school, given that this would ensure that all youth in Sri Lanka acquire these marketable skills (Anderson 2018).
- Update pedagogical practices and teacher capacity so that both are aligned with the realities of work in the age of information, international communication, and ICT in order to enable higher levels of personal agency among graduates.
- Provide TVET and STEM teacher mentoring in gender-equitable teaching strategies and pedagogies that shift away from lecture formats toward student-centered learning.
- Enhance job information and job placement services in school and community settings, with an increased emphasis on job centers in rural areas, and support the career counseling and placement function of high schools and universities, using trained counselors.
- Expand TVET programs and strengthen the National Vocational Qualification (NVQ) system, with island-wide accreditation of providers, including private sector providers (the government's efforts to expand the NVQ system and link to rural-based providers should ease some of the constraints experienced by rural women in accessing TVET).
- Ensure the presence of accommodation facilities for girls and women at vocational and technical training colleges and other TVET providers.
- Develop a national communication channel conveying information and resources that support women's LFP and networking, such as male and female role models that demonstrate success in achieving work-life balance; information on available training and resources for women's entrepreneurial and employment advancement; campaign updates on private and public agency accountability around family-friendly, gender-equitable policies; general education on the effective use of technology; and resources for computer science learning opportunities (Anderson 2018).

- Provide one-stop-shop job centers that coordinate job vacancy and TVET information and training services, while providing post-training assistance, such as peer group counseling for adult job seekers.
- Strengthen the relevant skill sets of women who are interested in obtaining high-skill, highly paid foreign employment by providing language skills and scholarships along with skills training.

PRIORITY AREA FOUR: (1) Ensure gender equity in labor legislation and nondiscriminatory workplace environments, and (2) undertake affirmative action and ethical branding initiatives to expand women's share of employment and firm ownership in emerging sectors

Improving women's LFP and employment in Sri Lanka also requires an enhanced review and enforcement of labor laws, antiharassment measures, and maternity leave—especially leave provisions in the private sector. Recommended activities include the following:

- Review labor laws for clauses that restrict women's rights to paid employment and consider amending them.
- Expand the application of maternity leave legislation to include enforcement in the private sector.
- Enhance safety regulation and labor monitoring audits of the workplace and sector-specific approaches, such as the promotion of child-safe tourism, and incorporate mechanisms for women to report crimes.
- Implement a zero-tolerance policy toward sexual harassment and other gender-based violence in the workplace and include male community leaders in public campaigns and advocacy for ending practices that objectify or intimidate women.
- Reward companies and programs that enforce gender-equitable hiring and workforce practices.
- Develop messaging around the proven high return on investment from a diverse work environment and workforce. This could include encouraging TVET institutes and colleges to reach out to employers about skilled female graduates, and encouraging companies to set diversity goals to address the underrepresentation of women and minorities in the workplace (Anderson 2018).

Direct support for women's expanded employment and firm ownership in emerging sectors could include the following areas:

- Provide subsidies and tax incentives to firms that support women's employment (for example, firms that hire and retain new female graduates or that participate in vocational training programs for women).
- Institute preferential government procurement for goods and services offered by women-owned firms or those with female-majority management.

- Establish public-private partnerships that contribute to verified certification and the ethical branding of firms as gender responsive, including creating safe and rewarding environments in which women can be employed.
- Improve business development and financial services for women's enterprises.

Notes

1. Findings from the key informant interviews with more than two dozen experts, conducted in 2018, are presented in the background paper developed for this book (Anderson 2018). Details on the book's primary qualitative and quantitative research can be found in appendixes B and E.

2. The Sri Lanka Systematic Country Diagnostic (World Bank 2015) cites pockets of high poverty rates in Monaragala district, the estate sector, and the north and east of Sri Lanka.

References

Anderson, Siri S. 2018. "Getting to Work Supplement: Inspiring Sri Lanka's Growing Economic Prosperity." Unpublished background paper for the current book. World Bank, Washington, DC.

IFC (International Finance Corporation). 2017. *Tackling Childcare: The Business Case for Employer-Supported Child Care*. Washington, DC: IFC.

IFC (International Finance Corporation), and UNICEF Sri Lanka. 2018. *Tackling Childcare: The Business Case for Employer-Supported Child Care in Sri Lanka*. Washington, DC: IFC. https://www.ifc.org/wps/wcm/connect/a0120dd6-f15c-405f -9bdf-e6a1ef6a4bc5/Report.pdf?MOD=AJPERES.

Niethammer, Carmen. 2017. "The Business Case for Tackling Childcare: Good for Employees and Employers, Good for Sri Lanka." *Financial Times*, Sri Lanka. October 3. http://www.ft.lk/columns/The-business-case-for-tackling-childcare--good-for -employees -and-employers--good-for-Sri-Lanka/4-640772.

World Bank. 2015. *Sri Lanka—Ending Poverty and Promoting Shared Prosperity: A Systematic Country Diagnostic*. Washington, DC: World Bank.

CHAPTER 5

Findings and Recommended Good Practices for Five Private Sector Industries

This chapter focuses on five private sector industries that were strongly represented in the three districts where primary data were collected. These five industries are regarded as a mix of emerging and traditional drivers of the economy: information and communication technology (ICT), tea estates, tourism, the garment sector, and commercial agriculture. The following discussion summarizes basic information about women's involvement in these industries—as well as barriers to their entry—and then offers recommendations and good practice examples to increase this involvement. Many of these recommendations can be applied to other industries, with the overall intent of achieving much greater participation by women in Sri Lanka's private sector. Common across the industry recommendations is the need to focus on women's safety in transportation, which is a crucial factor in raising female labor force participation (FLFP) rates and actually "getting women to work."

Information and Communication Technology

A fast-growing and relatively new industry in Sri Lanka, ICT has not yet been fully gender typed as "men's work" and thus, compared with other industries, may have potentially lower barriers to entry for skilled women. With higher education institutions consistently providing less than half the number of ICT graduates needed in the industry, information technology (IT) companies face the challenge of finding suitably trained professionals to fill vacancies (LIRNEasia 2006; Senewiratne 2011, quoted in Morgan 2012).

Unfortunately, women's entry into the sector is restricted by the narrow range of study and training courses considered to be gender appropriate, perceptions of parents and employers (as discussed earlier in this report), and limited English language skills (Jayaweera et al. 2007; Anderson 2018). Labour Force Survey data confirm this pattern: Women working in ICT are already becoming locked into jobs associated with lower-skill and lower-paying "women's work"; these jobs also generally lack decision-making authority. In 2009 and 2015, men outnumbered women in nearly all ICT occupations, with the greatest gender gaps occurring among science and engineering professionals and technicians. Women employed in the sector largely choose (or are slotted into) customer-facing positions that require limited technical skills (Anderson 2018). Although some of these women are in lower-skilled jobs because of their limited technical education, the majority occupy lower-level positions than their male counterparts, despite comparable education and skills attainment (Morgan 2012). The presumed value addition occurring within the industry is concentrated at occupational tiers within which women are not represented. Consequently, studies have found gender differences across all salary bands among ICT professionals in Sri Lanka, with a larger percentage of women than men in the lower pay bands (Jayaweera and Wanasundera 2006, quoted in Jayaweera et al. 2007; Gamage 2004, quoted in Morgan 2012). Women are also starkly absent in ICT decision-making structures, including boards, senior management levels of private firms, and ministries responsible for ICT policy and regulatory institutions (DCS 2016; Jayaweera and Wanasundera 2006).

The workflow of the software industry, which is designed in Sri Lanka to involve long hours of work, makes it especially hard for women with young children to seek or retain employment in the sector (Anderson 2018). Earlier studies have also identified that ICT employers prefer male applicants because they are reluctant to invest in "extra facilities" for women employees to accommodate the social norms around caretaking, mobility constraints, and the like (Morgan 2012; Ranasinghe 2004). One young woman from Gampaha in the ICT study site stated, "Women who are mothers of small children face a difficult situation in having to choose between employment and caring for their child. Often home responsibilities take precedence."[1] These trends in the ICT industry, which are a cause for concern, reflect barriers to women's entry and promotion, but these barriers could be reversed by taking a number of simultaneous actions. Recommended intervention areas include the following:

- *Create an enabling policy environment for increasing women's participation in ICT.* It is important that the government of Sri Lanka and IT companies acknowledge the lower share of women in the sector and encourage the development of a formal strategy for actively recruiting women. Collection of gender-disaggregated data should be required for planning and policy-making processes, and attention to gender equity should be increased throughout all national programs and projects that seek to promote the use of IT. Measures could be put in place to ensure adequate representation of women in decision-making bodies tasked with developing IT policy and strategy. Organizations with a good understanding of the opportunities, needs, and constraints experienced by women in the sector, as well as private sector stakeholders, should be involved in policy and strategy formulation, implementation, monitoring, and evaluation.

- *Make hiring criteria for ICT employment clear and transparent.* Government and industry leaders need to work together to determine and publicize objective hiring and advancement standards (namely, education, skills, and experience) to ensure that deserving female applicants and employees are not overlooked in employment and promotion opportunities. Making ICT employers accountable for gender-neutral hiring standards will help minimize gender discrimination.

- *Introduce, formalize, and publicize worker benefits and amenities that support women.* Such benefits and amenities include on-site childcare, sex-segregated washroom facilities, maternity leave (which may not be enforced in private sector firms, particularly informal ones), and flexible, part-time work options. The lack of a gender-focused policy among ICT employers increases their reliance on informal or piecemeal mechanisms that may not be sufficient to transform male-biased employment dynamics. FLFP in the industry would likely increase were ICT employers to introduce set schedules (as opposed to the current norm of fluctuating shift work), on-site childcare (which, according to research, contributes to reduced rates of sick leave, absenteeism, and turnover among employees [IFC 2017]), and flexible work hours, which would give women the option of working when children are at school—on a part-time basis—or in the evenings, as long as safe transportation to and from the work site is ensured. These interventions would allow women who want to work to plan their employment around their domestic and other responsibilities.

- *Increase female enrollment in ICT education by integrating a K-12 curriculum that makes digital and computational literacies as fundamental to education as reading, writing, and math.* Sri Lanka has the advantage of a ready platform to make computational literacy universal through its national curriculum, which is available to all students. Introducing computer science education as a compulsory subject in secondary school, or even earlier, would help make the subject more gender neutral and may be the fastest route to ensuring that girls, as well as boys, are acquiring these important technical skills for their futures. This could be coupled with professional development for all teachers to shift focus from simply delivering content to facilitating critical thinking and learning among students (Anderson 2018). A school-wide curriculum in ICT is a measure that a range of governments—including in India and several European and South American countries—have either considered instituting or have fully instituted to address pipeline shortages of employees adequately equipped with skills required in varied ICT sectors (Reddy 2015; Yadav, Hong, and Stephenson 2016; Grover and Pea 2013).

- *Promote the scaling up of science, technology, engineering, and math (STEM) to girls.* Providing STEM mentoring and peer support would also encourage girls to pursue careers in ICT over traditional "female" occupational streams. A critical companion to school-based ICT-awareness campaigns would be widespread efforts to discard the gendered presentation of roles, duties, and employment as female or male. Students should learn about all existing options in the job market and be encouraged by teachers, school administrators, and educational policies to pursue further studies and choose careers according to their interests and abilities and to labor market demand. Students in computer programming courses could be asked to create applications that facilitate improved community outcomes and their participation encouraged through programs such as Technovations, which equip girls with the skills they need to emerge as tech entrepreneurs and leaders. For instance, an app that allows a woman to anonymously report a sexual assault or harassment could quickly provide aggregated data about locations that need additional oversight and protection. Vocational training programs and universities, in particular, will need to improve their marketing of ICT-related courses to female trainees and students. Marketing such courses as spaces where learners collaborate to create solutions to existing community problems (rather than as places to learn a particular programming language or database processing skills) will attract more female students (Anderson 2018). Short of taking this measure, governments have less costly options as well. Female-targeted awareness-raising campaigns could be embedded at the basic education level.

- *Expand industry-linked internships and school-based business incubator and exposure programs for female students at the secondary school level.* After-school and extracurricular activities can enhance girls' familiarity with skills development and jobs.[2] Expanding internships and work experience opportunities for secondary students also can deepen students' on-the-job experience, clarify career goals, and make graduates more attractive to future employers in ICT and other growth industries. This effort could include attention to a range of technical opportunities and exposure to the government's "sectors of focus," such as tourism and construction.[3]

- *Provide career counseling and job market information in higher education.* A number of school-based interventions can be provided to promote increased FLFP in ICT, including internship placements with ICT employers and mentoring relationships with higher-skilled workers and managers (especially female ones). Mentoring and peer group support for girls in STEM areas as well as in business can reduce gender streaming in education and occupational choice, so that women increasingly pursue traditional "male" careers such as engineering, ICT, and business.[4] At the university level, Sri Lanka has experimented with supporting arts graduates in setting up their own business enterprises as entrepreneurs—and helping students plan for related coursework—while they are still enrolled. Success rates (including the persistence of new firms over time) should be evaluated, and, if warranted, the intervention should be replicated, particularly for students with an O-level or A-level education. Schools can consider partnerships with nongovernmental organizations or private sector technical and vocational education and training (TVET) providers to increase career exposure for youth (especially young women and school leavers) to expose them to a wider range of employment opportunities in a number of sectors. Such enhanced recruitment and retention of female technology professionals in ICT would help the sector reach its growth targets (GoSL 2012).

- *Encourage employers to establish special on-the-job training and mentoring opportunities for female ICT workers, and enable some work teams that are all or primarily female to rise into leadership roles.* Formalized leadership and technical training, as well as mentorship programs with managers (especially female ones), can encourage female ICT employees to stay in the industry and seek advancement while providing them with clearer paths to vertical mobility. This approach is especially important given evidence of employers "guiding" women into particular job roles on the "softer" side of computing— such as technical writing, quality assurance, and training—even when those women express an interest in working in more technical areas such as programming (Morgan 2012). Such factors also contribute to wage differences between men and women in ICT industries. Increasing women's access to training in more technical aspects of ICT work can help remedy female employees' overwhelming presence in low-skill jobs and low pay bands (Ranasinghe 2004).

- *Identify role models, also known as "deviant case studies," in IT sector jobs.* Given gender norms in Sri Lanka around appropriate male and female adult roles, students in secondary school and their parents would benefit from access to female role models from nontraditional postsecondary fields (Anderson 2018). The power of role models to influence girls' choice of postsecondary study or employment has been well documented across many cultural and national contexts (Holmes et al. 2012; Liston, Peterson, and Ragan 2008; Lyon and Jafri 2010). Thus, interventions targeting children and early adolescents are more likely to be successful over the long term; compared with adults, youth can more easily change their conceptual formations and shape their personal identities around STEM "roles" (Diekman, Weisgram, and Belanger 2015). To be effective, these role models should be relatively young, of the same ethnicity as the students, and personable to learners. Key informants interviewed suggested creating a database of Sri Lankan role models who could share their personal interests, activities, and job successes as well as challenges (in person or virtually) as a useful and cost-effective intervention to encourage students. Several centralized databases have been created for similar purposes and can be used as templates, such as FabFems, SheWorks UK, Techsploration, SciGirls Role Models, Women in STEM, and Women at Google.

- *Ensure Internet access or affordable access to data via phones in schools around the country.* Teachers cannot evolve their instructional practices around available online curriculum materials if they cannot consistently access the Internet (Anderson 2018). In addition to improvements in road infrastructure, prioritize high-speed access to the Internet in school settings by rewarding companies that facilitate those connections. Facilitate partnerships between private companies and schools to get affordable computing hardware into school settings.

- *Encourage education and vocational training institutions to invite input from ICT employers when developing education and training curricula and improve the instructional efficacy of educators by enabling a conducive learning environment.* Proactive involvement of ICT sector representatives in designing computer science curricula can equip young women and men with a better sense of both the technical and soft skills sought by employers and help prepare students for working in the often-coeducational environment of the ICT workplace. To effectively reach girls and other populations marginalized from success in hard sciences and computer science, teachers can be taught to use curricula and pedagogical strategies proven to make the content accessible and of interest to girls, also known as gender-equitable teaching strategies (TPT 2013; MacLain et al. 2018; Klawe 2014). For instance, according to Diekman, Weisgram, and Belanger (2015), teachers integrating computational thinking into their curricula benefit from understanding the communal orientation of girls and young women and fostering either a "helping" or "collaborative" learning experience. Thus, critical to the possibility of offering inclusive computer science education in schools is the ability of teachers to also gain the knowledge and skills necessary to deliver computer science curricula in ways that are meaningful and relevant to diverse students (Ryoo, Goode, and Margolis 2016). An examination of privilege, identity, interests, and access are themes among successful ICT programs for women and girls and other marginalized learners (DeJaeghere and Wiger 2013; Ryoo, Goode, and Margolis 2016; Stout and Tamer 2016; Margolis and Fisher 2002). According to key informants interviewed, exploring what women actually value and find relevant to their interests is especially pertinent in Sri Lanka, where wounds from the 30-year civil conflict are still raw (Anderson 2018).

Tea Estates

Although women in the tea estates have higher odds of working than women elsewhere, the poor quality of their working conditions, low wages, and declining interest in this work among the younger generation signal the need for intervention either to improve their working conditions or to provide them with alternative livelihoods outside of estate work. In collaboration with the United Nations Development Programme, the Ministry of Hill Country New Villages, Infrastructure and Community Development has developed a "Ten Year National Plan of Action for the Social Development of the Plantation Community 2016–2025" (GoSL and UNDP 2015). The document presents a comprehensive strategy for improving working conditions and living standards for women and men in Sri Lanka's estate community. With its prioritization of development interventions and detailed action plans that address successive life-cycle stages starting with early childhood development, the plan has little need for improvement. This discussion shares a few observations from the qualitative field research that are relevant to improvements in women's work and living conditions in the sector—particularly those observations concerning the quality of their work, wages, and opportunities for advancement.

The qualitative research finds that women in the estate sector tend to hold more nuanced views than other women (and men) regarding the social desirability of women's labor force participation. Respondents point out that women have no choice but to enter the workforce because men on the estates cannot be relied upon to earn for the household. Although the social ideal that women should not work still holds in the estate sector, it may not be adhered to because of economic necessity. Recommended intervention areas include the following:

- *Build upon the strong presence of women in the plantation estate sector to obtain "quick wins" through the promotion of women into management positions through the use of role models.* The fact that social biases against women's work have broken down is a solid starting point for improving labor market outcomes for women in the estate sector, as is the sector's tendency to offer more flexible working conditions than most other sectors. Tea sector employers' reported plans to increase the number of female workers could serve as an effective entry point for advancing better terms of employment for women. Regular jobs in the tea sector, of all sectors studied, also offer the highest number of employer-provided benefits (such as maternity leave and childcare) and facilities (dedicated transportation and separate toilets) for women.

- *Adopt new practices that promote women's technical training and access to higher-skill work, group leader positions, and middle- to upper-level management jobs that are associated with greater pay and enhanced decision-making responsibilities.* Where the tea estates fail women at work is in the types of jobs to which most are confined: low skill and low pay, with little to no decision-making responsibility and scarce opportunities for advancement. The primary fieldwork suggests that women's representation in management is lowest in the tea sector (3 percent) among all sectors studied. The "Ten Year National Plan of Action for the Social Development of the Plantation Community 2016–2025" covers these issues, recognizing that women need to be better represented at all levels of decision-making authority (GoSL and UNDP 2015). The high penetration of cell phones in estate communities is a promising avenue for improving access to distance learning and education and helping to develop the skills and capacity of the existing workforce (Anderson 2018). This upgrading of technical skills is also aligned with the government's objective of modernizing and improving the efficiency, competitiveness, profitability, employment creation, and social, economic, and environmental sustainability of the tea plantation estate sector.

• *Increase awareness of sexual and gender-based violence (SGBV) redress mechanisms and improve the ability of these mechanisms to respond to women workers in the estate sector.* Collaborative efforts between the National Committee on Women, the Sri Lankan police, and nongovernmental organizations have made substantial progress in developing programs to address and respond to SGBV in Sri Lanka, including engaging men and boys in prevention campaigns as well as providing timely response, referral, and legal assistance through 24-hour helplines. As acknowledged in the "2016–2020 Policy Framework and National Plan of Action to Address Sexual and Gender-Based Violence in Sri Lanka," expanding the outreach of these ongoing initiatives and increasing awareness of response services will be key to the well-being of estate sector workers, who experience relatively higher rates of SGBV compared with national averages (according to the 10-year plan for the plantation community) (GoSL and UNDP 2016). Labor unions' focus on improving work conditions and living wages, and more recently on the maternity needs of estate labor, could be expanded to highlight issues of SGBV and mobilize support for instituting robust redress systems (Anderson 2018).

• *Encourage women living in tea estates to pursue work outside the estate.* These women may prefer to work in the tea sector, combine this work with other employment outside the estate, or not be engaged in paid employment at all, according to the primary research. The estates function as self-contained social enclaves in many ways, and residents view the estates as their home, even if they migrate out for work (see also Gunetileke, Kuruppu, and Goonasekera 2008). Tensions arise, however, in the social stigma that estate residents face; and, according to the focus group discussions, many young residents avoid estate work because they fear such experience will prejudice their chances of employment outside the estate. Residents are increasingly seeking non-estate opportunities, including in small-scale horticulture and wage employment. In particular, women from the estates need support for livelihoods diversification. Such support could include approaches used by successful rural livelihoods programs that (1) organize women into savings groups, producer groups, and trade groups for the marketing and sale of horticulture or other products (such as the World Bank–supported rural livelihoods projects across South Asia that have so successfully helped women collectively save and use funds); and (2) provide them with technical and business-development skills training—especially if these women have access to credit programs. Ideally, programmatic interventions would be accompanied by policy interventions that improve women's ability to inherit, own, purchase, rent out, and sell land, or use it to generate income in other ways.

Tourism

The tourism industry's rapid expansion in recent years has made it the third-largest earner of foreign exchange in Sri Lanka. This growth is projected to continue: It is estimated that by 2020 the sector will add more than 600,000 new jobs through direct and indirect employment (Abeywardana and Priyadarshani 2017). Despite the high demand for workers, shortages exist at both the top and bottom ends of the sector: Highly trained, technically proficient, and multilingual workers are needed to develop and manage the institutions that will make tourism possible, just as waiters, housekeeping, and groundskeepers are needed to run everyday operations (Gunatilaka et al. 2017). Unlike the tea estate sector, however, where representation of women is higher than the average share of women in the employed population, the share of female employees is much lower than average in the tourism industry. The position of tourism as a promising growth sector in the Sri Lankan economy makes it an important space in which to investigate and overcome challenges to women's labor force participation.

Key informant interviews reveal some of the obstacles to women's employment in the sector: poor English speaking and listening skills, as well as an underdeveloped understanding of the wide variety of careers and opportunities available across the industry (Anderson 2018). Primary among the constraints identified is the perceived—and real—vulnerability of tourism to potential labor abuses and criminal activity, including the sexual abuse and trafficking of women and children. The survey results in the primary research confirm this finding: Women themselves, as well as their parents and husbands, fear for their safety in tourism, which tends to inhibit them from considering this sector for work opportunities. Among the employers interviewed for the primary research, those from the tourism sector (85 percent) are most likely to identify marriage as the reason for women's exit from the workforce. The industry will need to provide greater incentives to potential female employees to help overcome risks to safety and the associated stigma and to help women balance work and household responsibilities, for example, by providing on-site activities for their employees' children during school holidays.

Stigmatization of tourism jobs for women may be one factor in the notable lack of female trainees in related job skills programs, where such programs exist. Another factor is the lack of such programs in the country. In Trincomalee district, focus group discussion participants note that, despite demand from the tourism sector for workers, there is a dearth of local skilled workers because of higher school dropout rates and an accompanying lack of TVET options for the local populace. These spatial disparities in TVET service provision particularly affect women, who are less likely than men to enroll in and travel to programs located far from home—either because they are relatively time poor and cash poor or because of safety concerns and the social stigma associated with young women traveling long distances. According to a young female member of the focus group in Trincomalee, "Most of the big establishments, like tourist hotels, have been set up by outsiders, who [bring] skilled workers from outside. Because training facilities are not available locally in Trincomalee, those who wish to acquire skills have to go to Colombo, which costs a lot of money."[5]

Despite high social barriers to women's participation in the tourism industry—many of which appear to emanate from the labor supply side—the sector has relatively low demand-side barriers to entry (at least in the unskilled and semiskilled job tiers) and to the promotion of women. In fact, more than any of the other four sectors studied, the tourism industry is seeking a greater share of women as employees and is willing to make efforts to accommodate them. First, among all employers surveyed for this study's primary research, tourism sector employers are most likely to report that women are better and more reliable workers than men. Second, among all five sectors, tourism has the highest representation of women in management (31 percent). Third, the tourism sector is more likely to offer maternity leave (74 percent) and separate toilet facilities for women (91 percent), compared with other sectors on which respondents reported. Fourth, tourism employers are the most willing to make contributions for childcare: Tourism employers contribute 39 percent of costs, compared with employers in other sectors studied, where average contributions tend to be 10 percent or less. Tourism industry leaders, as well as policy makers and practitioners, need to take advantage of employers' relatively strong, positive attitude toward employing women by tackling supply-side constraints on female participation in the sector and by scaling up the attractive attributes of the demand side. Recommended intervention areas include the following:

• *Address supply-side labor constraints caused by stigma and fear of the tourism industry as a potential employer for women, and publicize these improvements.* Ensuring greater safety in tourism industry workplaces would require collective and sustained engagement between hotels, catering operations, and tourism enterprises and their owners to agree on the uniform application of equal opportunity policies and practices (Baum 2013). Firms within the sector's supply chain, whether large hotels or small handicrafts industry suppliers, should be required to adopt a zero-tolerance policy against child labor, sexual harassment, and other forms of SGBV. Implementing such measures would include required gender-sensitivity training for all employees and management. Similar training for banking sector employees in Pakistan—through the International Finance Corporation's Banking on Women program—has shown measurable improvements in the attitudes and behaviors of men and women working together (Hamm et al. 2017). Industry leaders also need to work with law enforcement and the legal sector to strengthen safeguards for women employed in the sector (UN Women 2011). Such legal protections would include the establishment and enforcement of laws pertaining to minimum wages, maximum work hours, and equal pay for equal work, as well as safe working conditions (Kamal and Woodbury 2016; UN Women 2011). Once these protections are in place, leaders also should work with the concerned government agencies and private sector media to increase public knowledge of these improvements and to promote a positive image of women in the tourism industry. These steps could be coupled with messages to enhance awareness of women's important economic role in the tourism sector (UN Women 2011). Awareness-raising campaigns using radio and television, social media, and even community-based, in-person transactions can be quite effective in reaching large populations and changing their perceptions.

- *Engage women in identifying concerns about working in the tourism industry and finding solutions to those concerns.* A central finding of this book is that the lack of perceived or actual "dignity" in tourism industry labor, along with threats to the safety of women and youth, are formidable obstacles to both recruitment and retention of employees. Involving women workers and potential workers in unpacking these safety and respect issues in specific settings and seeking their feedback for redress would help mitigate areas of concern and instill greater confidence in the sector as a suitable employer for women. Opportunities for existing employees to voice and share their apprehensions should be numerous and without sanction. These opportunities can be provided by well-functioning workplace grievance redress mechanisms that are publicized so that women know where and how to report discrimination or harassment (Kamal and Woodbury 2016).

- *Recognize and meet the transportation needs of women.* Law enforcement should be included when addressing another fear of the tourism sector for women: the distances required to travel to the industry's worksites, especially on public transportation. Some 90 percent of women and girls in Sri Lanka experience sexual harassment while using public transportation (UNFPA 2017). Perera, Gunawardane, and Jayasuriya (2011), in their review of evidence on SGBV in Sri Lanka, find that sexual harassment on buses triggers anxiety among women regarding the use of public transportation. Employers need to ensure that women who commute daily to jobs in tourism are provided with secure, comfortable, and affordable transportation. Transportation providers, moreover, also will need to be held accountable for a zero-tolerance policy for SGBV of any sort on the transport itself and at transport stops and stations. They also will need to receive training on how to recognize and confront harassment and other SGBV being perpetrated by others. If public transportation on an individual basis is not an option, the tourism sector can help organize collective transportation for workers and build residences for women who have no means of transportation from home or those who live far from their places of work (Baum 2013; Karkkainen 2011). More crowd-sourced transportation could be seeded, such as affordably rented cars and scooters that can be found and mobilized with GPS and phone blue-tooth systems.

- *Take advantage of tourism employers' acceptance of the need for childcare services and other benefits, and their willingness to help pay for them.* Policy makers and practitioners can build on employers' amenability by helping organize and certify childcare providers to operate in or near sites of tourism activity, or in sites near workers' residences. Introducing tax breaks for tourism enterprises that take more responsibility for the welfare of their employees—such as by providing free or low-cost childcare—is one means of providing incentives to hotels and other firms operating in the tourism industry to hire more women (Karkkainen 2011; Ferguson 2011; Baum 2013). Similarly, implementation of maternity leave requirements, work-from-home options, and flexible workplace hours would also help draw more women into tourism jobs.

- *Encourage entrepreneurship of women in the tourism sector.* Entrepreneurship may be another attractive option for women with childcare responsibilities— self-employment may allow them to work out of their homes or at least close to home. Facilitating mechanisms include the improvement of women's access to land, other property, and credit as well as training in how to responsibly manage funds and create (and sustain) enterprises with them (UN Women 2011). Ecotourism, in particular, can be a very hospitable subsector for women working in the industry (ADB 2013).

- *Facilitate the industry's participation in school and TVET settings to create clear pathways for careers in tourism.* If tourism is to absorb large numbers of female workers, as envisaged by national human resources strategies like Sri Lanka's *2012 National Human Resources and Employment Policy* (GoSL 2012), tertiary-level education and vocational training opportunities will need to be better oriented toward careers in tourism. The active engagement of tourism and hospitality-focused enterprises in higher educational institutions and TVET centers could help educators understand industry needs and expose young people to the tremendous range of opportunities available in the tourism industry, including marketing, financial planning, client services, environmental protection, and other operational functions. Sector representatives could serve as advisory board members—in both regular secondary and TVET settings—and help expand perceptions of what is acceptable work for women in this sector through paid internships, school visits, and interactive English listening and speaking practice through using free online tools (Anderson 2018).

- *Increase access to training and skills that are marketable in tourism.* In addition to aligning skills development to industry needs, training programs linked to tourism jobs will also need to be greatly expanded (so that women in rural and remote areas have greater access), as will improving the skills of women who are already employed in different parts of the sector. Women typically get trapped in jobs that reflect traditional gender roles—such as cooking, cleaning, and small-scale handicrafts—and that tend to be highly labor intensive, yet yield products for which markets are saturated. Women need to be provided with training in areas beyond these gender-stereotyped occupations, such as through work-based training programs in hotels. Requiring quotas for women in training would promote incentives for enhanced hotel outreach to women (Karkkainen 2011).

- *Develop a strategy and involve women in every part of its planning and execution.* Multiple actors will need to come together and make concerted efforts to encourage women to fill employment gender gaps in the tourism sector. Chief among these are the concerned ministries in the central government; private sector leaders of the hotel, catering, and tourism industries and other enterprises operating in the tourism sector; those tasked with designing TVET curricula and certifying providers; and those who run job search mechanisms, whether based in social or traditional media or in-person job placement centers, so that trainees can be linked with jobs requiring the skills they have acquired, and employers' needs can be met through the administration of industry-informed training curricula. Together, these actors will need to ensure that women are represented in all groups and at all stages of the strategy, including the development of any tourism legislation and policies and, moreover, the development of action plans that involve targets for women's participation across all subsectors within the tourism industry (UN Women 2011).

Garments

As with tourism, garment sector work appears to carry a stigma for female employees (Ariyarathne et al. 2012). According to the primary research, both tourism and the garment industry are maligned even more by men than women, which implies that fathers and husbands may steer their daughters and wives away from such work; moreover, unmarried women may be less inclined to seek these jobs for fear of jeopardizing their marriage prospects. In spite of the stigma associated with it, however, more than 70 percent of apparel workers in Sri Lanka were women as of 2015, according to Labour Force Survey data. With the garment industry rebounding and expanding since the end of the civil war, even more workers are needed to fill labor shortages—and thus there is ample space for an influx of female as well as male workers. According to one study there were about 30,000 vacancies for women in the garment sector, especially in the export processing zones (EPZs) (Prasanna and Kuruppuge 2013). In fact, as found in this book's primary research, research from 2009 suggests that employers in Sri Lanka's export-oriented garment sector preferred hiring women because they regarded women as being more flexible and manageable and "as having patience conducive to the smooth running of labour-intensive production processes than men" (Madurawala 2009, quoted in ILO 2016, 59). To attract more women, employers and other stakeholders in the industry will need to address the stigma-related barriers to their entry, as well as improve working conditions for women by addressing gender-related skills, pay, and promotion gaps in this highly segregated industry. Recommended intervention areas include the following:

- *Have women who are more highly placed in the garment industry act as role models.* A large proportion of garment employment occurs in EPZs. Typically hired right out of secondary school (whether having graduated or dropped out), women in EPZs are the majority among worker cadres, whereas men hold most supervisory and technical as well as top administrative positions. Although the garment sector employs far more women than men, men historically have tended to obtain the higher-paying jobs and rise more quickly to positions with decision-making authority. Until 2009, men occupied the majority of management positions; however, 2015 Labour Force Survey data reveal a shift in this pattern, with greater representation of women in production and specialized services management positions. The industry needs to build on these successes in women's advancement, though they are still far from the norm, by engaging women who have risen to higher positions as role models and as mentors to other female employees, and in outreach efforts that target potential female applicants. Industry leaders also should take advantage of the relatively high education levels of their female employees (80 percent of garment workers have A-level or O-level educations) to provide them with on-the-job training in higher-skill work as well as greater opportunities for promotion into management positions.

- *Communicate the success of companies following progressive labor policies.* Recognizing and publicizing the efforts of industry leaders and firms such as Brandix, Hela Clothing, and MAS Holdings—all of which model gender-equitable practices and demonstrate financial success—can encourage other businesses to follow suit. The garment sector launched efforts to attract more women employees, including a 55 million Sri Lankan rupee (US$490,000) campaign in 2011, but these efforts have not yielded the anticipated boost in women workers (Samath 2011). Perhaps this and similar campaigns did not sufficiently reflect improvements made to the industry that would provide women with better incentives to consider working there. The sector can better market itself to potential female employees by advertising its relatively generous maternity leave benefits. If the industry could offer flexible work alternatives to allow women to take leave or even work from home during school breaks, that would further attract an otherwise unavailable group of women. According to garment employees in Gampaha, firms allow maternity leave of up to 84 days for their employees, as required by law. Unlike many private sector firms, garment sector firms also tend to comply with other requirements, including provisions for pregnant women (slightly shorter working hours and freedom from hazardous work) and for nursing mothers (permitting daily visits and travel time with nursing infants). A Gampaha firm worker said, "Some women opt to [remain] employed after availing their maternity leave, because of the nutrition they can obtain from the factory-supplied meals, which they cannot afford at home."[6]

- *Improve workplace conditions for women and raise awareness among workers about their entitlements.* Formal sector garment firms provide better benefits than informal ones; however, the vast majority of employment in Sri Lanka remains located in the informal sector, where poorer working conditions can constrain women's entry and persistence in the workforce. Similar requirements should be made of informal sector garment firms as formal firms: ensuring that workplaces are comfortable (that is, having separate restrooms for women) and safe (for example, requiring gender-sensitivity training for all management and staff as well as mandating a zero-tolerance policy for sexual harassment). Incentives should be given to garment sector firms— both formal and informal—to share the costs of childcare services with workers and to provide flexible work hours for women. The global Sri Lankan textile and apparel manufacturer MAS Holdings reports that once it made on-site childcare available in one of its factories in Jordan, the incidence of sick leave fell by 9 percent after a mere eight months, and production lines were more stabilized (Niethammer 2017; IFC 2017). Increasing workers' awareness of their rights would also contribute to holding garment industry employers accountable for providing proper worker benefits and pay and decent working conditions. Finally, improving wages—even marginally—for women workers would further encourage women to seek jobs in the sector. A one-percent boost in Sri Lanka's expected garment industry wage would increase the odds of women's labor force participation by 89 percent (Lopez-Acevedo and Robertson 2016).

- *Design and staff regional Maker Spaces[7] to spur entrepreneurial activity.* Establishing regionally distributed safe spaces where women could connect with one another and use their talents to collaboratively produce and sell their own garments would be a potential launching pad for many sorts of innovation in the Sri Lankan economy. Community-owned Maker Spaces are often partners with universities and private sector employees, with at least some of the time reserved for use by members. A Maker Space collectively owns digital, manufacturing, and analog tools that members can use to solve a problem or create something new. In a publicly accessible Maker Space, women could learn applied skills in new technologies, gain support for launching a small business, and facilitate income generation that aligns with their focus on raising children. By providing women the opportunities and resources to explore new possibilities in garment manufacturing through leading technologies—such as 3D printing and laser cutting—in the progressive field of wearable e-textiles, these spaces could help foster women's leadership skills, successful entrepreneurship, and innovation. Maker Spaces also could help develop specialized knowledge and expertise in niche areas, such as environmentally sustainable garment production and reuse to give Sri Lanka a leading edge in capturing and holding on to growth areas in the international garment industry market (Anderson 2018).

- *Enforce transparent labor recruitment standards to reduce discrimination against married and older female workers.* Shortly after the end of the civil war, the participation of married women in the garment sector workforce was reported to be as low as 10 percent (Meyer and Scott 2011, quoted by Ariyarathne et al. 2012). This low rate is partly due to self-selection out of the sector as a result of the industry stigma as well as married women's increased domestic and caretaking responsibilities. Research also reveals management preferences for young unmarried workers in the recruitment process, however—due in large part to a desire to avoid worker "challenges" related to pregnancy and childcare (Prasanna and Kuruppuge 2013). The enforcement of labor standards that minimize such bias and allow women to balance their caregiving and other domestic responsibilities with employment is needed to provide equal work opportunities for married and older women who wish to sustain their employment in the sector.

- *Establish garment factories in remote areas of Sri Lanka in collaboration with local and foreign investors.* Given the need for expanded job opportunities in rural and remote regions, such as the conflict-affected areas, the garment industry needs greater incentives to move into these regions. Rural areas would be conducive to increasing garment sector work in grassroots-level job markets, where women would be able to work from their homesteads and better balance work and household responsibilities.

- *Finally, as in most sectors, providing women with dedicated, safe transportation to and from garment sector jobs—or providing secure and comfortable nearby living accommodations to those who cannot make the daily commute—is imperative for attracting and retaining more women in the industry.* Investments in female-worker housing and transportation would address some of the safety concerns of women and their families and lower the cultural barriers to women's work in the sector (Ariyarathne et al. 2012). These services would not only open up new employment options for women but also promote the long-term growth of the industry, given the large number of workers the sector is looking to recruit to meet increasing international demand.

Commercial Agriculture

Even though respondents to the primary survey tend to feel that commercial agriculture presents the fewest social barriers for work-seeking women, employers from this sector are most likely (80 percent) to report that they do not have plans to hire women. They also are among the employers most likely to express the opinion that men are better workers than women. Policy makers, practitioners, and development partners need to make concerted efforts to improve opportunities for women in agricultural value chains; once these opportunities come to fruition, the attitudes of those working in the sector may start to change. Recommended intervention areas include the following:

- *Agricultural development programs that emphasize diversification to higher-value crops should work closely with the government to develop and pilot schemes that help women practicing subsistence farming make the transition to more profitable crops and markets.* Investments in modern machinery that women farmers can use at various stages of production, along with technical training to improve efficiency, yield higher-quality products. Greater efficiency also eases the time poverty of women, allowing them more time for household responsibilities, and higher-quality products fetch higher prices in product markets. At the same time, addressing female farmers' consistent disadvantage in access to markets may be remedied to a large extent by expanding women-friendly and affordable transport links and increasing women's representation in farmer, producer, and marketing groups.

• *Commercial agriculture is a valuable entry point for reaching some of the most vulnerable groups of women,* such as those who are heads of households (many of whom are war widows in Sri Lanka); other women living in the impoverished, conflict-affected areas of northern and eastern Sri Lanka; and women who aspire to supplement or replace their income from their low-reward work in estate sector jobs. Agricultural development programs should incorporate explicit provisions to address constraints on the participation of women who are resource poor or otherwise marginalized because of, for example, household status, ethnicity, or lack of education. Such provisions could include intensive outreach and training for these marginalized groups as well as efforts to address the lack of childcare or other household responsibilities that tend to keep women from engaging in paid work. The use of female extension trainers to work with women in more conservative communities—especially those that value restrictions on women's mobility—can ensure the success of programs in these communities. Also important is ensuring that professional mobilizers and trainers have the resources required for targeted outreach and training.

• *The private sector needs to be provided with greater incentives to invest in rural industries.* Expansion and promotion of agro-based and off-farm industries at the rural level could focus on local opportunities in the garment industry (for example, as suppliers of materials to larger actors that are further along in value chains), other cottage industries, food and beverage production, light engineering, and eco-tourism.

• *Finally, interventions to improve women's participation in and remuneration from commercial agriculture must take into account its lack of worker benefits that support women as well as the lack of protections for women.* Any improvements that can be made to ease the time poverty of women (for example, through providing child and elder care support, greater access to electricity and water, and reliable transportation to and from markets) and lower the risk of harassment and other violence against women working in agriculture (for instance, through community-level awareness raising and provision of safe and dedicated transportation) are likely to yield a substantial increase in women's participation in the sector. Fortunately (and somewhat surprisingly), according to the employer and household surveys, commercial agriculture, compared with other sectors, is reported to have the most formal procedural responses in place to address workplace sexual harassment. Thus, compared with other sectors, commercial agriculture provides a stronger foundation on which to address the threat of SGBV.

Notes

1. Unemployed female, 28 years old, A-level pass, married—Yaithena village, Gampaha district.

2. The Junior Achievement program in the United States, for example, orients students to business and entrepreneurship activities while enhancing financial literacy. The Girl Scouts and Girl Guides programs have related activities in the area of girls' business and career acumen that could be further supported in the Sri Lankan context (CGO 2012).

3. The Tertiary and Vocational Education Commission is the Ministry of Education agency that oversees accreditation of training providers. Training requirements out-pace available spaces in such industry areas as hotels and tourism (1,960 training places for 28,000 jobs to be filled), building and construction (4,538 places for 25,000 jobs), and metal and light engineering (4,300 places for 16,000 positions) (GoSL 2009).

4. Authors in Sri Lanka have cited gender constraints faced by female students at the university level, particularly with regard to mentoring, professional development, and educational streaming (Gunawardena 2003; Gunawardena et al. 2006). More generally, we note that there appear not to have been studies in Sri Lanka regarding the presence of gender-regressive practices in the classroom setting—for example, teachers exhibiting favoritism toward male students—despite research elsewhere pointing to such subtle or overt practices. A study of South Asian countries finds school-based peer support groups to have been quite effective at retaining female students—especially those who belong to ethnic minority groups—once they already are enrolled in STEM courses (Asian Development Bank 2012).

5. Female hotel worker, 29 years old, O-level pass, married—Kumburupitty village, Trincomalee district.

6. Male machine operator in garment factory, 26 years old, O-level pass—Henegama village, Gampaha district.

7. An emerging context in which to perform project-based learning is the Maker Space, where typically a variety of materials—such as textiles, cardboard, production tools, and high-end digital fabrication technology (such as 3D printers, sensors, and computerization tools)—provide a place where open-ended projects can be designed, prototyped, and constructed (Halverson and Sheridan 2014; Holman 2015; Pines, Sullivan, and Nogales 2015).

References

Abeywardana. H., and I. Priyadarshani. 2017. "Barriers to Recruiting and Retaining Youth, Including Women, to the Hospitality Industry in Sri Lanka." Chrysalis.

Asian Development Bank. 2012. *Innovative Strategies in Technical and Vocational Education and Training for Accelerated Human Resource Development in South Asia*. Manila: ADB.

ADB (Asian Development Bank). 2013. *Gender Equality in the Labor Market in the Philippines*. Manila: Asian Development Bank.

Anderson, Siri S. 2018. "Getting to Work Supplement: Inspiring Sri Lanka's Growing Economic Prosperity." Unpublished background paper for the current book. World Bank, Washington, DC.

Ariyarathne, Tehani, Gayathri Lokuge, Nadhiya Najab, and Priyanthi Fernando. 2012. "The Vulnerability of Women in the Economy." *Economic Review*, People's Bank, Colombo. Vol. 38. http://www.cepa.lk/uploads/4bae1bc28cb6cbe73a08a2bf084b8fa3-120830 -ER-The-vulnerability-of-women-in-the-economy---CEPA.pdf.

Baum, T. 2013. *International Perspectives on Women and Work in Hotels, Catering and Tourism*. Geneva: International Labour Organization.

CGO (Center for Gender in Organizations). 2012. "Dreaming Big: What's Gender Got to Do with It? The Impact of Gender Stereotypes on Career Aspirations of Middle Schoolers." CGO Briefing Note 35, Center for Gender in Organizations, Simmons College, Boston. http://www.simmons.edu/som/docs/insights_35_v2_%282%29.pdf.

DCS (Department of Census and Statistics). 2016. *Sri Lanka Labour Force Survey, Annual Report 2015*. Colombo: DCS. http://www.statistics.gov.lk/samplesurvey /LFS_Annual%20Report_2015.pdf.

DeJaeghere, J., and N. P. Wiger. 2013. "Gender Discourses in an NGO Education Project: Openings for Transformation toward Gender Equality in Bangladesh." *International Journal of Educational Development* 33(6): 557–65.

Diekman, Amanda B., Erica S. Weisgram, and Aimee L. Belanger. 2015. "New Routes to Recruiting and Retaining Women in STEM: Policy Implications of a Communal Goal Congruity Perspective." *Social Issues and Policy Review* 9 (1): 52–88.

Ferguson, L. 2011. "Promoting Gender Equality and Empowering Women? Tourism and the Third Millennium Development Goal." *Current Issues in Tourism* 14 (3): 235–49.

Gamage, G. 2004. "Gender and ICT: A Sri Lankan Perspective." Paper presented at the "9th National Convention on Women's Studies," Colombo, Sri Lanka, March.

GoSL (Government of Sri Lanka). 2009. *Labour and Social Trends in Sri Lanka*. Ministry of Labour Relations and Manpower, Central Bank of Sri Lanka and Department of Census and Statistics. Colombo: GoSL.

———. 2012. *The National Human Resources and Employment Policy for Sri Lanka*. Secretariat for Senior Ministers. Colombo: GoSL.

GoSL (Government of Sri Lanka), and UNDP (United Nations Development Programme). 2015. "Ten Year National Plan of Action for the Social Development of the Plantation Community 2016–2025." Ministry of Plantation Infrastructure Development, GoSL, Colombo.

Grover, Suchi, and Roy Pea. 2013. "Computational Thinking in K-12: A Review of the State of the Field." *Educational Researcher* 42 (1): 38–43.

Gunatilaka, R., D. Bandaranaike, N. Arunatilake, A. deSilva, D. Gunewardena, and C. Wijebandara. 2017. "Increasing Women's Participation in Sri Lanka Labour Market." Policy Brief.

Gunawardena, Chandra. 2003. "Gender Equity in Higher Education in Sri Lanka: A Mismatch between Access and Outcomes." *McGill Journal of Education* 38 (3): 437–50.

Gunawardena, Chandra, Yoga Rasanayagam, Tressir Leitan, Kanchana Bulumulle, and Asha Abeyasekera-Van Dort. 2006. "Quantitative and Qualitative Dimensions of

Gender Equity in Sri Lankan Higher Education." *Women's Studies International Forum* 29: 562–71.

Gunetileke, Neranjana, Sanjana Kuruppu, and Susrutha Goonasekera. 2008. *The Estate Workers' Dilemma: Tensions and Changes in the Tea and Rubber Plantations in Sri Lanka.* Study Series 4. Colombo: CEPA.

Halverson, Erica Rosenfeld, and Kimberly Sheridan. 2014. "The Maker Movement in Education." *Harvard Educational Review* 84 (4): 495–504.

Hamm, Kathrin, Mathai Joseph Roshin, Sebastian Veit, and Sandeep Singh. 2017. *Gender Intelligence for Banks: Moving the Needle on Gender Equality.* Washington, DC: International Finance Corporation.

Holman, Will. 2015. "Makerspace: Towards a New Civic Infrastructure." *Places Journal*, November. https://placesjournal.org/article/makerspace-towards-a-new-civic-infrastr ucture/?gclid=CLGj2N3t1dACFQ8vaQodg5wN5A.

Holmes, Stephanie, Adrienne Redmond, Julie Thomas, and Karen High. 2012. "Girls Helping Girls: Assessing the Influence of College Student Mentors in an Afterschool Engineering Program." *Mentoring and Tutoring: Partnership in Learning* 20 (1): 137–50.

Iaccino, Ludovica. 2014. "Top Five Countries with Highest Rates of Child Prostitution." *International Business Times*, February 6. http://www.ibtimes.co.uk/top-five -countries-highest-rates-child-prostitution-1435448.

IFC (International Finance Corporation). 2017. *Tackling Childcare: The Business Case for Employer-Supported Child Care.* Washington, DC: IFC.

ILO (International Labour Organization). 2016. *Factors Affecting Women's Labour Force Participation in Sri Lanka.* Colombo: ILO.

Jayaweera, S., and L. Wanasundera. 2006. "Gender and ICT in Sri Lanka: An Overview." Paper presented at the 10th National Convention on Women's Studies, April, Colombo.

Jayaweera, S., Hiranthi Wijemanne, Leelangi Wanasundera, and Kamini Meedeniya Vitarana. 2007. *Gender Dimensions of the Millennium Development Goals in Sri Lanka.* Colombo: UNDP and Centre for Women's Research. http://www.undp.org/content /dam/srilanka/docs/mdg/Gender_Dimensions%20of%20Sri%20Lanka.pdf.

Kamal, A., and L. Woodbury. 2016. *Emerging Opportunities for Women in Khyber Pakhtunkhwa: Industry (Manufacturing and Construction), Mining, Tourism, and Agriculture.* London: International Growth Center, London School of Economics and Political Science.

Karkkainen, O. 2011. *Women and Work in Tunisia: Tourism and ICT Sectors—A Case Study.* Turin: European Training Foundation.

Klawe, Maria. 2014. "The Science behind Graduating a Class with Majority Women Engineers." *Forbes*, July 10. https://www.forbes.com/sites/mariaklawe/2014/07/10 /the-science-behind-graduating-a-class-with-majority-women-engineers/#182d521a4c9e.

LIRNEasia. 2006. "A Baseline Sector Analysis of the Business Process Outsourcing Industry in Sri Lanka." Information and Communication Technology Agency of Sri Lanka, Colombo.

Liston, Carrie, Karen Peterson, and Vicky Ragan. 2008. "Evaluating Promising Practices in Informal Information Technology (IT) Education for Girls." National Center for Women in Technology and Girl Scouts of the USA, New York.

Lopez-Acevedo, G., and R. Robertson. 2016. *Stitches to Riches? Apparel Employment, Trade, and Economic Development in South Asia.* Washington, DC: World Bank.

Lyon, Gabrielle, and Jameela Jafri. 2010. "Project Exploration's Sisters4Science: Involving Urban Girls of Color in Science Out of School." *Afterschool Matters* 11: 15–23.

Madurawala, D.S.P. 2009. "Labour Force Participation of Women in Child-Bearing Ages, Sri Lanka." *Sri Lanka Journal of Population Studies* 11: 1–38.

Margolis, J., and A. Fisher. 2002. *Unlocking the Clubhouse Door: Women in Computing.* Cambridge, MA: MIT Press.

McLain, B., T. McLain, T. Chachon, and A. Smith. 2018. "Final Report: SciGirls Strategies Executive Summary. XSci Experiential Science Education Research Collaborative at University of Colorado, Boulder." http://www.scigirlsconnect.org /wp-content/uploads/2019/01/SciGirls-Final-Report-FINAL-REPORT -Executive-Summ.pdf.

Meyer, R., and H. Scott. 2011. "Women in the Global Factory—The Garment Industry in Sri Lanka." Accessed August 23, 2012. http://www.utexas.edu/cola/insts /southasia/_files.

Morgan, Sharon. 2012. "Women's ICT Sector Employment in Developing Countries: Dualism of Rhetoric vs. Reality in the Case of Sri Lanka." Development Informatics Working Paper No. 49, Centre for Development Informatics, Institute for Development Policy and Management, SED, University of Manchester.

Niethammer, Carmen. 2017. "The Business Case for Tackling Childcare: Good for Employees and Employers, Good for Sri Lanka." *Financial Times*, Sri Lanka, October 3. http://www.ft.lk/columns/The-business-case-for-tackling-childcare--good-for -employees-and-employers--good-for-Sri-Lanka/4-640772.

Perera, Jennifer, Nalika Gunawardane, and Vathsala Jayasuriya, eds. 2011. *Review of Research Evidence on Gender Based Violence (GBV) in Sri Lanka.* Colombo: Sri Lanka Medical Association.

Pines, E., P. Sullivan, and L. Nogales. 2015. "Broadening Participation through Engagement in the Makerspace Movement." Paper presented at the 122nd ASEE Annual Conference & Exposition, Seattle, Washington, June 14–17. Accessed online at https://www.asee .org/public/conferences/56/papers/11287/view.

Prasanna, R. P. I. R., and R. H. Kuruppuge. 2013. "General Wage Situation of Apparel Industry Workers in Sri Lanka." Asia Floor Wage Alliance. http://asia.floorwage.org /resources/wage-reports/general-wage-situation-of-apparel-industry-workers-in -sri-lanka.

Ranasinghe, Athula Lakshman. 2004. "ICT and Decent Work: An Assessment of the Labour Market Impacts of the Advent of Information and Communication Technology in Sri Lanka." Department of Economics, University of Colombo, Sri Lanka. Prepared for and presented at the JILPT/ILO Networking of National Institutes for Labour Studies: Meeting on Joint Investigative Studies for "Determining the Impact of Information and Communications Technology on Decent Work in the Asia and Pacific Region," Bangkok, Thailand, December 2–3.

Reddy, R. Ravikanth. 2015. "Computer Education May Be Made Mandatory." *The Hindu*, January 20. http://www.thehindu.com/news/cities/Hyderabad/computer-education -may-be-made-mandatory/article6800774.ece.

Ryoo, J., J. Goode, and J. Margolis. 2016. "It Takes a Village: Supporting Inquiry- and Equity-Oriented Computer Science Pedagogy through a Professional Learning Community." *Computer Science Education* 25 (4): 351–70.

Samath, Feizal. 2011. "Sri Lanka: Garment Industry Woos Women Workers." Inter Press Service News Agency, February 10. http://www.ipsnews.net/2011/02/sri-lanka-garment-industry-woos-women-workers/.

Senewiratne, Hiran H. 2011. "Lanka Needs More Graduates for IT Industry Growth." *The Island Newspaper*, Colombo, Sri Lanka. http://www.island.lk/index.php?page_cat=article-details&page=article-details&code_title=24351.

Stout, J., and B. Tamer. 2016. "Collaborative Learning Eliminates the Negative Impact of Gender Stereotypes on Women's Self-Concept." Proceedings of the 47th ACM Technical Symposium on Computing Science Education (p. 496). Association for Computing Machinery. Accessed online at http://cra.org/cerp/wp-content/uploads/sites/4/2016/03/Final-draft_blind_ASEE_for-website.pdf.

TPT (Twin Cities Public Television). 2013. "SciGirls Seven: How to Engage Girls in STEM." St. Paul, MN. http://tpt.vo.llnwd.net/o26/scigirls/ScigirlsSeven_Print.pdf.

UNDP (United Nations Development Programme) and Ministry of Women and Child Affairs. 2016. *Policy Framework and National Plan of Action to Address Sexual and Ggender-Based Violence in Sri Lanka.* Colombo: UNDP.

UNFPA (United Nations Population Fund). 2017. "Sexual Harassment on Public Buses and Trains in Sri Lanka." UNFPA, Colombo, Sri Lanka. https://www.unfpa.org/news/ninety-cent-sri-lankan-women-endure-sexual-harassment-public-transport-unfpa-study-shows.

UN Women. 2011. *Global Report on Women in Tourism 2010.* New York: United Nations.

Yadav, Aman, Hai Hong, and Chris Stephenson. 2016. "Computational Thinking for All: Pedagogical Approaches to Embedding 21st Century Problem Solving in K–12 Classrooms." *TechTrends* 60: 565–68.

Sri Lanka: Country Gender Profile

This country profile presents an overview of Sri Lanka's status and progress across a range of social, political, and economic development indicators from a gender perspective. The following sections examine gender implications of the country's legal context, along with sex-disaggregated data and an analysis of key human development outcomes, from health and nutrition, education, and economic participation to voice and agency. The concluding section notes observed gaps in the available data.

Sri Lanka performs well across several social and human development indicators and is cited as a model for gender equity in the South Asia region. It ranks 76th out of 189 countries on the Human Development Index, outperforming all other South Asian countries (UNDP 2018). Its score of 0.35 on the UN Gender Inequality Index (see figure A.1) is among the lowest in the region, second only to the Maldives.[1] In fact, in a number of dimensions, Sri Lanka's performance is closer to that of upper-middle-income countries such as Malaysia (which is in the East Asia and Pacific region), ranked 62nd on the Gender Inequality Index (UNDP 2018) (see table A.1).

Legal and Political Context

Sri Lankan General Law formally recognizes gender equality. The 1978 Constitution provides equal rights without discrimination on the basis of sex, and Sri Lanka is a signatory to the UN Convention on the Elimination of all Forms of a Discrimination against Women (CEDAW). All married and unmarried women and men have equal rights to apply for a passport, obtain a national ID, travel outside their home or outside the country, choose where to live, and be heads of a household or family. The law also applies equally to men and women in financial, commercial, and property-related transactions, such as signing a contract, registering a business, opening a bank account, obtaining a job, and pursuing a trade or profession. Parental rights over children, although equal, tend to advantage male legal guardianship of children (ADB 2015). Moreover, personal laws as

Figure A.1 Gender Inequality Index, 2018

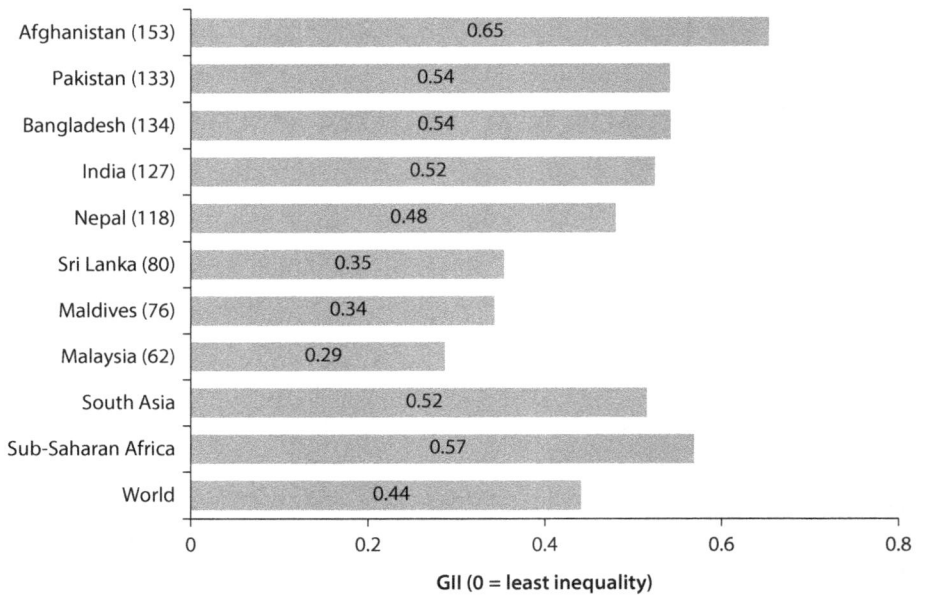

Source: UNDP 2018.
Note: Gender Inequality Index (GII) rank among 189 countries. Rank shown in parentheses.

Table A.1 Human Development Indicators of Gender Equality: Sri Lanka Compared with South Asia and Upper-Middle-Income Country Averages

Indicator	Sri Lanka	South Asia	Upper-middle-income countries
Gender Inequality Index (a)	0.35	0.52	—
Life expectancy at birth (years) females/males (b)	79/72	71/67	78/73
Youth literacy rate (% of those age 15–24): girls/boys (c)	99/98	86/90	98/98
Population, females (% of total) (d)	52	48	50

Sources: (a) UNDP 2018; (b) World Bank Data Center 2019; (c) UNESCO 2019; (d) World Bank Data Center 2018.
Note: — = not available.

interpreted in each religious community contain provisions regarding marriage, divorce, financial transactions, and property that disadvantage women at varying levels (ADB 2015). Until recently, women were denied equal rights to land in state-assisted resettlement in Sri Lanka; the Land Development Ordinance (1935) continues to contain provisions that give preference to male heirs over female heirs.[2]

Gender implications of labor law: Sri Lanka's labor legislation for women's health and safety, wage benefits, and maternity leave conform to international standards. However, the law is only applicable to the formal sector and does not cover the more than two-thirds of Sri Lanka's male and female workers who are employed in the informal sector. Provisions under the law mandate paid maternity leave of 84 days, with the employer paying for 100 percent of benefits and wages during this time. Although the law requires that employers provide break time for nursing mothers, mothers are not guaranteed an equivalent position of employment after returning from maternity leave, and parents are not entitled to flexible or part-time schedules. Furthermore, although laws prohibit the dismissal of pregnant workers, they do not prohibit prospective employers from asking about family status. Laws also do not prohibit gender-based discrimination in hiring, nor do they guarantee equal remuneration for work of equal value. The regulatory regime prohibits women's nighttime work and limits overtime, which could be a disincentive for employers to hire women. Sri Lanka provides few tax incentives for women to work and little job protection. There are no childcare tax deductions or credits specific to men or women; the government does not support or provide childcare services or a childcare allowance for parents; and most employers do not provide leave to care for sick relatives.

Legal protections against gender-based violence: Legislation on domestic violence prescribes clear criminal penalties and a specialized court and procedure for addressing cases of such violence are in place. Additionally, this legislation encompasses the physical, sexual, emotional, and economic aspects of domestic violence, and protects family members, former spouses, and unmarried intimate partners. Protection orders for domestic violence provide for the removal of the perpetrator from the home. Furthermore, they prohibit the perpetrator's contact with the survivor and ensure that they maintain a geographic distance from them. However, no legislation explicitly criminalizes marital rape. Sri Lanka also possesses legislation that specifically addresses sexual harassment. This legislation prescribes criminal penalties and covers sexual harassment in places of employment and education, but not in public places more broadly.

Health

Summary of current status: Sri Lanka performs well on many indicators of health. Life expectancy is higher for females than males (78.8 and 72.1 years, respectively), outperforming the regional female average of 70.5 years. The female under-five mortality rate is 8 deaths per 1,000 live births, significantly lower than the regional average of 44.5 deaths per 1,000 live births. Sri Lanka also does well on maternal health indicators in comparison with other South Asian countries. Nearly all pregnant women receive prenatal care and have births attended by skilled staff in a health facility (DCS 2017). Sri Lanka's maternal mortality ratio is the lowest in South Asia, at 30 per 100,000 live births, and contraceptive prevalence among women age 15–49 is among the highest in the region. Sri Lanka's total fertility rate and adolescent fertility rate have declined and are considerably lower than regional averages.

Although the prevalence of malnutrition in Sri Lanka is not as high as in other South Asian countries, or even some middle-income countries, there has been little improvement in overall child malnutrition rates over the past decade. Among the under-five population, stunting rates have remained stagnant, at 17 percent, between 2006 and 2016 (DCS 2017). During the same period, the proportion of underweight children declined only marginally, from 21.1 percent to 20.5 percent (DCS 2017). Additional details on indicators of health and nutrition in Sri Lanka are provided in table A.2.

Table A.2 Key Health and Nutrition Indicators by Sex

Indicator	Total % of age-relevant population	Female	Male	Regional average (Female)
Life expectancy at birth (years) (a)	75.5 (2017)	78.8 (2017)	72.1 (2017)	70.5 (2017)
Sex ratio at birth (male births per female births) (a)	1.04 (2017)	—	—	1.1 (2017)
Under-5 mortality rate (per 1,000 live births), by sex (a)	8.8 (2017)	8.0 (2017)	9.6 (2017)	44.5 (2017)
Fertility rate, total (births per woman) (a, b)	—	2.0 (2017)	—	2.4 (2017)
Adolescent fertility rate (births per 1,000 women age 15–19) (a)	—	14.1 (2017)	—	32.2 (2017)
Age at first marriage among ever-married women (b)	—	23.0 (2016)	—	—
Women who were first married by age 18 (% of women age 25–49) (b)	—	12 (2016)	—	—
Ever-married women receiving antenatal care from a skilled provider for the most recent birth (%) (b)	—	99.2 (2016)	—	—
Births attended by skilled provider (% of total) (b, a)	—	99.3 (2016)	—	75.6 (2014)
Maternal mortality ratio (modeled estimate, per 100,000 live births) (a)	—	30 (2015)	—	182 (2015)
Contraceptive prevalence rate among women who are married or in a union (% of women age 15–49) (a)	—	61.7 (2016)	—	51.8 (2014)
Percentage of children age 12–23 months who did not receive specific vaccines by the time of survey, by sex (b)	0.8 (2016)	0.8 (2016)	0.8 (2016)	—
Underweight prevalence, weight for age (% of all children under 5) (b)	20.5 (2016)	20.5 (2016)	20.5 (2016)	—
Stunting prevalence, height for age (% of all children under 5) (b)	17.3 (2016)	16.6 (2016)	17.9 (2016)	—
Women's share of population age 15+ living with HIV (%) (a)	—	33.7 (2017)	—	36.2 (2017)

Sources: (a) World Development Indicators (http://wdi.worldbank.org/tables); (b) Sri Lanka Demographic and Health Survey 2016.
Note: — = not available; HIV = human immunodeficiency virus.

Trends through time. Sri Lanka's health indicators have traditionally been among the best in the region, and most reflect the large reduction in gender disparities that has occurred over the past several decades. Between 1962 and 2017, sex ratios at birth remained constant, at 1.04.[3] The total fertility rate has dropped in recent decades, from 5.5 births per woman in 1960 to 2.0 births in 2017. In the same period, the adolescent fertility rate has declined significantly, from 99 to 14 births per 1,000 women between the ages of 15 and 19.

The proportion of pregnant women receiving prenatal care rose from 94 percent in 1987 to 99.2 percent in 2016, as did the proportion of births attended by skilled health staff—from 87 percent in 1987 to 99.3 percent in 2016. Correspondingly, the maternal mortality ratio fell from 75 deaths per 100,000 live births in 1990 to 30 deaths in 2016. However, the proportion of female adults with HIV increased from 23.1 to 33.7 percent between 1987 and 2017.

Both female and male under-five mortality rates dropped by more than half between 1990 and 2013—from 19.4 to 8.0 deaths (per 1,000 live births) for girls, and from 23.1 to 9.6 deaths for boys. Malnutrition prevalence indicators also improved for both girls and boys—particularly stunting (malnutrition measured as height for age), which dropped from 30.5 percent for girls and 32.7 percent for boys (1987) to 16.6 and 17.9 percent, respectively (2016).

Education

Summary of current status. Sri Lankans have the highest average number of years of schooling of any country in South Asia (UNDP 2018; Dundar et al. 2017). Girls and boys alike have benefited from Sri Lanka's approach to education as a basic right for more than seven decades, with free and equal access to primary, secondary, and tertiary education since 1945. The 1997 Compulsory Education Regulation Act made school enrollment and attendance compulsory for all children between the ages of 5 and 14. In 2016, the provisions of this regulation were extended to children up to age 16. As a result, gender parity in education exists at most levels. The ratio of female-to-male primary enrollment is 98.6 percent, and the ratio of female-to-male secondary enrollment is greater than 100 percent. The ratio of female-to-male tertiary enrollment is an extraordinary 151.2 percent, reflecting women's high levels of participation in university education in Sri Lanka. According to statistics provided by the University Grants Commission, 66 percent of all undergraduate degrees and 55 percent of all postgraduate degrees conferred by universities and higher educational institutions established under the Universities Act were awarded to women (University Grants Commission 2017). Additional details on key education indicators in Sri Lanka are provided in table A.3.

Trends through time. Over the course of the past 40 years, Sri Lanka has seen increasing gender equality in indicators related to education. The ratio of young literate females to males improved from 98.2 percent in 1981 to 100.6 percent in 2017. The ratio of female-to-male gross primary enrollment rates rose from

Table A.3 Key Education Indicators by Sex

Indicator	Country rate or female-to male-ratio	Regional average or female-to-male ratio
Literacy		
Youth literacy rate (% of population age 15–24) (a)	98.7 (2017)	88.3 (2016)
Ratio of young literate females to males (% age 15–24) (a)	100.6 (2017)	95.0 (2016)
Enrollment		
Primary		
Total gross primary enrollment rate (% of age-relevant population) (b)	101.9 (2017)	111.7 (2017)
Ratio of female-to-male gross primary enrollment rates (%) (b)	98.6 (2017)	109.6 (2017)
Secondary		
Total gross secondary enrollment rate (% of age-relevant population) (b)	98.0 (2017)	70.7 (2017)
Ratio of female-to-male gross secondary enrollment rates (%) (b)	105.2 (2017)	100.5 (2017)
Tertiary		
Total gross tertiary enrollment rate (% of age-relevant population) (b)	19.0 (2017)	23.3 (2017)
Ratio of female-to-male gross tertiary enrollment rates (%) (b)	151.20 (2017)	96.0 (2017)
Completion		
Completion rate, primary (% of total age-relevant population) (b)	101.9 (2017)	95.2 (2017)
Ratio of female-to-male primary completion rates (%) (b)	98.5 (2017)	101.4 (2017)
Male-female gap in primary completion rates (% male minus female rates) (b)	1.5 (2017)	−1.3 (2017)
Completion rate, lower secondary (% of total age-relevant population) (b)	96.5 (2017)	80.7 (2017)
Ratio of female-to-male lower secondary completion rates (%) (b)	99.2 (2017)	104.6 (2017)
Male-female gap in lower secondary completion rates (% male minus female rates) (b)	0.7 (2017)	−3.7 (2017)

Sources: (a) UNESCO (http://uis.unesco.org/country/LK); (b) World Development Indicators (http://wdi.worldbank.org/tables)

91 percent in 1970 to 98.6 percent in 2017; at the secondary level, this ratio has remained largely constant and close to parity. Yet the ratio of female-to-male gross tertiary enrollment rates has over time become highly skewed toward females, moving from 78.8 percent in 1970 to 151.2 percent in 2017, indicating an emerging gender differential that favors young women.

Primary and secondary completion rates have improved considerably for both females and males, from about 63 percent for girls and 64 percent for boys in

1970 to 101.2 and 102.7 percent, respectively, in 2017. Between 1970 and 2017, the ratio of female-to-male primary completion rates remained in the range of 97 to 100 percent. Lower secondary completion rates rose between 1970 and 2016, from 38.9 to 96.1 percent for girls, and from 35.7 to 96.8 percent for boys during the same period.

Economic Opportunity: Labor Force Participation and Employment, and Access to Finance

Summary of current status. Despite favorable education and health outcomes for women, Sri Lanka performs worse than expected for its gross national income per capita level on key indicators of women's income-earning opportunities, financial inclusion, and use of productive assets. Women make up only 35 percent of the labor force. In comparison with men's rates, not only are female labor force participation rates significantly lower, but women's unemployment rates are more than twice as high as men's. Gender disparities in labor force participation, unemployment, and employment-to-population ratios are also in evidence among Sri Lanka's youth, as shown in table A.4. Both women and men are most likely to work as wage and salaried workers. Yet men are more likely than women to be own-account workers or employers, whereas women are more likely than men to be unpaid contributing family workers.

Table A.4 Key Economic Opportunity Indicators by Sex

Indicator	Total % of age-relevant population	Sri Lanka		Regional average	
		Females	Males	Females	Males
Labor force participation and employment					
Labor force, female (% of total labor force) (a)	—	35.0 (2018)	—	24.1 (2018)	—
Total labor force participation rate for age 15–64 (%) (national estimate) (b)	51.8 (2018)	—	—	—	—
Labor force participation rate, by sex (% of female or male population age 15+) (national estimate) (b)	—	33.6 (2018)	73.0 (2018)	—	—
Labor force participation rate for age 15–24, by sex (%) (national estimate) (c)	33.0 (2017)	24.1 (2017)	42.4 (2017)	—	—
Employment					
Employment-to-population ratio, age 15+, by sex (%) (modeled ILO estimate) (a)	50.2 (2018)	32.4 (2018)	70.0 (2018)	25.3 (2018)	77.3 (2018)
Employment to population ratio, age 15–24, by sex (%) (modeled ILO estimate) (a)	19.9 (2018)	11.6 (2018)	28.3 (2018)	15.0 (2018)	45.5 (2018)
Unemployment					
Unemployment, total (% of total labor force) and by sex (national estimate) (b)	4.4 (2018)	7.1 (2018)	3.0 (2018)	—	—
Ratio of female unemployment rate to male unemployment rate (national estimate) (b)	236.7 (2018)	—	—	—	—

table continues next page

Getting to Work • http://dx.doi.org/10.1596/978-1-4648-1067-1

Table A.4 Key Economic Opportunity Indicators by Sex *(continued)*

Indicator	Total % of age-relevant population	Females	Males	Regional average Females	Males
Unemployment, youth total and by sex (% of total labor force ages 15–24) (national estimate) (b)	21.4 (2018)	30.0 (2018)	16.8 (2018)	—	—
Ratio of youth female unemployment rate to youth male unemployment rate (national estimate) (b)	178.6 (2018)	—	—	—	—
Type (status) of employment					
Employee (% of employed) by sex (national estimate) (b)	—	55.7 (2017)	58.8 (2017)	—	—
Own-account worker (% of employed), by sex (national estimate) (b)	31.3 (2017)	25.6 (2017)	34.5 (2017)	—	—
Contributing family worker (% of employed), by sex (national estimate) (b)	8.0 (2017)	17.7 (2017)	2.6 (2017)	—	—
Employer (% of employed), by sex (national estimate) (b)	3.0 (2017)	1.1 (2017)	4.1 (2017)	—	—
Vulnerable employment (modeled ILO estimate, % of employed age 15+), by sex (a)	38.9 (2018)	42.8 (2018)	36.9 (2018)	78.5 (2018)	70.8 (2018)
Sector of employment					
Employment in agriculture, by sex (modeled ILO estimate, % of female or male employment) (a)	25.9 (2018)	29.2 (2018)	24.2 (2018)	59.5 (2018)	38.6 (2018)
Employment in services, by sex (modeled ILO estimate, % of female or male employment) (a)	45.8 (2018)	43.9 (2018)	46.8 (2018)	23.0 (2018)	35.6 (2018)
Employment in industry, by sex (modeled ILO estimate, % of female or male employment) (a)	28.3 (2018)	26.9 (2018)	29.1 (2018)	17.4 (2018)	25.7 (2018)
Access to finance					
Account ownership at a financial institution or with a mobile-money-service provider, by sex (% of population age 15+) (d)	73.6 (2017)	73.4 (2017)	73.8 (2017)	64.2 (2017)	74.8 (2017)

Sources: (a) WDI (http://wdi.worldbank.org/tables); (b) Sri Lanka Labour Force Survey 2018 bulletin; (c) Sri Lanka Labour Force Survey 2017; (d) Demirgüç-Kunt et al. 2018.
Note: — = not available; ILO = International Labour Organization.

Although a considerable proportion of men (37 percent) hold vulnerable jobs, the share of women in such jobs is higher (43 percent). Men are better represented than women in the services sector (47 percent, as compared with 44 percent), whereas women constitute a higher share of those employed in agriculture (29 percent versus 24 percent). The proportions of women and men employed in industry are roughly similar at 27 percent and 29 percent, respectively.

Microfinance institution coverage of women borrowers is lower in Sri Lanka than in other South Asia countries except Pakistan and Afghanistan (figure A.2). Women's opportunities for success in entrepreneurship in Sri Lanka— including in the agricultural and rural sectors—remain constrained by their lack of access to and control over productive assets such as land and credit. Research suggests that even when women microenterprise owners in Sri Lanka receive one-time

Figure A.2 Active Microfinance Borrowers, by South Asian Country

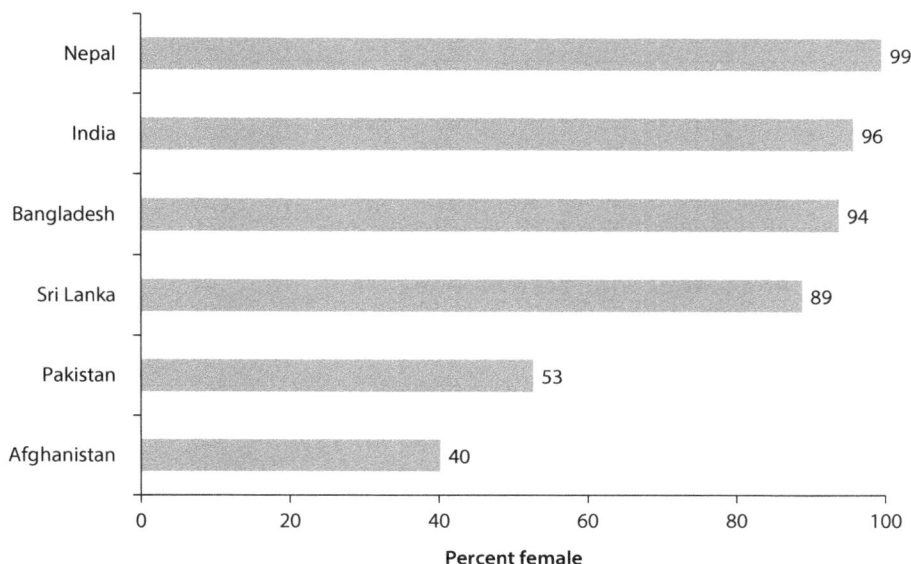

Source: Mix Market microfinance institution data, March 2015.

grants, there is no measurable short- or long-term benefit for the enterprise, as there is for male-owned microenterprises that receive similar one-time grants (de Mel et al. 2008). Additional details on key indicators of economic opportunity in Sri Lanka are provided in table A.4.

Trends through time. Labor force participation patterns and trends in Sri Lanka have not progressed toward parity in the past three decades. Between 1990 and 2018, the total labor force participation rate saw an overall decline, from 61 percent to 52 percent, with female labor force participation rates falling by more than 10 percentage points over the past decade. Hence, the ratio of female-to-male labor force participation rates dropped from 52 percent to 46 percent between 2006 and 2018. Among young workers (age 15–24), labor force participation rates for both women and men dropped between 1990 and 2017, from 45 to 24 percent among young women, and from 60 to 42 percent among young men. This drop may reflect the fact that more young adults have attended school in recent years. The employment-to-population ratio for women (age 15+) decreased slightly—from 33 percent in 2006 to 32 percent in 2017. For men, the same indicator increased from 65 percent in 2006 to 70 percent in 2017.

Voice and Agency

Summary of current status. Women's political participation remains relatively low in Sri Lanka. Women in Sri Lanka were granted equal rights to contest elections in 1931 and have served as elected leaders since 1960.

Table A.5 Key Voice and Agency Indicators by Sex

Indicator	Sri Lanka	Regional average
Political representation and voice and agency		
Proportion of seats held by women in the national parliament (%) (a)	5.8 (2018)	18.3 (2018)
Ever-married women who participate in household decisions (own health care, major household purchases, and visiting family) (%) (b)	85.0 (2016)	—
Female-headed households (% of households with a female head) (b)	23.9 (2016)	—
Women who were first married by age 18 (% of women age 20–24) (b)	9.8 (2016)	—
Gender-based violence		
Proportion of women age 15–49 subjected to domestic violence in the past 12 months by an intimate partner (%) (b)	17.0 (2016)	—
Proportion of women age 15–49 subjected to sexual violence in the past 12 months (% among women subjected to domestic violence) (b)	15.0 (2016)	—

Sources: (a) World Development Indicators (http://wdi.worldbank.org/tables); (b) Sri Lanka Demographic and Health Survey 2016.
Note: — = not available.

Women's representation in political bodies remains low at both local and national levels, however. At just 5.8 percent, the proportion of national parliament seats held by women in Sri Lanka is the lowest in South Asia and is considerably below the regional average of 18.3 percent (Inter-Parliamentary Union 2018; World Development Indicators). At local levels of government, female participation fares worse. Additional details on key indicators of voice and agency in Sri Lanka are provided in table A.5.

Trends through time. In recent decades, Sri Lankan women seem to have made limited progress in the area of voice and agency. The proportion of women who were first married by the age of 18 declined modestly, from 13.7 percent in 1987 to 9.8 percent in 2016. The proportion of seats held by women in the national parliament only rose from 4.9 to 5.8 percent between 1990 and 2018. The absence of reliable data on gender-based violence and attitudes toward intimate partner violence challenges assessment of trends in these areas.

Data Gaps

Sri Lanka possesses largely complete data on indicators of health and education; however, the data available on the type (status) and sector of employment, financial inclusion, and various indicators of voice and agency are limited. Data are especially lacking on the prevalence of and attitudes toward various forms of gender-based violence, including trafficking, sexual harassment, and intimate partner violence.

Notes

1. The Gender Inequality Index is a composite measure of reproductive health (maternal mortality ratio and adolescent fertility rate), empowerment (share of parliamentary seats held by each sex, and female and male secondary educational attainment rates), and labor force participation rate (share of women and men in the labor force). The index ranges from 0 to 1, with 1 indicating the highest degree of gender inequality.
2. CEDAW Committee report on Sri Lanka, 48th Session of the UN General Assembly, 2011. CEDAW/C/LKA/CO/7.
3. Sex ratio at birth is defined as the number of male births per female births. The indicator is used as a measure of sex discrimination.

References

ADB (Asian Development Bank). 2015. *Sri Lanka Country Gender Assessment: An Update.* Manila: Asian Development Bank and Deutsche Gesellschaft für Internationale Zusammenarbeit GmbH.

De Mel, Suresh, David McKenzie, and Christopher Woodruff. 2008. "Returns to Capital in Microenterprises: Evidence from a Field Experiment." *Quarterly Journal of Economics* 123 (4): 1329–72.

Demirgüç-Kunt, Asli, Leora Klapper, Dorothe Singer, Saniya Ansar, and Jake Hess. 2018. *The Global Findex Database 2017: Measuring Financial Inclusion and the Fintech Revolution.* Washington, DC: World Bank.

DCS (Department of Census and Statistics). 2017. *Sri Lanka Demographic Health Survey (DHS) 2016.* Colombo: Department of Census and Statistics and Ministry of National Policies and Economic Affairs. http://www.statistics.gov.lk/social/SLDHS%20 2016%20Report%20Final%20Full%2010%20Oct%202017.pdf.

———. 2019. *Sri Lanka Labour Force Survey 2018 Annual Bulletin.* Colombo: DCS. http://www.statistics.gov.lk/samplesurvey/LFS_Annual%20Bulletin_2018.pdf.

Dundar, Halil, Benoit Millot, Michelle Riboud, Mari Shojo, Harsha Aturupane, Sangeeta Goyal, and Dhushyanth Raju. 2017. *Sri Lanka Education Sector Assessment: Achievements, Challenges, and Policy Options.* Directions in Development—Human Development. Washington, DC: World Bank.

University Grant Commission, Sri Lanka. 2017. "Report on Graduate Outputs." http://www.ugc.ac.lk/downloads/statistics/stat_2017/Chapter%204.pdf.

UNDP (United Nations Development Programme). 2018. *Human Development Indices and Indicators: 2018 Statistical Update.* New York: United Nations Development Programme. http://www.hdr.undp.org/sites/default/files/2018_human_development _statistical_update.pdf.

UNESCO. 2016. UNESCO Institute for Statistics (UIS). UNESCO, Montreal. http://uis .unesco.org/country/LK.

UNICEF. 2014. *The State of the World's Children 2015: Reimagine the Future–Innovation for Every Child.* New York: UNICEF.

World Bank. 2018. World Development Indicators (WDI) Database. World Bank, Washington, DC. http://wdi.worldbank.org/tables.

APPENDIX B

Data and Methods

This book uses both quantitative and qualitative approaches to examine determinants of labor market outcomes for men and women in Sri Lanka. It undertakes descriptive and econometric analyses of the Sri Lanka Labour Force Surveys (LFS) 2006–15 and the Integrated Household Income and Expenditure Surveys (HIES) 2009–10 and 2012–13 to identify broader labor market trends and determinants of gender gaps in labor market outcomes (labor force participation, unemployment, wages, and working as a paid employee) that are representative at the national level. The secondary data analysis is supplemented with primary data collected from 556 households and 157 employers to gain deeper insights into the social environment and norms that shape men's and women's labor market outcomes in Sri Lanka. Primary data, both quantitative and qualitative, were collected in Gampaha, Badulla, and Trincomalee districts in 2012 and focused specifically on five growth sectors in Sri Lanka: tea estates, commercial agriculture, garments, tourism, and information and communication technology. Focus group discussions (FGDs) and key informant interviews (KIIs) complemented the surveys. In addition, KIIs were conducted in 2018 with select labor market experts, practitioners in the field of education, and industry leaders to further inform findings from the primary and secondary analysis (see appendix E for a list of the key informants interviewed in 2018). These findings help identify practical actions and recommendations for improving women's labor market participation in growth sectors of the Sri Lankan economy.

Secondary Data and Methods

The analyses of LFS and HIES data rigorously explore three key hypotheses to explain gender gaps in labor market outcomes:[1] household roles and responsibilities, human capital and skills mismatch, and gender bias. A detailed discussion of these hypotheses is provided in the conceptual framework section in chapter 2 of this book. The secondary data analyses investigate four key outcome variables: labor market participation, odds of becoming a paid employee, unemployment, and earnings for persons age 15–64. Before 2011, the LFS did not include data on all provinces in the country because of the prevailing civil conflict. The quantitative analysis of national survey data is conducted twice for each survey year—first using the full sample (all provinces) from that year, and then using a sample without the districts and provinces not included in surveys from years before 2011—to allow for comparability across the years.

The quantitative data analysis estimates probit models using maximum likelihood methods, with sample selection corrected to address selectivity bias. The estimations are undertaken first for the entire sample and then separately for women and men—nationally, and also disaggregated by the urban and rural-estate sectors. Standard Mincer regressions are used to examine the determinants of earnings and to estimate returns to education and marital status, among other characteristics. Finally, Oaxaca-Blinder decompositions use 2006–15 LFS data to estimate the contribution of unobserved factors (including gender discrimination) on two outcome areas of interest: labor market participation and earnings.[2] Regression results from secondary data analysis are presented in tables C1–C21 of appendix C.

Primary Data and Methods

The analysis of secondary data provides broad evidence to support the three hypotheses advanced to explain women's low rates of labor force participation and other poor labor market outcomes in Sri Lanka; however, the analysis does not capture underlying norms and beliefs that shape the outcomes observed, largely for two reasons. First, the LFS focuses primarily on the characteristics of the working population and on the types and conditions of work, making it difficult to determine who remains outside the workforce and possible barriers that prevent their participation in labor markets. Second, the secondary quantitative data do not reflect the sociocultural environment that shapes the labor market behavior of both men and women. For example, the secondary data do not necessarily explain why household responsibilities fall disproportionately on women, why women choose educational tracks and careers that put them at a disadvantage in the labor market, and why work conditions or employer preferences limit women's labor market choices or may undermine their persistence in the workforce. The primary data have thus been collected and analyzed with a view toward illuminating prevailing perceptions, beliefs, and norms, which in turn affect the labor market behavior of Sri Lankan women and their potential employers.

The primary data are from a mixed methods approach involving both quantitative and qualitative primary data collection. The quantitative data collection includes three discrete components: an employer survey, a worker survey, and a household survey. All three surveys were administered in Sri Lanka in 2012.

The employer survey was administered in firms identified from selected sectors of interest—that is, tea estates, commercial agriculture, tourism, garments, and information and communication technology—in three districts:

Badulla, Trincomalee, and Gampaha.[3] The team ensured that large, medium, and small firms were represented in each sector by conducting a participatory firm-ranking exercise, with employers to select firms from all size tiers for administration of the questionnaire. Overall, 157 employers were interviewed from the five sectors in nearly the same proportion. The employer survey collected information from firm owners or senior managers on the prevailing practices in hiring workers, employer perceptions of worker characteristics and attributes, specific working conditions and benefits available in the firm, and constraints faced by the employers with regard to the labor market. See appendix D, table D.5, for a detailed description of employer characteristics.

The worker survey was intended to collect information on working conditions, job prospects, and perceptions of workers on employment and other variables of interest to understand labor supply factors. The survey interviewed workers with different skill levels (managerial, skilled, and unskilled) and their households (worker households), which were identified with the help of firms from selected sectors of interest. From the same locality (villages), comparison households (that is, nonworker households) were chosen using household wealth-ranking techniques to identify whether there were systematic differences between the household groups. In all, the household and worker surveys collected information from 556 households: 405 worker households and 151 nonworker households—totaling 1,590 and 649 individuals, respectively. The survey collected data on demographics, education, employment, assets, and housing, as well as on outcomes of interest related to household decision-making, nutrition, and perceptions on schooling and work. Both men and women workers were purposely selected to ensure a gender balance in respondents, making up 58.8 percent and 41.3 percent, respectively, of the overall sample. The questionnaire also included modules that were specific to women and youth (age 15–29) to examine issues of job market entry and exit, job search, and perceptions of future employment in this age group. See appendix D, tables D.1–D.4, for a detailed description of the survey sample.

The mixed methods approach also entailed qualitative data collection to enrich the interpretation of survey findings. The qualitative methods included focus group discussions with male and female workers and unemployed persons, KIIs, and participatory rural appraisal exercises—all conducted in 2012. In addition, KIIs were conducted in 2018 (see next section). Focus group discussions and KIIs were intended to triangulate the findings of the surveys and to gain a deeper understanding of prevailing norms and perceptions regarding women's labor market outcomes.

KIIs with Select Labor Market Experts, Education Practitioners, and Industry Leaders

Additional KIIs were conducted in 2018 with the intent of gathering recommendations for next steps in growing the Sri Lankan economy by addressing obstacles to women's labor force participation. Purposeful sampling of leaders in relevant areas elicited qualitative data on practical actions that could improve economic returns to women in Sri Lanka's workforce. Recommended actions also are intended to provide incentives to key industries to make adjustments so that women will be more inclined to choose work that meets their potential. In turn, women can expect to receive remuneration appropriate to their educational and skills attainment. The 2018 KIIs focused in particular on eliciting suggestions for facilitating women's improved employment participation and outcomes in the fields of information and communication technologies, the garment industry, tourism, and tea estates—as well as inputs that could support cross-sector opportunities for expanding women's participation and economic success. The findings from KIIs, together with findings from a review of secondary literature, are included in chapters 4 and 5 of this book.

Notes

1. The LFS and HIES are conducted by the Department of Census and Statistics, Sri Lanka (DCS), on a regular basis. The surveys are representative at the district level and at the level of the urban, rural, and estate sectors. The LFS collects information on the characteristics of the labor force, while the HIES focuses on consumption expenditures by households.

2. The models control for such factors as education, age, gender, household characteristics, province, and household income level. Variables representing family and household-level factors include (1) proportion of children under age 5 in the household, (2) proportion of elderly above age 64 in the household, (3) membership in a female-headed household, (4) female household headship status, and (5) marital status. Detailed data on educational attainment and on age are used as proxies for skills. A dummy variable for gender is used in regressions on the entire sample, and separate estimations for female-only samples provide information on the contribution of gender difference to worker outcomes.

3. The study area consisted of three districts—Gampaha, Badulla, and Trincomalee— representing three main geographical regions of Sri Lanka: western, estate, and eastern regions, respectively. Field research was conducted in two sites per district in Gampaha and Badulla, one site representing an emerging industrial sector and the other a traditional sector in which women's labor force participation has traditionally been high. In Trincomalee, however, only an emerging industrial sector was covered, with a total of five sectors being selected for the research.

Full Regression Results from Secondary Data Analysis of Labor Market Outcomes

Table C.1 Labor Force Participation Regressions, 2015

Labor force participation	All	All males	All females	Urban, all	Urban, males	Urban, females	Estate and rural, all	Estate and rural, male	Estate and rural, female
	(1)	(2)	(3)	(4)	(5)	(6)	(7)	(8)	(9)
Household characteristics									
Children under age 5	-0.0265***	0.00392	-0.0743***	-0.00617	0.0299**	-0.0617***	-0.0310***	-0.00216	-0.0766***
	(0.00314)	(0.00444)	(0.00519)	(0.00730)	(0.0123)	(0.0116)	(0.00355)	(0.00458)	(0.00594)
Elderly over age 64	0.00815**	0.0104***	0.0111**	0.00613	0.0135	0.00814	0.00895**	0.0111***	0.0117**
	(0.00329)	(0.00399)	(0.00494)	(0.00852)	(0.0116)	(0.0114)	(0.00355)	(0.00421)	(0.00544)
The head of the household is female	-0.0537***	-0.0194***	-0.0604***	-0.0598***	-0.00653	-0.0822***	-0.0520***	-0.0223***	-0.0546***
	(0.00627)	(0.00664)	(0.00960)	(0.0146)	(0.0168)	(0.0222)	(0.00689)	(0.00713)	(0.0106)
Individual characteristics									
Female	-0.378***						-0.375***		
(0 = male, 1 = female)	(0.00285)						(0.00368)		
Female and head of household	0.106***		0.119***	0.105***		0.0970***	0.107***		0.126***
	(0.0101)		(0.0130)	(0.0252)		(0.0304)	(0.0111)		(0.0147)
Married	0.0316***	0.110***	-0.0436***	-0.0219	0.103***	-0.111***	0.0410***	0.109***	-0.0296***
	(0.00542)	(0.00623)	(0.00799)	(0.0142)	(0.0171)	(0.0192)	(0.00603)	(0.00674)	(0.00911)
Potential experience	0.0273***	0.0239***	0.0240***	0.0283***	0.0283***	0.0197***	0.0272***	0.0233***	0.0249***
	(0.000442)	(0.000462)	(0.000670)	(0.00125)	(0.00133)	(0.00185)	(0.000485)	(0.000492)	(0.000763)
Potential experience squared	-0.000477***	-0.000420***	-0.000450***	-0.000522***	-0.000527***	-0.000404***	-0.000471***	-0.000404***	-0.000459***
	(7.24e–06)	(7.89e–06)	(1.12e–05)	(2.22e–05)	(2.47e–05)	(3.26e–05)	(7.84e–06)	(8.45e–06)	(1.25e–05)
Education									
Below grade 6	-0.0102	0.0588***	-0.0548***	0.00975	0.0716	-0.00655	-0.0105	0.0571***	-0.0574***
	(0.0150)	(0.0211)	(0.0190)	(0.0527)	(0.0718)	(0.0648)	(0.0158)	(0.0216)	(0.0208)
Grades 7 to 9	-0.0780***	-0.000295	-0.137***	-0.0618	-0.00431	-0.0885	-0.0746***	0.00371	-0.138***
	(0.0153)	(0.0213)	(0.0197)	(0.0523)	(0.0705)	(0.0625)	(0.0161)	(0.0217)	(0.0215)
O-levels completed	-0.115***	-0.0196	-0.192***	-0.100**	-0.0149	-0.165***	-0.109***	-0.0129	-0.188***
	(0.0153)	(0.0213)	(0.0193)	(0.0507)	(0.0700)	(0.0619)	(0.0165)	(0.0220)	(0.0218)
A-levels completed	-0.0492***	-0.0281	-0.0836***	-0.0151	-0.00465	-0.0422	-0.0480***	-0.0278	-0.0820***

table continues next page

Table C.1 Labor Force Participation Regressions, 2015 *(continued)*

Labor force participation	All	All males	All females	Urban, all	Urban, males	Urban, females	Estate and rural, all	Estate and rural, male	Estate and rural, female
	(1)	(2)	(3)	(4)	(5)	(6)	(7)	(8)	(9)
	(0.0159)	(0.0219)	(0.0204)	(0.0517)	(0.0714)	(0.0639)	(0.0171)	(0.0226)	(0.0226)
University	0.204***	0.0355	0.258***	0.187***	0.0312	0.238***	0.227***	0.0497*	0.274***
	(0.0209)	(0.0263)	(0.0263)	(0.0565)	(0.0769)	(0.0695)	(0.0234)	(0.0290)	(0.0298)
Ethnicity									
Sri Lankan Tamil	-0.0333***	-0.00325	-0.0590***	-0.0329**	0.0417**	-0.0975***	-0.0343***	-0.0238**	-0.0407**
	(0.00777)	(0.00952)	(0.0134)	(0.0159)	(0.0212)	(0.0263)	(0.0108)	(0.0114)	(0.0197)
Indian Tamil	0.0260**	-0.0265**	0.0603***	0.0646*	0.121***	0.0203	0.0231	-0.0344**	0.0650***
	(0.0107)	(0.0125)	(0.0150)	(0.0386)	(0.0413)	(0.0522)	(0.0151)	(0.0147)	(0.0203)
Sri Lankan Moor	-0.105***	-0.000509	-0.230***	-0.0920***	0.0322**	-0.228***	-0.111***	-0.0119	-0.229***
	(0.00647)	(0.00801)	(0.0127)	(0.0134)	(0.0163)	(0.0235)	(0.00883)	(0.00916)	(0.0178)
Malay	-0.00212	0.0942**	-0.107*	0.0507	0.157***	-0.0594	0.00412	0.0823	-0.0838
	(0.0382)	(0.0432)	(0.0650)	(0.0372)	(0.0563)	(0.0531)	(0.0904)	(0.0784)	(0.189)
Burgher	-0.0727	0.0235	-0.153	-0.0861	0.0111	-0.171	-0.0768	0.0215	-0.146
	(0.0465)	(0.0498)	(0.100)	(0.0565)	(0.0618)	(0.105)	(0.0752)	(0.0865)	(0.170)
Other	-0.260***	-0.0123		-0.275***	-0.0499		-0.281*		
	(0.0689)	(0.0856)		(0.0801)	(0.0979)		(0.145)		
Sector and province									
Urban sector	-0.0339***	-0.0281***	-0.0407***						
	(0.00527)	(0.00617)	(0.00866)						
Central Province	0.0347***	0.0159**	0.0487***	0.00915	-0.000598	0.0103	0.0395***	0.0200**	0.0529***
	(0.00638)	(0.00773)	(0.00992)	(0.0160)	(0.0265)	(0.0319)	(0.00891)	(0.00846)	(0.0140)

table continues next page

Table C.1 Labor Force Participation Regressions, 2015 *(continued)*

Labor force participation	All	All males	All females	Urban, all	Urban, males	Urban, females	Estate and rural, all	Estate and rural, male	Estate and rural, female
	(1)	(2)	(3)	(4)	(5)	(6)	(7)	(8)	(9)
Southern Province	0.0155***	0.0146**	0.0145	-0.0237	-0.0298	-0.00895	0.0216***	0.0207***	0.0191
	(0.00599)	(0.00716)	(0.00931)	(0.0160)	(0.0224)	(0.0240)	(0.00807)	(0.00801)	(0.0126)
Northern Province	-0.0136	0.0145	-0.0526***	0.00502	-0.0164	0.0228	-0.0114	0.0349**	-0.0724***
	(0.00964)	(0.0118)	(0.0168)	(0.0248)	(0.0305)	(0.0406)	(0.0134)	(0.0141)	(0.0248)
Eastern Province	-0.0247***	0.00450	-0.0607***	-0.0168	-0.0228	-2.41e-05	-0.0218*	0.0196*	-0.0758***
	(0.00765)	(0.00932)	(0.0140)	(0.0158)	(0.0213)	(0.0255)	(0.0115)	(0.0114)	(0.0220)
North Western Province	0.0382***	0.0184**	0.0506***	0.0643***	0.0748**	0.0710*	0.0403***	0.0194**	0.0531***
	(0.00651)	(0.00784)	(0.0101)	(0.0209)	(0.0334)	(0.0410)	(0.00838)	(0.00787)	(0.0132)
North Central Province	0.0686***	0.0393***	0.0878***	-0.0765	-0.0643	-0.0153	0.0740***	0.0444***	0.0922***
	(0.00936)	(0.0112)	(0.0133)	(0.0718)	(0.0496)	(0.0991)	(0.0126)	(0.0119)	(0.0185)
Uva Province	0.0768***	0.0326***	0.110***	0.0321	0.00307	0.0610	0.0805***	0.0361***	0.114***
	(0.00929)	(0.0106)	(0.0135)	(0.0260)	(0.0267)	(0.0491)	(0.0131)	(0.0119)	(0.0188)
Sabaragamuwa Province	0.0453***	0.0186**	0.0645***	0.0726**	0.0770**	0.0740**	0.0463***	0.0183**	0.0658***
	(0.00661)	(0.00772)	(0.00994)	(0.0282)	(0.0359)	(0.0347)	(0.00851)	(0.00867)	(0.0129)
Household income proxy	Yes	Yes	Yes	Yes	Yes	Yes	Yes	Yes	Yes
Observations	55,897	26,565	29,320	8,712	4,146	4,556	47,185	22,417	24,764

Source: Labour Force Survey 2015. The sample includes population age 15 and older in all districts. The labor force was defined as those identified as employed and unemployed. Unemployment includes those who were not employed in the reference period but had found a job or enterprise or expected to do a paid job or had looked for a job in the past four weeks.

Note: Standard errors in parentheses.

*** $p < 0.01$, ** $p < 0.05$, * $p < 0.1$.

Table C.2 Labor Force Participation Regressions, 2013

Labor force participation	All	All males	All females	Urban, all	Urban, males	Urban, females	Estate and rural, all	Estate and rural, Male	Estate and rural, female
	(1)	(2)	(3)	(4)	(5)	(6)	(7)	(8)	(9)
Household characteristics									
Children under age 5	-0.0272***	-0.00747**	-0.0614***	-0.00792	-0.00929	-0.0311**	-0.0314***	-0.00737*	-0.0674***
	(0.00290)	(0.00356)	(0.00469)	(0.00729)	(0.00864)	(0.0121)	(0.00314)	(0.00388)	(0.00506)
Elderly over age 64	0.00235	0.000489	0.0131***	0.0120	0.0154	0.0190*	0.000625	-0.00192	0.0115**
	(0.00301)	(0.00373)	(0.00417)	(0.00825)	(0.01000)	(0.0101)	(0.00318)	(0.00401)	(0.00459)
The head of the household is female	-0.0509***	-0.0317***	-0.0463***	-0.0723***	-0.0377***	-0.0744***	-0.0447***	-0.0305***	-0.0380***
	(0.00550)	(0.00566)	(0.00838)	(0.0133)	(0.0136)	(0.0194)	(0.00597)	(0.00619)	(0.00929)
Individual characteristics									
Female	-0.314***			-0.337***			-0.309***		
	(0.00331)			(0.00702)			(0.00371)		
Female and head of household	0.0979***		0.127***	0.0282		0.0450	0.113***		0.146***
	(0.0101)		(0.0122)	(0.0252)		(0.0288)	(0.0109)		(0.0134)
Married	0.0429***	0.106***	-0.0150*	-0.0175	0.103***	-0.110***	0.0539***	0.104***	0.00374
	(0.00525)	(0.00631)	(0.00769)	(0.0129)	(0.0151)	(0.0175)	(0.00569)	(0.00698)	(0.00839)
Potential experience	0.0317***	0.0284***	0.0267***	0.0345***	0.0316***	0.0267***	0.0312***	0.0278***	0.0268***
	(0.000388)	(0.000428)	(0.000584)	(0.00115)	(0.00114)	(0.00162)	(0.000409)	(0.000462)	(0.000627)
Potential experience squared	-0.000485***	-0.000441***	-0.000435***	-0.000580***	-0.000543***	-0.000481***	-0.000469***	-0.000423***	-0.000429***
	(7.06e-06)	(7.96e-06)	(1.03e-05)	(2.17e-05)	(2.19e-05)	(3.20e-05)	(7.35e-06)	(8.42e-06)	(1.09e-05)
Education									
Below grade 6	-0.0519***	0.0123	-0.0808***	-0.120***	-0.0812	-0.118**	-0.0424***	0.0214	-0.0717***
	(0.0109)	(0.0131)	(0.0142)	(0.0367)	(0.0513)	(0.0478)	(0.0112)	(0.0132)	(0.0149)
Grades 7 to 9	-0.0415***	0.0272**	-0.102***	-0.0934***	-0.0477	-0.124***	-0.0314***	0.0372***	-0.0918***
	(0.0111)	(0.0133)	(0.0148)	(0.0360)	(0.0506)	(0.0467)	(0.0115)	(0.0134)	(0.0157)
O-levels completed	0.0418***	0.122***	-0.0492***	-0.0308	0.0182	-0.0845*	0.0559***	0.137***	-0.0370**
	(0.0109)	(0.0132)	(0.0143)	(0.0353)	(0.0500)	(0.0450)	(0.0113)	(0.0134)	(0.0151)
A-levels completed	0.134***	0.143***	0.0745***	0.0479	0.0361	0.0336	0.152***	0.158***	0.0884***

table continues next page

Table C.2 Labor Force Participation Regressions, 2013 (continued)

Labor force participation	All	All males	All females	Urban, all	Urban, males	Urban, females	Estate and rural, all	Estate and rural, Male	Estate and rural, female
	(1)	(2)	(3)	(4)	(5)	(6)	(7)	(8)	(9)
	(0.0117)	(0.0141)	(0.0151)	(0.0367)	(0.0517)	(0.0469)	(0.0123)	(0.0145)	(0.0161)
University	0.341***	0.197***	0.343***	0.216***	0.0964*	0.228***	0.384***	0.213***	0.390***
	(0.0174)	(0.0210)	(0.0218)	(0.0420)	(0.0559)	(0.0533)	(0.0196)	(0.0245)	(0.0242)
Ethnicity									
Sri Lankan Tamil	0.00343	0.0105	-0.0107	-0.0171	0.0283	-0.0606***	0.0135	-0.000644	0.0246
	(0.00877)	(0.00902)	(0.0140)	(0.0161)	(0.0173)	(0.0226)	(0.00959)	(0.0103)	(0.0162)
Indian Tamil	0.0703***	-0.00675	0.121***	0.0618*	-0.0135	0.121***	0.0717***	-0.00603	0.123***
	(0.0107)	(0.00946)	(0.0137)	(0.0363)	(0.0383)	(0.0384)	(0.0112)	(0.00967)	(0.0148)
Sri Lankan Moor	-0.0477***	0.0151**	-0.133***	-0.0341***	0.0325**	-0.0963***	-0.0579***	0.00256	-0.148***
	(0.00711)	(0.00714)	(0.0135)	(0.0114)	(0.0140)	(0.0184)	(0.00872)	(0.00794)	(0.0179)
Malay	-0.0308	-0.0326	-0.0499	0.000353	-0.0279	0.00518	-0.0774	-0.0396	-0.114
	(0.0432)	(0.0463)	(0.0901)	(0.0566)	(0.0643)	(0.105)	(0.0554)	(0.0543)	(0.118)
Burgher	-0.0331	-0.0262	-0.0327	0.00973	0.0345	0.0175	-0.104**	-0.104*	-0.0939
	(0.0336)	(0.0403)	(0.0540)	(0.0438)	(0.0351)	(0.0643)	(0.0491)	(0.0600)	(0.0738)
Other	0.0110	0.0641	-0.0380	-0.0247	0.0391	-0.0762	0.0357	0.162	-0.0146
	(0.0565)	(0.0988)	(0.0673)	(0.106)	(0.134)	(0.136)	(0.0558)	(0.109)	(0.0579)
Sector and province									
Urban sector	-0.0407***	-0.0184***	-0.0596***						
	(0.00560)	(0.00612)	(0.00846)						
Central Province	0.0271***	0.0157**	0.0336***	0.00518	-0.00255	0.0142	0.0324***	0.0231***	0.0348***
	(0.00696)	(0.00701)	(0.0103)	(0.0143)	(0.0171)	(0.0196)	(0.00775)	(0.00767)	(0.0116)
Southern Province	0.0399***	0.0307***	0.0444***	-0.0117	-0.00782	-0.0102	0.0477***	0.0382***	0.0504***
	(0.00675)	(0.00718)	(0.00942)	(0.0122)	(0.0178)	(0.0167)	(0.00756)	(0.00776)	(0.0107)
Northern Province	-0.0256**	0.0199*	-0.0840***	-0.00293	-0.0204	0.0152	-0.0321***	0.0394***	-0.127***
	(0.0106)	(0.0109)	(0.0186)	(0.0194)	(0.0248)	(0.0335)	(0.0119)	(0.0123)	(0.0212)
Eastern Province	-0.00708	0.0237***	-0.0550***	-0.00599	-0.0177	0.00211	-0.00498	0.0433***	-0.0809***

table continues next page

Table C.2 Labor Force Participation Regressions, 2013 *(continued)*

Labor force participation	All	All males	All females	Urban, all	Urban, males	Urban, females	Estate and rural, all	Estate and rural, Male	Estate and rural, female
	(1)	(2)	(3)	(4)	(5)	(6)	(7)	(8)	(9)
	(0.00827)	(0.00846)	(0.0152)	(0.0135)	(0.0169)	(0.0216)	(0.00995)	(0.00969)	(0.0186)
North Western Province	0.0568***	0.0295***	0.0733***	0.0302	0.0181	0.0338	0.0613***	0.0355***	0.0761***
	(0.00746)	(0.00765)	(0.0108)	(0.0293)	(0.0378)	(0.0280)	(0.00795)	(0.00804)	(0.0116)
North Central Province	0.0819***	0.0578***	0.0945***	0.0225	0.0201	0.0258	0.0878***	0.0652***	0.0981***
	(0.0113)	(0.0104)	(0.0159)	(0.0574)	(0.0337)	(0.0597)	(0.0117)	(0.0107)	(0.0167)
Uva Province	0.0722***	0.0464***	0.0828***	0.0191	0.00700	0.0426	0.0785***	0.0548***	0.0856***
	(0.00971)	(0.00944)	(0.0138)	(0.0321)	(0.0475)	(0.0336)	(0.0103)	(0.00981)	(0.0148)
Sabaragamuwa Province	0.0413***	0.0379***	0.0427***	0.0132	0.0420*	0.00237	0.0445***	0.0417***	0.0437***
	(0.00754)	(0.00751)	(0.0106)	(0.0333)	(0.0216)	(0.0489)	(0.00804)	(0.00802)	(0.0114)
Household income proxy	Yes	Yes	Yes	Yes	Yes	Yes	Yes	Yes	Yes
Observations	66,307	31,928	34,379	10,651	5,107	5,532	55,656	26,815	28,841

Source: Labour Force Survey 2013. The sample includes population age 15 and older in all districts. The labor force was defined as those identified as employed and unemployed. Unemployment includes those who were not employed in the reference period but had found a job or enterprise or expected to do a paid job or had looked for a job in the past four weeks. Sri Lanka is reweighting Labour Force Survey aggregates and microdata using revised Sri Lanka and subnational population estimates consistent with the 2012 Census; however, data are not available to us for 2013. Therefore, we used a simple linear population projection to adjust the 2013 population indicators.

Note: Standard errors in parentheses.

*** p < 0.01, ** p < 0.05, * p < 0.1.

Table C.3 Labor Force Participation Regressions, 2011

Labor force participation	All	All males	All females	Urban, all	Urban, males	Urban, females	Estate and rural, all	Estate and rural, Male	Estate and rural, female
	(1)	(2)	(3)	(4)	(5)	(6)	(7)	(8)	(9)
Household characteristics									
Children under age 5	-0.0228***	-0.00909**	-0.0522***	-0.0116*	0.0106	-0.0436***	-0.0253***	-0.0129***	-0.0539***
	(0.00344)	(0.00448)	(0.00557)	(0.00689)	(0.00999)	(0.0124)	(0.00370)	(0.00477)	(0.00595)
Elderly over age 64	-0.00284	0.00233	0.00179	-0.0160*	-0.0117	-0.00609	0.000311	0.00555	0.00395
	(0.00375)	(0.00478)	(0.00523)	(0.00942)	(0.0117)	(0.0132)	(0.00403)	(0.00497)	(0.00570)
The head of the household is female	-0.0449***	-0.0249***	-0.0446***	-0.0494***	-0.0353*	-0.0470*	-0.0428***	-0.0225***	-0.0427***
	(0.00634)	(0.00696)	(0.00941)	(0.0160)	(0.0208)	(0.0243)	(0.00704)	(0.00724)	(0.0106)
Individual characteristics									
Female	-0.317***			-0.340***			-0.314***		
	(0.00334)			(0.0102)			(0.00440)		
Female and head of household	0.0877***		0.106***	0.0671**		0.0857**	0.0936***		0.112***
	(0.0116)		(0.0137)	(0.0309)		(0.0342)	(0.0129)		(0.0154)
Married	0.0263***	0.0989***	-0.0343***	-0.0322*	0.0577**	-0.0918***	0.0348***	0.104***	-0.0252**
	(0.00645)	(0.00778)	(0.00908)	(0.0184)	(0.0225)	(0.0242)	(0.00693)	(0.00824)	(0.0102)
Potential experience	0.0328***	0.0302***	0.0275***	0.0349***	0.0356***	0.0248***	0.0324***	0.0294***	0.0277***
	(0.000468)	(0.000521)	(0.000700)	(0.00138)	(0.00160)	(0.00210)	(0.000501)	(0.000555)	(0.000775)
Potential experience squared	-0.000503***	-0.000473***	-0.000445***	-0.000568***	-0.000594***	-0.000428***	-0.000493***	-0.000457***	-0.000444***
	(8.43e-06)	(9.54e-06)	(1.27e-05)	(2.57e-05)	(3.11e-05)	(3.77e-05)	(9.22e-06)	(1.02e-05)	(1.41e-05)
Education									
Below grade 6	-0.0428***	-0.00352	-0.0519***	-0.0900**	-0.0544	-0.0916***	-0.0356***	0.00125	-0.0441***
	(0.0119)	(0.0161)	(0.0154)	(0.0377)	(0.0450)	(0.0413)	(0.0125)	(0.0161)	(0.0161)
Grades 7 to 9	-0.0150	0.0357**	-0.0590***	-0.0405	0.0257	-0.114***	-0.00828	0.0379**	-0.0484***
	(0.0121)	(0.0162)	(0.0159)	(0.0356)	(0.0484)	(0.0386)	(0.0127)	(0.0164)	(0.0170)
O-levels completed	0.0553***	0.115***	-0.0198	-0.00259	0.0781*	-0.108***	0.0673***	0.121***	-0.00252
	(0.0120)	(0.0158)	(0.0155)	(0.0369)	(0.0470)	(0.0370)	(0.0130)	(0.0158)	(0.0171)
A-levels completed	0.152***	0.144***	0.103***	0.122***	0.110**	0.0562	0.159***	0.149***	0.111***

table continues next page

Table C.3 Labor Force Participation Regressions, 2011 *(continued)*

	All	All males	All females	Urban, all	Urban, males	Urban, females	Estate and rural, all	Estate and rural, Male	Estate and rural, female
	(1)	(2)	(3)	(4)	(5)	(6)	(7)	(8)	(9)
Labor force participation									
	(0.0129)	(0.0170)	(0.0166)	(0.0378)	(0.0487)	(0.0379)	(0.0141)	(0.0175)	(0.0180)
University	0.354***	0.182***	0.377***	0.252***	0.114*	0.248***	0.389***	0.211***	0.401***
	(0.0207)	(0.0257)	(0.0252)	(0.0489)	(0.0601)	(0.0505)	(0.0244)	(0.0303)	(0.0282)
Ethnicity									
Sri Lankan Tamil	0.00588	0.00509	0.00579	-0.00721	0.0163	-0.0206	0.0130	0.00657	0.0153
	(0.00942)	(0.0105)	(0.0143)	(0.0172)	(0.0231)	(0.0209)	(0.0146)	(0.0134)	(0.0215)
Indian Tamil	0.0437***	-0.0277**	0.0892***	0.0692*	0.105**	0.0134	0.0406***	-0.0348***	0.0935***
	(0.0102)	(0.0108)	(0.0134)	(0.0364)	(0.0492)	(0.0451)	(0.0140)	(0.0134)	(0.0187)
Sri Lankan Moor	-0.0692***	-0.00753	-0.155***	-0.0315*	0.0372*	-0.121***	-0.0803***	-0.0209**	-0.162***
	(0.00719)	(0.00859)	(0.0137)	(0.0174)	(0.0206)	(0.0250)	(0.00960)	(0.0104)	(0.0172)
Malay	-0.0519	0.0732	-0.172**	0.00386	0.0727	-0.0455	-0.103*	0.0873	-0.293**
	(0.0433)	(0.0666)	(0.0853)	(0.0554)	(0.0987)	(0.0992)	(0.0623)	(0.0596)	(0.132)
Burgher	-0.0169	0.0382	-0.0838	-0.0217	0.0303	-0.0597	0.00157	0.0753	-0.105
	(0.0615)	(0.0985)	(0.103)	(0.0808)	(0.145)	(0.103)	(0.0935)	(0.0710)	(0.191)
Other	-0.101***	-0.00877	-0.345*	-0.140***	0.0266		-0.106	-0.122***	-0.116
	(0.0310)	(0.0461)	(0.199)	(0.0283)	(0.0590)		(0.0790)	(0.0160)	(0.232)
Sector and province									
Urban sector	-0.0235***	-0.00404	-0.0392***						
	(0.00647)	(0.00759)	(0.00995)						
Central Province	0.0579***	0.0418***	0.0729***	-0.0566*	-0.0116	-0.0940***	0.0729***	0.0522***	0.0918***
	(0.00755)	(0.00884)	(0.0111)	(0.0287)	(0.0323)	(0.0336)	(0.00987)	(0.0101)	(0.0149)
Southern Province	0.0560***	0.0522***	0.0585***	0.0411**	0.0344	0.0190	0.0631***	0.0585***	0.0686***

table continues next page

Table C.3 Labor Force Participation Regressions, 2011 (continued)

Labor force participation	All (1)	All males (2)	All females (3)	Urban, all (4)	Urban, males (5)	Urban, females (6)	Estate and rural, all (7)	Estate and rural, Male (8)	Estate and rural, female (9)
	(0.00690)	(0.00804)	(0.00991)	(0.0191)	(0.0346)	(0.0226)	(0.00867)	(0.00901)	(0.0126)
Northern Province	−0.0162	0.0393***	−0.0886***	−0.0389**	−0.0143	−0.0878***	−0.00789	0.0551***	−0.0845***
	(0.0110)	(0.0127)	(0.0175)	(0.0188)	(0.0264)	(0.0263)	(0.0171)	(0.0158)	(0.0266)
Eastern Province	0.0212**	0.0594***	−0.0350**	0.0133	0.0246	−0.0262	0.0291**	0.0718***	−0.0312
	(0.00863)	(0.0103)	(0.0148)	(0.0186)	(0.0258)	(0.0254)	(0.0115)	(0.0119)	(0.0204)
North Western Province	0.0579***	0.0648***	0.0481***	0.0456	0.0498	0.0330	0.0659***	0.0718***	0.0581***
	(0.00710)	(0.00860)	(0.0106)	(0.0324)	(0.0379)	(0.0663)	(0.00947)	(0.00952)	(0.0142)
North Central Province	0.102***	0.0813***	0.119***	−0.0146	−0.0415*	0.0163	0.114***	0.0930***	0.133***
	(0.00873)	(0.0104)	(0.0121)	(0.0305)	(0.0219)	(0.0267)	(0.0126)	(0.0117)	(0.0179)
Uva Province	0.120***	0.0774***	0.146***	0.00884	0.0166	0.0114	0.132***	0.0861***	0.161***
	(0.00924)	(0.0106)	(0.0123)	(0.0342)	(0.0240)	(0.0423)	(0.0135)	(0.0141)	(0.0176)
Sabaragamuwa Province	0.0648***	0.0476***	0.0835***	−0.0276	0.0195	−0.0802	0.0738***	0.0538***	0.0965***
	(0.00763)	(0.00917)	(0.0110)	(0.0272)	(0.0352)	(0.0500)	(0.00998)	(0.0109)	(0.0140)
Household Income Proxy	Yes	Yes	Yes	Yes	Yes	Yes	Yes	Yes	Yes
Observations	47,430	23,156	24,274	6,206	3,025	3,167	41,224	20,131	21,093

Source: Labour Force Survey 2011. The sample includes population age 15 and older in all districts. The labor force was defined as those identified as employed and unemployed. Unemployment includes those who were not employed in the reference period but had found a job or enterprise or expected to do a paid job or had looked for a job in the past four weeks. Sri Lanka is reweighting Labour Force Survey aggregates and microdata, using revised Sri Lanka and subnational population estimates consistent with the 2012 census; however, the data are not available for us for the year 2011. Therefore, we used a simple linear population projection to adjust the 2011 population indicators.

Note: Standard errors in parentheses.

*** $p < 0.01$, ** $p < 0.05$, * $p < 0.1$.

Table C.4 Labor Force Participation Regressions, 2009, Excluding Northern Province

Labor force participation	All	All males	All females	Urban, all	Urban, males	Urban, females	Estate and rural, all	Estate and rural, Male	Estate and rural, female
	(1)	(2)	(3)	(4)	(5)	(6)	(7)	(8)	(9)
Household characteristics									
Children under age 5	-0.0294***	-0.00363	-0.0695***	-0.0274***	-0.0192	-0.0585***	-0.0294***	-0.00195	-0.0700***
	(0.00329)	(0.00441)	(0.00538)	(0.00943)	(0.0142)	(0.0152)	(0.00352)	(0.00463)	(0.00571)
Elderly over age 64	0.00731**	0.0135***	0.0121**	0.00344	0.00308	0.0275*	0.00819***	0.0158***	0.0102*
	(0.00363)	(0.00426)	(0.00561)	(0.00944)	(0.0121)	(0.0146)	(0.00391)	(0.00453)	(0.00601)
The head of the household is female	-0.0501***	-0.00711	-0.0700***	-0.0635***	-0.0119	-0.0929***	-0.0465***	-0.00521	-0.0644***
	(0.00665)	(0.00686)	(0.0100)	(0.0171)	(0.0181)	(0.0241)	(0.00717)	(0.00739)	(0.0109)
Individual characteristics									
Female	-0.366***			-0.389***			-0.362***		
	(0.00311)			(0.00841)			(0.00333)		
Female and head of household	0.0965***		0.0892***	0.0927***		0.0699**	0.0981***		0.0932***
	(0.0112)		(0.0140)	(0.0298)		(0.0334)	(0.0121)		(0.0153)
Married	0.0335***	0.143***	-0.0596***	-0.0242	0.144***	-0.136***	0.0402***	0.140***	-0.0488***
	(0.00581)	(0.00709)	(0.00848)	(0.0163)	(0.0224)	(0.0219)	(0.00620)	(0.00748)	(0.00914)
Potential experience	0.0266***	0.0220***	0.0244***	0.0274***	0.0259***	0.0211***	0.0266***	0.0219***	0.0249***
	(0.000665)	(0.000539)	(0.000730)	(0.00160)	(0.00182)	(0.00213)	(0.000512)	(0.000561)	(0.000774)
Potential experience squared	-0.000478***	-0.000413***	-0.000466***	-0.000519***	-0.000525***	-0.000427***	-0.000475***	-0.000404***	-0.000470***
	(8.05e-06)	(8.77e-06)	(1.24e-05)	(2.83e-05)	(3.15e-05)	(3.85e-05)	(8.36e-06)	(9.04e-06)	(1.30e-05)
Education									
Below grade 6	-1.79e-05	0.0686***	-0.0290*	0.0978*	0.276***	-0.0255	-0.00645	0.0518**	-0.0299*
	(0.0130)	(0.0197)	(0.0166)	(0.0508)	(0.0647)	(0.0591)	(0.0133)	(0.0202)	(0.0173)
Grades 7 to 9	-0.0578***	0.00813	-0.101***	-0.00665	0.162***	-0.146**	-0.0577***	-0.00153	-0.0933***
	(0.0131)	(0.0193)	(0.0174)	(0.0500)	(0.0577)	(0.0583)	(0.0136)	(0.0200)	(0.0183)
O-levels completed	-0.0940***	-0.0206	-0.153***	-0.0427	0.108*	-0.186***	-0.0917***	-0.0247	-0.144***
	(0.0130)	(0.0193)	(0.0170)	(0.0487)	(0.0559)	(0.0569)	(0.0135)	(0.0201)	(0.0179)
A-levels completed	-0.0216	-0.0262	-0.0359*	0.0561	0.120**	-0.0289	-0.0229	-0.0337	-0.0322*

table continues next page

Table C.4 **Labor Force Participation Regressions, 2009, Excluding Northern Province** *(continued)*

Labor force participation	All	All males	All females	Urban, all	Urban, males	Urban, females	Estate and rural, all	Estate and rural, Male	Estate and rural, female
	(1)	(2)	(3)	(4)	(5)	(6)	(7)	(8)	(9)
	(0.0139)	(0.0201)	(0.0185)	(0.0505)	(0.0587)	(0.0593)	(0.0145)	(0.0210)	(0.0196)
University	0.167***	0.243	0.220***	0.220***	0.179***	0.211***	0.172***	0.0118	0.224***
	(0.0205)	(0.0254)	(0.0262)	(0.0586)	(0.0650)	(0.0703)	(0.0224)	(0.0275)	(0.0286)
Ethnicity									
Sri Lankan Tamil	−0.0263***	−0.0114	−0.0418***	−0.0505***	0.0285	−0.114***	−0.0192*	−0.0240**	−0.0192
	(0.00856)	(0.00996)	(0.0138)	(0.0162)	(0.0210)	(0.0254)	(0.0101)	(0.0115)	(0.0160)
Indian Tamil	0.0378***	−0.0401***	0.0974***	0.118**	0.169***	0.0967*	0.0329**	−0.0487***	0.0976***
	(0.0135)	(0.0137)	(0.0213)	(0.0461)	(0.0592)	(0.0578)	(0.0139)	(0.0138)	(0.0224)
Sri Lankan Moor	−0.0959***	−0.0167*	−0.188***	−0.0815***	0.00118	−0.150***	−0.102***	−0.0221**	−0.200***
	(0.00688)	(0.00891)	(0.0138)	(0.0142)	(0.0197)	(0.0249)	(0.00793)	(0.0102)	(0.0161)
Malay	−0.0381	0.0309	−0.122*	−0.0358	0.0730	−0.153	−0.0297	0.0218	−0.0964
	(0.0356)	(0.0477)	(0.0720)	(0.0484)	(0.0757)	(0.119)	(0.0416)	(0.0647)	(0.0776)
Burger	0.0200	0.00238	0.0151	−0.0509	0.0171	−0.122	0.0569	0.0330	0.0605
	(0.0393)	(0.0534)	(0.0678)	(0.0530)	(0.0838)	(0.0769)	(0.0565)	(0.0714)	(0.0973)
Other	−0.139***	−0.0555	−0.174**	0.0219	0.125	−0.0804	−0.183***	−0.0968***	−0.217***
	(0.0439)	(0.0411)	(0.0689)	(0.0868)	(0.0801)	(0.110)	(0.0404)	(0.0370)	(0.0792)
Sector and province									
Urban sector	−0.0251***	−0.0187**	−0.0327***						
	(0.00633)	(0.00725)	(0.0104)						
Central Province	0.0414***	0.0154**	0.0668***	−0.0265	−0.00686	−0.0506	0.0507***	0.0222***	0.0798***
	(0.00695)	(0.00779)	(0.0111)	(0.0191)	(0.0273)	(0.0313)	(0.00741)	(0.00815)	(0.0119)
Southern Province	0.0470***	0.0333***	0.0577***	−0.0256	−0.0231	−0.0303	0.0554***	0.0393***	0.0687***
	(0.00627)	(0.00725)	(0.00957)	(0.0191)	(0.0239)	(0.0253)	(0.00667)	(0.00757)	(0.0104)
Northern Province	—	—	—	—	—	—	—	—	—
Eastern Province	0.0144*	0.0513***	−0.0221	0.0118	−0.00531	0.0298	0.0194**	0.0659***	−0.0249

table continues next page

Table C.4 Labor Force Participation Regressions, 2009, Excluding Northern Province *(continued)*

Labor force participation	All	All males	All females	Urban, all	Urban, males	Urban, females	Estate and rural, all	Estate and rural, Male	Estate and rural, female
	(1)	(2)	(3)	(4)	(5)	(6)	(7)	(8)	(9)
	(0.00795)	(0.00997)	(0.0143)	(0.0166)	(0.0216)	(0.0271)	(0.00913)	(0.0114)	(0.0165)
North Western Province	0.0444***	0.0394***	0.0480***	0.0745**	0.0294	0.0953**	0.0487***	0.0432***	0.0537***
	(0.00676)	(0.00799)	(0.0105)	(0.0321)	(0.0428)	(0.0421)	(0.00698)	(0.00807)	(0.0110)
North Central Province	0.0982***	0.0609***	0.129***	−0.00163	0.0369	−0.0133	0.105***	0.0665***	0.138***
	(0.00857)	(0.0101)	(0.0126)	(0.0380)	(0.0698)	(0.0454)	(0.00882)	(0.0103)	(0.0131)
Uva Province	0.121***	0.0485***	0.178***	0.170***	0.0996*	0.158***	0.125***	0.0524***	0.184***
	(0.00930)	(0.0106)	(0.0133)	(0.0387)	(0.0521)	(0.0437)	(0.00953)	(0.0107)	(0.0139)
Sabaragamuwa Province	0.0629***	0.0242***	0.0950***	−0.00123	−0.0202	−0.00287	0.0684***	0.0285***	0.103***
	(0.00702)	(0.00830)	(0.0106)	(0.0230)	(0.0313)	(0.0469)	(0.00724)	(0.00838)	(0.0111)
Household income proxy	Yes	Yes	Yes	Yes	Yes	Yes	Yes	Yes	Yes
Observations	49,516	23,641	25,875	6,499	3,072	3,425	43,017	20,567	22,450

Source: Labour Force Survey 2009. The sample includes population age 15 and older in all districts except Northern Province. The labor force was defined as those identified as employed and unemployed. Unemployment includes those who were not employed in the reference period but had found a job or enterprise or expected to do a paid job or had looked for a job in the past four weeks.

Note: Standard errors in parentheses.

*** $p < 0.01$, ** $p < 0.05$, * $p < 0.1$

Table C.5 Labor Force Participation Regressions, 2006, Excluding Northern and Eastern Provinces

	All	All males	All females	Urban, all	Urban, males	Urban, females	Estate and rural, all	Estate and rural, Male	Estate and rural, female
Labor force participation	(1)	(2)	(3)	(4)	(5)	(6)	(7)	(8)	(9)
Household characteristics									
Children under age 5	-0.0293***	-0.00122	-0.0766***	-0.00609	0.00733	-0.0364**	-0.0346***	-0.00366	-0.0839***
	(0.00328)	(0.00437)	(0.00562)	(0.00847)	(0.0131)	(0.0144)	(0.00356)	(0.00471)	(0.00601)
Elderly over age 64	0.00268	0.0154***	0.00145	-0.0107	0.0197	-0.0164	0.00564	0.0159***	0.00574
	(0.00378)	(0.00441)	(0.00593)	(0.00993)	(0.0131)	(0.0146)	(0.00407)	(0.00466)	(0.00642)
The head of the household is female	-0.0375***	-0.000226	-0.0572***	-0.0554***	-0.0117	-0.0728***	-0.0330***	0.00313	-0.0536***
	(0.00648)	(0.00652)	(0.0102)	(0.0162)	(0.0177)	(0.0230)	(0.00700)	(0.00700)	(0.0110)
Individual characteristics									
Female	-0.355***			-0.418***			-0.344***		
	(0.00318)			(0.00719)			(0.00345)		
Female and head of household	0.0874***		0.0812***E158	0.0638**		0.0656**	0.0945***		0.0881***
	(0.0109)		(0.0141)	(0.0264)		(0.0318)	(0.0119)		(0.0155)
Married	0.0189***	0.137***	-0.0792***	-0.0454***	0.147***	-0.170***	0.0271***	0.132***	-0.0644***
	(0.00578)	(0.00706)	(0.00864)	(0.0161)	(0.0202)	(0.0217)	(0.00617)	(0.00754)	(0.00932)
Potential experience	0.0256***	0.0215***	0.0234***	0.0272***	0.0255***	0.0187***	0.0257***	0.0215***	0.0242***
	(0.000502)	(0.000549)	(0.000767)	(0.00154)	(0.00164)	(0.00212)	(0.000528)	(0.000577)	(0.000822)
Potential experience squared	-0.000461***	-0.000398***	-0.000457***	-0.000525***	-0.000520***	-0.000408***	-0.000457***	-0.000390***	-0.000466***
	(8.26e-06)	(8.98e-06)	(1.30e-05)	(2.70e-05)	(2.78e-05)	(3.91e-05)	(8.62e-06)	(9.29e-06)	(1.39e-05)
Education									
Below grade 6	0.00427	0.0746***	-0.0371**	-0.00354	0.0497	-0.0454	0.00835	0.0783***	-0.0344*
	(0.0127)	(0.0171)	(0.0167)	(0.0441)	(0.0537)	(0.0545)	(0.0132)	(0.0176)	(0.0175)
Grades 7 to 9	-0.0442***	0.0421**	-0.113***	-0.0381	0.0338	-0.0985*	-0.0380***	0.0489***	-0.110***
	(0.0129)	(0.0170)	(0.0175)	(0.0427)	(0.0527)	(0.0517)	(0.0135)	(0.0176)	(0.0186)
O-levels completed	-0.0675***	0.0314*	-0.153***	-0.0879**	-0.0106	-0.181***	-0.0568***	0.0445**	-0.142***
	(0.0130)	(0.0171)	(0.0173)	(0.0418)	(0.0507)	(0.0524)	(0.0136)	(0.0178)	(0.0184)
A-levels completed	0.0246*	0.0456**	-0.0190	-0.00326	0.0128	-0.0584	0.0361**	0.0570***	-0.00672

table continues next page

Table C.5 Labor Force Participation Regressions, 2006, Excluding Northern and Eastern Provinces *(continued)*

	All	All males	All females	Urban, all	Urban, males	Urban, females	Estate and rural, all	Estate and rural, Male	Estate and rural, female
	(1)	(2)	(3)	(4)	(5)	(6)	(7)	(8)	(9)
Labor force participation									
	(0.0140)	(0.0180)	(0.0191)	(0.0441)	(0.0530)	(0.0549)	(0.0148)	(0.0189)	(0.0204)
University	0.172***	0.0461*	0.213***	0.121**	−0.00200	0.118*	0.194***	0.0588**	0.242***
	(0.0211)	(0.0239)	(0.0277)	(0.0527)	(0.0619)	(0.0645)	(0.0237)	(0.0260)	(0.0314)
Ethnicity									
Sri Lankan Tamil	−0.00475	−0.0116	−0.00819	−0.0351**	0.0275	−0.102***	0.0178	−0.0316**	0.0556***
	(0.0102)	(0.0116)	(0.0167)	(0.0169)	(0.0192)	(0.0246)	(0.0131)	(0.0145)	(0.0210)
Indian Tamil	0.0653***	−0.0164	0.128***	0.0667	0.0613	0.0425	0.0665***	−0.0211*	0.140***
	(0.0107)	(0.0118)	(0.0154)	(0.0492)	(0.0613)	(0.0503)	(0.0108)	(0.0119)	(0.0162)
Sri Lankan Moor	−0.129***	−0.0297***	−0.266***	−0.108***	0.00701	−0.227***	−0.148***	−0.0461***	−0.284***
	(0.00769)	(0.00890)	(0.0167)	(0.0149)	(0.0168)	(0.0266)	(0.00894)	(0.0105)	(0.0201)
Malay	−0.120***	−0.0266	−0.226***	−0.145***	−0.0266	−0.256***	−0.0743	0.0344	−0.172
	(0.0315)	(0.0398)	(0.0700)	(0.0388)	(0.0511)	(0.0712)	(0.0506)	(0.0618)	(0.135)
Burger	−0.0486	−0.00751	−0.105	0.0736	0.146	0.0414	−0.130***	−0.0813	−0.194***
	(0.0365)	(0.0541)	(0.0753)	(0.0596)	(0.0986)	(0.129)	(0.0464)	(0.0704)	(0.0675)
Other	−0.0767	−0.0996	−0.0722	−0.0597	0.122	−0.234***	−0.0837	−0.192	0.0359
	(0.102)	(0.123)	(0.156)	(0.0525)	(0.0955)	(0.0601)	(0.164)	(0.133)	(0.271)
Sector and province									
Urban sector	−0.0422***	−0.00809	−0.0814***						
	(0.00657)	(0.00761)	(0.0110)						
Central Province	0.0182***	0.00934	0.0324***	0.0291	0.0229	0.0389	0.0212***	0.0138*	0.0324***
	(0.00677)	(0.00765)	(0.0109)	(0.0223)	(0.0268)	(0.0323)	(0.00715)	(0.00803)	(0.0117)

table continues next page

Table C.5 Labor Force Participation Regressions, 2006, Excluding Northern and Eastern Provinces *(continued)*

Labor force participation	All	All males	All females	Urban, all	Urban, males	Urban, females	Estate and rural, all	Estate and rural, Male	Estate and rural, female
	(1)	(2)	(3)	(4)	(5)	(6)	(7)	(8)	(9)
Southern Province	0.0323***	0.0268***	0.0364***	−0.0339**	−0.0119	−0.0519*	0.0372***	0.0300***	0.0431***
	(0.00618)	(0.00714)	(0.00955)	(0.0167)	(0.0218)	(0.0267)	(0.00659)	(0.00754)	(0.0103)
Northern Province	—	—	—	—	—	—	—	—	—
Eastern Province	—	—	—	—	—	—	—	—	—
North Western Province	0.0464***	0.0328***	0.0606***	0.0102	−0.000834	0.0274	0.0496***	0.0359***	0.0640***
	(0.00664)	(0.00804)	(0.0103)	(0.0238)	(0.0355)	(0.0395)	(0.00685)	(0.00822)	(0.0108)
North Central Province	0.0545***	0.0518***	0.0578***	0.0752***	0.0695*	0.0771*	0.0579***	0.0540***	0.0618***
	(0.00825)	(0.00972)	(0.0128)	(0.0280)	(0.0385)	(0.0402)	(0.00850)	(0.00992)	(0.0135)
Uva Province	0.101***	0.0618***	0.133***	0.0691	0.0283	0.0816	0.103***	0.0656***	0.136***
	(0.00913)	(0.0105)	(0.0133)	(0.0420)	(0.0563)	(0.0614)	(0.00932)	(0.0105)	(0.0139)
Sabaragamuwa Province	0.0255***	0.0203***	0.0311***	0.0627**	0.0359	0.0855**	0.0268***	0.0228***	0.0310***
	(0.00678)	(0.00780)	(0.0106)	(0.0319)	(0.0369)	(0.0429)	(0.00697)	(0.00795)	(0.0111)
Household income proxy	Yes	Yes	Yes	Yes	Yes	Yes	Yes	Yes	Yes
Observations	48,347	23,392	24,955	6,260	2,942	3,311	42,087	20,446	21,641

Source: Labour Force Survey 2006. The sample includes population age 15 and older in all districts except Northern and Eastern Provinces. The labor force was defined as those identified as employed and unemployed. Unemployment includes those who were not employed in the reference period but they had found a job or enterprise or expected to do a paid job or had looked for a job in the past four weeks.

Note: Standard errors in parentheses.

*** $p < 0.01$, ** $p < 0.05$, * $p < 0.1$.

Table C.6 Mincer Earnings Regression, 2015: OLS and Heckman Selection Maximum Likelihood Estimates

	All			Female			Male		
	OLS	Heckman		OLS	Heckman		OLS	Heckman	
	Log of earnings	Log of earnings	Be a paid employee	Log of earnings	Log of earnings	Be a paid employee	Log of earnings	Log of earnings	Be a paid employee
Variables	(1)	(2)	(3)	(1)	(2)	(3)	(1)	(2)	(3)
Household characteristics									
Children under age 5 living in the household	0.00477	−0.000230	0.00333	−0.0236	−0.0237	−0.0114	0.00677	0.00125	−0.00523
	(0.0109)	(0.00900)	(0.0158)	(0.0224)	(0.0169)	(0.0275)	(0.0111)	(0.00968)	(0.0188)
People over age 64 living in the household	−0.000460	0.00438	0.0354**	−0.00236	0.0123	0.0177	−0.00447	−0.00695	0.0381*
	(0.0111)	(0.00845)	(0.0160)	(0.0181)	(0.0119)	(0.0242)	(0.0133)	(0.0110)	(0.0201)
Member of female-headed household	−0.0249	−0.0206	−0.113***	−0.0155	−0.0167	−0.123***	−0.0257	−0.0160	−0.0795**
	(0.0191)	(0.0144)	(0.0290)	(0.0320)	(0.0220)	(0.0474)	(0.0216)	(0.0185)	(0.0367)
Individual characteristics									
Female	−0.317***	−0.312***	−0.0344						
	(0.0182)	(0.0133)	(0.0255)						
Head of household	0.1000***	0.103***	0.0757***	−0.0408	−0.00416	−0.0973*	0.0844***	0.0799***	0.0297
	(0.0180)	(0.0147)	(0.0279)	(0.0504)	(0.0324)	(0.0573)	(0.0195)	(0.0176)	(0.0351)
Female head of household	−0.125**	−0.0924***	−0.0983*						
	(0.0511)	(0.0325)	(0.0557)						
Married	0.105***	0.105***	−0.109***	−0.00285	0.0186	−0.262***	0.187***	0.176***	0.0249
	(0.0182)	(0.0133)	(0.0256)	(0.0280)	(0.0204)	(0.0370)	(0.0226)	(0.0171)	(0.0343)
Potential experience	0.0211***	0.0192***	0.00394	0.0186***	0.0146***	0.0116***	0.0212***	0.0208***	−0.00123
	(0.00199)	(0.00152)	(0.00249)	(0.00322)	(0.00222)	(0.00391)	(0.00243)	(0.00199)	(0.00318)

table continues next page

129

Table C.6 Mincer Earnings Regression, 2015: OLS and Heckman Selection Maximum Likelihood Estimates *(continued)*

	All			Female			Male		
	OLS	Heckman		OLS	Heckman		OLS	Heckman	
Variables	Log of earnings	Log of earnings	Be a paid employee	Log of earnings	Log of earnings	Be a paid employee	Log of earnings	Log of earnings	Be a paid employee
	(1)	*(2)*	*(3)*	*(1)*	*(2)*	*(3)*	*(1)*	*(2)*	*(3)*
Potential experience squared	−0.000411***	−0.000392***	−0.000317***	−0.000303***	−0.000250***	−0.000454***	−0.000436***	−0.000434***	−0.000237***
	(3.26e−05)	(2.64e−05)	(3.93e−05)	(5.57e−05)	(4.14e−05)	(6.70e−05)	(3.93e−05)	(3.36e−05)	(4.78e−05)
Education									
Below grade 6	−0.0617	−0.0577	−0.243***	−0.127**	−0.0617	−0.224**	0.0550	0.0107	−0.213**
	(0.0464)	(0.0399)	(0.0676)	(0.0603)	(0.0490)	(0.0953)	(0.0720)	(0.0604)	(0.0906)
Grades 7 to 9	−0.0542	−0.0578	−0.406***	−0.0947	−0.0562	−0.465***	0.0557	0.0209	−0.330***
	(0.0467)	(0.0409)	(0.0678)	(0.0649)	(0.0557)	(0.101)	(0.0714)	(0.0603)	(0.0906)
O-levels completed	0.0228	0.0201	−0.442***	0.00937	0.0460	−0.653***	0.123*	0.0943	−0.311***
	(0.0461)	(0.0409)	(0.0691)	(0.0622)	(0.0554)	(0.102)	(0.0710)	(0.0599)	(0.0906)
A-levels completed	0.227***	0.245***	−0.0927	0.216***	0.254***	−0.274***	0.318***	0.319***	0.0374
	(0.0479)	(0.0422)	(0.0716)	(0.0695)	(0.0584)	(0.106)	(0.0729)	(0.0610)	(0.0931)
University	0.544***	0.564***	0.597***	0.499***	0.522***	0.445***	0.645***	0.657***	0.696***
	(0.0532)	(0.0475)	(0.0852)	(0.0751)	(0.0664)	(0.123)	(0.0814)	(0.0684)	(0.110)
Ethnicity									
Sri Lankan Tamil	−0.0552*	−0.0618***	0.0831	−0.0576	−0.0494	0.212***	−0.0430	−0.0615**	0.0222
	(0.0295)	(0.0232)	(0.0513)	(0.0643)	(0.0416)	(0.0819)	(0.0279)	(0.0258)	(0.0597)
Indian Tamil	−0.0485	−0.0370	0.365***	−0.0386	−0.0492	0.572***	−0.0696	−0.0505	0.220**
	(0.0423)	(0.0403)	(0.0947)	(0.0517)	(0.0546)	(0.127)	(0.0551)	(0.0501)	(0.106)
Sri Lankan Moor	0.0375	0.00935	−0.208***	0.00646	−0.0442	−0.496***	0.0169	−0.00470	−0.161***
	(0.0242)	(0.0228)	(0.0423)	(0.0582)	(0.0535)	(0.0828)	(0.0248)	(0.0244)	(0.0465)
Malay	0.136	0.118	0.120	−0.193	−0.234	−0.467	0.204	0.198	0.328
	(0.170)	(0.166)	(0.203)	(0.299)	(0.299)	(0.366)	(0.152)	(0.149)	(0.235)
Burgher	0.180	0.153	0.0439	−0.0350	−0.0972	0.0593	0.248	0.233	0.0835
	(0.141)	(0.140)	(0.222)	(0.134)	(0.121)	(0.412)	(0.174)	(0.174)	(0.286)

table continues next page

Table C.6 Mincer Earnings Regression, 2015: OLS and Heckman Selection Maximum Likelihood Estimates *(continued)*

	All			Female			Male		
	OLS	Heckman		OLS	Heckman		OLS	Heckman	
	Log of earnings	Log of earnings	Be a paid employee	Log of earnings	Log of earnings	Be a paid employee	Log of earnings	Log of earnings	Be a paid employee
Variables	(1)	(2)	(3)	(1)	(2)	(3)	(1)	(2)	(3)
Industry type, sector and province									
Public sector	0.454***	0.445***		0.759***	0.752***		0.306***	0.297***	
	(0.0189)	(0.0157)		(0.0344)	(0.0287)		(0.0203)	(0.0161)	
Private formal	0.325***	0.324***		0.547***	0.560***		0.237***	0.229***	
	(0.0164)	(0.0138)		(0.0304)	(0.0243)		(0.0174)	(0.0153)	
Urban sector	0.286***	0.288***	−0.833***	0.263***	0.319***	−0.906***	0.326***	0.301***	−0.755***
	(0.0494)	(0.0418)	(0.0997)	(0.0726)	(0.0539)	(0.131)	(0.0580)	(0.0503)	(0.110)
Rural sector	0.196***	0.169***	−0.851***	0.122*	0.141***	−0.999***	0.254***	0.207***	−0.735***
	(0.0458)	(0.0403)	(0.0969)	(0.0639)	(0.0511)	(0.127)	(0.0554)	(0.0489)	(0.106)
Central Province	−0.192***	−0.137***	−0.293***	−0.248***	−0.142***	−0.297***	−0.168***	−0.145***	−0.288***
	(0.0269)	(0.0193)	(0.0373)	(0.0473)	(0.0300)	(0.0550)	(0.0262)	(0.0213)	(0.0434)
Southern Province	−0.137***	−0.120***	−0.341***	−0.158***	−0.125***	−0.274***	−0.143***	−0.133***	−0.381***
	(0.0241)	(0.0210)	(0.0363)	(0.0362)	(0.0303)	(0.0527)	(0.0251)	(0.0228)	(0.0403)
Northern Province	−0.142***	−0.130***	−0.391***	−0.164**	−0.133*	−0.443***	−0.167***	−0.160***	−0.364***
	(0.0352)	(0.0308)	(0.0700)	(0.0761)	(0.0591)	(0.108)	(0.0331)	(0.0321)	(0.0785)
Eastern Province	−0.0830***	−0.0662***	−0.300***	−0.163**	−0.109*	−0.557***	−0.0669**	−0.0582***	−0.208***
	(0.0298)	(0.0241)	(0.0574)	(0.0809)	(0.0509)	(0.0872)	(0.0261)	(0.0252)	(0.0648)
North Western Province	−0.125***	−0.0831***	−0.233***	−0.145***	−0.0855***	−0.239***	−0.118***	−0.0837***	−0.228***
	(0.0264)	(0.0201)	(0.0394)	(0.0439)	(0.0321)	(0.0576)	(0.0290)	(0.0227)	(0.0445)
North Central Province	−0.0908***	−0.0918***	−0.504***	−0.0842**	−0.0725*	−0.580***	−0.0831***	−0.0872***	−0.449***

table continues next page

Table C.6 Mincer Earnings Regression, 2015: OLS and Heckman Selection Maximum Likelihood Estimates *(continued)*

	All			Female			Male		
	OLS	Heckman		OLS	Heckman		OLS	Heckman	
	Log of earnings	Log of earnings	Be a paid employee	Log of earnings	Log of earnings	Be a paid employee	Log of earnings	Log of earnings	Be a paid employee
Variables	(1)	(2)	(3)	(1)	(2)	(3)	(1)	(2)	(3)
	(0.0238)	(0.0236)	(0.0462)	(0.0402)	(0.0408)	(0.0739)	(0.0269)	(0.0276)	(0.0553)
Uva Province	−0.0892**	−0.0739***	−0.501***	−0.0680	−0.0554	−0.573***	−0.116**	−0.0904***	−0.442***
	(0.0368)	(0.0281)	(0.0561)	(0.0436)	(0.0417)	(0.0758)	(0.0488)	(0.0310)	(0.0661)
Sabaragamuwa Province	−0.239***	−0.240***	−0.193***	−0.252***	−0.244***	−0.129**	−0.229***	−0.233***	−0.225***
	(0.0264)	(0.0257)	(0.0414)	(0.0379)	(0.0363)	(0.0568)	(0.0287)	(0.0280)	(0.0484)
Constant	8.785***	8.803***	0.852***	8.479***	8.482***	1.058***	8.627***	8.659***	0.641***
	(0.0725)	(0.0659)	(0.127)	(0.0952)	(0.0805)	(0.173)	(0.103)	(0.0911)	(0.150)
Controls for income	Yes	Yes	Yes	Yes	Yes	Yes	Yes	Yes	Yes
Observations	14,652	32,646	32,646	5,431	11,588	11,588	9,221	21,058	21,058
R^2	0.344			0.363			0.325		
Rho		0.0541	0.0541		−0.00996	−0.00996		0.0895	0.0895
F-test	168.1	168.1	168.1		94.06	94.06		95.42	95.42
P-value	0	0	0		0	0		0	0

Source: Labour Force Survey 2015. The samples include population age 15 and older in all districts of all provinces. Earnings are defined as all earnings (including other benefits) reported by employees and own–account workers. Earnings are reported in logarithm and are in 2010 Sri Lanka rupee values. A discrete variable with nine categories of skill and industry for each member of the household was used as a proxy of family income.

Note: Standard errors in parentheses. OLS = ordinary least squares.

*** $p < 0.01$, ** $p < 0.05$, * $p < 0.1$.

Table C.7 Mincer Earnings Regression, 2013: OLS and Heckman Selection Maximum Likelihood Estimates

Variables	All				Female				Male		
	OLS	Heckman			OLS	Heckman			OLS	Heckman	
	Log of earnings	Log of earnings	Be a paid employee		Log of earnings	Log of earnings	Be a paid employee		Log of earnings	Log of earnings	Be a paid employee
	(1)	(2)	(3)		(1)	(2)	(3)		(1)	(2)	(3)
Household characteristics											
Children under age 5 living in the household	0.00419	0.00133	−0.0249		−0.0238	−0.0188	−0.0234		0.00653	0.000189	−0.0444**
	(0.0182)	(0.00969)	(0.0171)		(0.0324)	(0.0146)	(0.0291)		(0.0201)	(0.0118)	(0.0199)
People over age 64 living in the household	0.0186	0.00887	0.0692***		0.00873	−0.00148	0.101***		0.0264	0.0140	0.0319
	(0.0172)	(0.00885)	(0.0167)		(0.0209)	(0.0135)	(0.0253)		(0.0233)	(0.0106)	(0.0203)
Member of female-headed household	−0.00536	−0.0298*	−0.124***		0.0729	0.0208	−0.140***		−0.0509	−0.0548***	−0.0742*
	(0.0383)	(0.0155)	(0.0310)		(0.0723)	(0.0239)	(0.0505)		(0.0346)	(0.0189)	(0.0381)
Individual characteristics											
Female	−0.299***	−0.315***	−0.0124								
	(0.0294)	(0.0134)	(0.0247)								
Head of household	0.0899***	0.0850***	0.0637**		0.00177	0.0515	−0.143**		0.111***	0.0940***	−0.0263
	(0.0301)	(0.0153)	(0.0277)		(0.0906)	(0.0354)	(0.0611)		(0.0322)	(0.0186)	(0.0352)
Female head of household	−0.124	−0.0573*	−0.122**								
	(0.0816)	(0.0345)	(0.0572)								
Married	0.0894***	0.103***	−0.0602**		−0.0189	0.0187	−0.258***		0.161***	0.160***	0.120***
	(0.0274)	(0.0140)	(0.0256)		(0.0377)	(0.0212)	(0.0383)		(0.0349)	(0.0185)	(0.0348)
Potential experience	0.0266***	0.0210***	0.00744***		0.0246***	0.0171***	0.0154**		0.0251***	0.0215***	0.00335
	(0.00318)	(0.00157)	(0.00252)		(0.00414)	(0.00243)	(0.00398)		(0.00386)	(0.00199)	(0.00324)
Potential experience squared	−0.000471***	−0.000410***	−0.000377***		−0.000375***	−0.000282***	−0.000496***		−0.000484***	−0.000447***	−0.000317***
	(4.77e−05)	(2.73e−05)	(3.95e−05)		(7.02e−05)	(4.64e−05)	(6.69e−05)		(5.56e−05)	(3.23e−05)	(4.86e−05)
Education											
Below grade 6	−0.0409	−0.00608	−0.304***		−0.0165	0.0556	−0.286***		−0.0188	−0.0196	−0.246***
	(0.0569)	(0.0388)	(0.0638)		(0.0689)	(0.0590)	(0.0916)		(0.0980)	(0.0472)	(0.0866)

table continues next page

Table C.7 Mincer Earnings Regression, 2013: OLS and Heckman Selection Maximum Likelihood Estimates *(continued)*

	All			Female			Male		
	OLS	Heckman		OLS	Heckman		OLS	Heckman	
	Log of earnings	Log of earnings	Be a paid employee	Log of earnings	Log of earnings	Be a paid employee	Log of earnings	Log of earnings	Be a paid employee
Variables	*(1)*	*(2)*	*(3)*	*(1)*	*(2)*	*(3)*	*(1)*	*(2)*	*(3)*
Grades 7 to 9	−0.00542	0.00219	−0.472***	−0.0128	0.116*	−0.584***	0.0368	−0.0214	−0.350***
	(0.0575)	(0.0405)	(0.0651)	(0.0888)	(0.0645)	(0.0978)	(0.0938)	(0.0483)	(0.0870)
O-levels completed	0.128**	0.123***	−0.513***	0.161**	0.215***	−0.684***	0.151	0.106**	−0.365***
	(0.0558)	(0.0398)	(0.0649)	(0.0716)	(0.0650)	(0.0957)	(0.0932)	(0.0471)	(0.0868)
A-levels completed	0.354***	0.330***	−0.172**	0.447***	0.410***	−0.294***	0.331***	0.309***	−0.0475
	(0.0584)	(0.0412)	(0.0685)	(0.0784)	(0.0673)	(0.101)	(0.0968)	(0.0494)	(0.0906)
University	0.515***	0.549***	0.507***	0.578***	0.547***	0.496***	0.499***	0.584***	0.533***
	(0.0743)	(0.0460)	(0.0831)	(0.0928)	(0.0715)	(0.120)	(0.119)	(0.0584)	(0.110)
Ethnicity									
Sri Lankan Tamil	−0.0570	−0.0380*	0.131***	−0.0827	0.00879	0.220***	−0.0421	−0.0583**	0.111**
	(0.0684)	(0.0224)	(0.0474)	(0.118)	(0.0408)	(0.0830)	(0.0578)	(0.0246)	(0.0530)
Indian Tamil	−0.110**	−0.133***	0.426***	−0.115	−0.139***	0.511***	−0.0979**	−0.122***	0.378***
	(0.0443)	(0.0314)	(0.0754)	(0.0801)	(0.0482)	(0.110)	(0.0472)	(0.0393)	(0.0869)
Sri Lankan Moor	0.0472	−0.0123	−0.236***	0.0217	−0.0324	−0.324***	0.0403	−0.0238	−0.217***
	(0.0326)	(0.0244)	(0.0405)	(0.0646)	(0.0591)	(0.0813)	(0.0354)	(0.0245)	(0.0443)
Malay	0.265***	0.213**	−0.00722	0.177	0.0610	0.0786	0.287**	0.253**	−0.0405
	(0.0954)	(0.0972)	(0.227)	(0.113)	(0.117)	(0.440)	(0.121)	(0.124)	(0.264)
Burgher	0.261***	0.226*	0.396	0.101	0.0623	−0.0380	0.309***	0.289**	0.563**
	(0.0937)	(0.0924)	(0.254)	(0.167)	(0.156)	(0.349)	(0.114)	(0.113)	(0.274)
Industry type, sector and province									
Public sector	0.359***	0.356***		0.551***	0.618***		0.272***	0.240***	
	(0.0240)	(0.0149)		(0.0451)	(0.0297)		(0.0265)	(0.0160)	
Private formal	0.306***	0.305***		0.418***	0.513***		0.286***	0.224***	
	(0.0250)	(0.0132)		(0.0448)	(0.0239)		(0.0257)	(0.0150)	

table continues next page

Table C.7 Mincer Earnings Regression, 2013: OLS and Heckman Selection Maximum Likelihood Estimates *(continued)*

	All			Female			Male		
	OLS	Heckman		OLS	Heckman		OLS	Heckman	
	Log of earnings	Log of earnings	Be a paid employee	Log of earnings	Log of earnings	Be a paid employee	Log of earnings	Log of earnings	Be a paid employee
Variables	(1)	(2)	(3)	(1)	(2)	(3)	(1)	(2)	(3)
Urban sector	0.118**	0.159***	-0.880***	0.127	0.222***	-0.966***	0.140**	0.173***	-0.784***
	(0.0552)	(0.0362)	(0.0818)	(0.0980)	(0.0589)	(0.121)	(0.0561)	(0.0417)	(0.0932)
Rural sector	0.00218	0.0284	-0.877***	-0.0332	0.0422	-1.049***	0.0429	0.0647	-0.747***
	(0.0487)	(0.0346)	(0.0784)	(0.0893)	(0.0560)	(0.114)	(0.0497)	(0.0400)	(0.0892)
Central Province	-0.262***	-0.171***	-0.309***	-0.375***	-0.201***	-0.304***	-0.189***	-0.155***	-0.304***
	(0.0516)	(0.0172)	(0.0327)	(0.117)	(0.0301)	(0.0538)	(0.0334)	(0.0192)	(0.0380)
Southern Province	-0.157***	-0.144***	-0.331***	-0.137***	-0.138***	-0.293***	-0.179***	-0.159***	-0.348***
	(0.0269)	(0.0172)	(0.0300)	(0.0365)	(0.0286)	(0.0476)	(0.0346)	(0.0202)	(0.0352)
Northern Province	-0.146**	-0.203***	-0.488***	-0.260**	-0.349***	-0.577***	-0.120*	-0.168***	-0.471***
	(0.0736)	(0.0314)	(0.0595)	(0.128)	(0.0591)	(0.106)	(0.0628)	(0.0338)	(0.0672)
Eastern Province	-0.169***	-0.123***	-0.218***	-0.213**	-0.206***	-0.500***	-0.156***	-0.0987***	-0.140***
	(0.0535)	(0.0228)	(0.0433)	(0.0965)	(0.0517)	(0.0822)	(0.0549)	(0.0239)	(0.0481)
North Western Province	-0.145***	-0.144***	-0.208***	-0.199***	-0.165***	-0.172***	-0.112***	-0.134***	-0.221***
	(0.0260)	(0.0182)	(0.0321)	(0.0435)	(0.0288)	(0.0497)	(0.0292)	(0.0205)	(0.0377)
North Central Province	-0.128**	-0.113***	-0.561***	-0.174*	-0.116*	-0.745***	-0.109*	-0.112***	-0.443***
	(0.0519)	(0.0281)	(0.0434)	(0.101)	(0.0486)	(0.0712)	(0.0580)	(0.0312)	(0.0514)
Uva Province	-0.0782***	-0.0998***	-0.463***	-0.0776	-0.0835**	-0.509***	-0.0893***	-0.115***	-0.427***
	(0.0282)	(0.0237)	(0.0429)	(0.0518)	(0.0396)	(0.0662)	(0.0317)	(0.0281)	(0.0509)
Sabaragamuwa Province	-0.278***	-0.174***	-0.335***	-0.144***	-0.135***	-0.259***	-0.367***	-0.196***	-0.370***
	(0.0466)	(0.0218)	(0.0341)	(0.0475)	(0.0317)	(0.0544)	(0.0627)	(0.0262)	(0.0399)

table continues next page

Table C.7 Mincer Earnings Regression, 2013: OLS and Heckman Selection Maximum Likelihood Estimates *(continued)*

	All			Female			Male		
	OLS	Heckman		OLS	Heckman		OLS	Heckman	
	Log of earnings	Log of earnings	Be a paid employee	Log of earnings	Log of earnings	Be a paid employee	Log of earnings	Log of earnings	Be a paid employee
Variables	(1)	(2)	(3)	(1)	(2)	(3)	(1)	(2)	(3)
Constant	8.625***	8.723***	0.863***	8.301***	8.291***	1.093***	8.568***	8.687***	0.597***
	(0.0828)	(0.0547)	(0.110)	(0.113)	(0.0819)	(0.161)	(0.127)	(0.0661)	(0.136)
Controls for income	Yes	Yes	Yes	Yes	Yes	Yes	Yes	Yes	Yes
Observations	13,654	31,048	31,048	4,992	10,808	10,808	8,662	20,240	20,240
R^2	0.206			0.235			0.180		
Rho		0.00166	0.00166		−0.0652	−0.0652		0.0340	0.0340
F-test		155.2	155.2		81.54	81.54		92.93	92.93
P-value		0	0		0	0		0	0

Source: Labour Force Survey 2013. The samples include population age 15 and older in all districts of all provinces. Earnings are defined as all earnings (including other benefits) reported by employees and own-account workers. Earnings are reported in logarithm and are in 2010 Sri Lanka rupee values. A discrete variable with nine categories of skill and industry for each member of the household was used as a proxy of family income.

Note: Standard errors in parentheses. OLS = ordinary least squares.

*** $p < 0.01$, ** $p < 0.05$, * $p < 0.1$.

Table C.8 Mincer Earnings Regression, 2011: OLS and Heckman Selection Maximum Likelihood Estimates

	All			Female			Male		
	OLS	Heckman		OLS	Heckman		OLS	Heckman	
	Log of earnings	Log of earnings	Be a paid employee	Log of earnings	Log of earnings	Be a paid employee	Log of earnings	Log of earnings	Be a paid employee
Variables	(1)	(2)	(3)	(1)	(2)	(3)	(1)	(2)	(3)
Household characteristics									
Children under age 5 living in the household	0.0144	−0.00988	−0.00792	0.00706	0.0223	−0.0825**	0.00573	−0.0298**	0.00585
	(0.0253)	(0.0130)	(0.0206)	(0.0437)	(0.0223)	(0.0334)	(0.0270)	(0.0142)	(0.0246)
People over age 64 living in the household	0.0443**	0.00222	0.0551***	0.0155	0.0110	0.0344	0.0752***	0.00713	0.0522**
	(0.0202)	(0.0128)	(0.0203)	(0.0324)	(0.0204)	(0.0320)	(0.0252)	(0.0148)	(0.0254)
Member of female-headed household	−0.0859**	0.0370*	−0.184***	−0.154***	0.0660**	−0.296***	−0.0788	0.0179	−0.0878*
	(0.0343)	(0.0212)	(0.0369)	(0.0462)	(0.0313)	(0.0617)	(0.0507)	(0.0260)	(0.0465)
Individual characteristics									
Female	−0.283***	−0.304***	0.0639**						
	(0.0396)	(0.0189)	(0.0300)						
Head of household	0.0863**	0.0397*	0.128***	−0.204**	0.0363	−0.188**	0.148**	0.0638**	0.0382
	(0.0423)	(0.0226)	(0.0334)	(0.0797)	(0.0473)	(0.0739)	(0.0598)	(0.0256)	(0.0433)
Female head of household	−0.213**	−0.0648	−0.168**						
	(0.0859)	(0.0473)	(0.0704)						
Married	0.0917**	0.156***	−0.0883***	0.0452	0.180***	−0.245***	0.0914*	0.134***	0.0577
	(0.0400)	(0.0207)	(0.0319)	(0.0637)	(0.0339)	(0.0471)	(0.0478)	(0.0253)	(0.0439)
Potential experience	0.0266***	0.0128***	0.0114***	0.0315***	0.00425	0.0173***	0.0212***	0.0178***	0.00779*
	(0.00497)	(0.00246)	(0.00338)	(0.00807)	(0.00373)	(0.00514)	(0.00473)	(0.00300)	(0.00434)
Potential experience squared	−0.000468***	−0.000171***	−0.000406***	−0.000480***	4.25e−05	−0.000533***	−0.000409***	−0.000286***	−0.000338***
	(7.38e−05)	(4.38e−05)	(5.56e−05)	(0.000130)	(6.86e−05)	(8.91e−05)	(7.19e−05)	(5.29e−05)	(6.82e−05)

table continues next page

Table C.8 Mincer Earnings Regression, 2011: OLS and Heckman Selection Maximum Likelihood Estimates *(continued)*

Variables	All OLS — Log of earnings (1)	All Heckman — Log of earnings (2)	All Heckman — Be a paid employee (3)	Female OLS — Log of earnings (1)	Female Heckman — Log of earnings (2)	Female Heckman — Be a paid employee (3)	Male OLS — Log of earnings (1)	Male Heckman — Log of earnings (2)	Male Heckman — Be a paid employee (3)
Education									
Below grade 6	-0.0487	0.100**	-0.331***	-0.0165	0.0928	-0.269***	-0.0381	0.0925	-0.265***
	(0.0667)	(0.0501)	(0.0693)	(0.0826)	(0.0685)	(0.0939)	(0.104)	(0.0624)	(0.0991)
Grades 7 to 9	0.00847	0.204***	-0.448***	0.0365	0.271***	-0.485***	0.0184	0.153**	-0.323***
	(0.0712)	(0.0524)	(0.0724)	(0.0992)	(0.0737)	(0.104)	(0.107)	(0.0635)	(0.0997)
O-levels completed	0.124*	0.331***	-0.413***	0.240**	0.545***	-0.649***	0.106	0.232***	-0.216**
	(0.0726)	(0.0535)	(0.0731)	(0.0983)	(0.0800)	(0.106)	(0.104)	(0.0623)	(0.0989)
A-levels completed	0.325***	0.400***	-0.0227	0.366***	0.523***	-0.202*	0.335***	0.343***	0.157
	(0.0781)	(0.0552)	(0.0766)	(0.115)	(0.0805)	(0.111)	(0.107)	(0.0657)	(0.104)
University	0.634***	0.536***	0.552***	0.717***	0.651***	0.293**	0.588***	0.495***	0.806***
	(0.0965)	(0.0622)	(0.0954)	(0.130)	(0.0887)	(0.137)	(0.137)	(0.0770)	(0.129)
Ethnicity									
Sri Lankan Tamil	-0.0162	-0.152***	0.183***	-0.0320	-0.189***	0.268***	-0.0311	-0.141***	0.164**
	(0.0726)	(0.0353)	(0.0613)	(0.0895)	(0.0579)	(0.0881)	(0.0986)	(0.0366)	(0.0740)
Indian Tamil	-0.0305	-0.304***	0.589***	-0.0743	-0.418***	0.986***	-0.0247	-0.241***	0.311***
	(0.0660)	(0.0535)	(0.0860)	(0.0840)	(0.0730)	(0.130)	(0.0937)	(0.0600)	(0.117)
Sri Lankan Moor	0.102	0.0562	-0.112*	0.106	0.0901	-0.209*	0.0817	0.0432	-0.128*
	(0.0637)	(0.0379)	(0.0631)	(0.120)	(0.0766)	(0.116)	(0.0668)	(0.0382)	(0.0670)
Malay	0.247***	-0.0233	0.277	0.317**	0.361	-0.362	0.220*	-0.0919	0.487
	(0.0801)	(0.139)	(0.394)	(0.126)	(0.405)	(0.789)	(0.131)	(0.134)	(0.374)

table continues next page

Table C.8 Mincer Earnings Regression, 2011: OLS and Heckman Selection Maximum Likelihood Estimates *(continued)*

	All			Female			Male		
	OLS	Heckman		OLS	Heckman		OLS	Heckman	
Variables	Log of earnings	Log of earnings	Be a paid employee	Log of earnings	Log of earnings	Be a paid employee	Log of earnings	Log of earnings	Be a paid employee
	(1)	(2)	(3)	(1)	(2)	(3)	(1)	(2)	(3)
Burgher	−0.821	0.148	0.110	0.627*	0.394	0.555	−1.457	0.0400	−0.153
	(0.943)	(0.257)	(0.385)	(0.343)	(0.464)	(0.710)	(1.049)	(0.157)	(0.445)
Industry type, sector and province									
Public sector	0.481***	0.387***		0.782***	0.635***		0.343***	0.278***	
	(0.0450)	(0.0193)		(0.0817)	(0.0400)		(0.0514)	(0.0200)	
Private formal	0.434***	0.309***		0.709***	0.510***		0.322***	0.235***	
	(0.0353)	(0.0175)		(0.0699)	(0.0308)		(0.0378)	(0.0192)	
Urban sector	0.184**	0.455***	−0.694***	0.187*	0.449***	−0.641***	0.193	0.435***	−0.695***
	(0.0897)	(0.0598)	(0.0883)	(0.0979)	(0.0815)	(0.132)	(0.128)	(0.0679)	(0.119)
Rural sector	0.184**	0.410***	−0.765***	0.124	0.341***	−0.717***	0.229*	0.418***	−0.767***
	(0.0862)	(0.0564)	(0.0809)	(0.0897)	(0.0736)	(0.119)	(0.126)	(0.0663)	(0.114)
Central Province	−0.121***	0.0243	−0.416***	−0.249**	0.0470	−0.452***	−0.0585	−0.0241	−0.395***
	(0.0470)	(0.0337)	(0.0471)	(0.0969)	(0.0554)	(0.0667)	(0.0403)	(0.0351)	(0.0570)
Southern Province	−0.107***	−0.00572	−0.402***	−0.122**	0.0219	−0.393***	−0.110**	−0.0490	−0.410***
	(0.0352)	(0.0290)	(0.0439)	(0.0549)	(0.0461)	(0.0670)	(0.0433)	(0.0324)	(0.0507)
Northern Province	−0.0374	0.119**	−0.439***	−0.254**	0.0929	−0.630***	0.0304	0.0956*	−0.404***
	(0.0692)	(0.0507)	(0.0822)	(0.110)	(0.0941)	(0.119)	(0.0894)	(0.0504)	(0.0971)
Eastern Province	−0.172*	0.0586	−0.308***	−0.253	0.219***	−0.642***	−0.133	−0.000785	−0.202**
	(0.0944)	(0.0405)	(0.0747)	(0.165)	(0.0728)	(0.106)	(0.107)	(0.0409)	(0.0846)

table continues next page

Table C.8 Mincer Earnings Regression, 2011: OLS and Heckman Selection Maximum Likelihood Estimates *(continued)*

	All			Female			Male		
	OLS	Heckman		OLS	Heckman		OLS	Heckman	
	Log of earnings	Log of earnings	Be a paid employee	Log of earnings	Log of earnings	Be a paid employee	Log of earnings	Log of earnings	Be a paid employee
Variables	(1)	(2)	(3)	(1)	(2)	(3)	(1)	(2)	(3)
North Western Province	−0.0534	0.00141	−0.341***	−0.0249	0.0545	−0.439***	−0.0762*	−0.0494	−0.295***
	(0.0331)	(0.0297)	(0.0473)	(0.0498)	(0.0523)	(0.0733)	(0.0412)	(0.0308)	(0.0539)
North Central Province	−0.0783	0.158***	−0.663***	−0.156	0.240***	−0.863***	−0.0263	0.0983**	−0.54***
	(0.0562)	(0.0405)	(0.0550)	(0.111)	(0.0799)	(0.0853)	(0.0642)	(0.0399)	(0.0648)
Uva Province	−0.154***	0.115***	−0.707***	−0.241***	0.133*	−0.731***	−0.124*	0.0687	−0.678***
	(0.0589)	(0.0429)	(0.0658)	(0.0790)	(0.0733)	(0.0925)	(0.0745)	(0.0438)	(0.0746)
Sabaragamuwa Province	−0.278***	−0.0430	−0.304***	−0.233**	−0.00294	−0.220***	−0.313**	−0.0870*	−0.351***
	(0.100)	(0.0424)	(0.0584)	(0.100)	(0.0560)	(0.0828)	(0.122)	(0.0449)	(0.0663)
Constant	8.343***	8.836***	0.657***	8.035***	8.368***	0.924***	8.297***	8.795***	0.415**
	(0.122)	(0.0799)	(0.118)	(0.155)	(0.117)	(0.172)	(0.169)	(0.101)	(0.161)
Controls for income	Yes	Yes	Yes	Yes	Yes	Yes	Yes	Yes	Yes
Observations	9,380	22,032	22,032	3,326	7,411	7,411	6,054	14,621	14,621
R²	0.168			0.220			0.139		
Rho		−0.847	−0.847		−0.871	−0.871		−0.787	−0.787
F-test		76.63	76.63		49.12	49.12		50.76	50.76
P-value		0	0		0	0		0	0

Source: Labour Force Survey 2011. The samples include population age 15 and older in all districts of all provinces. Earnings are defined as all earnings (including other benefits) reported by employees and own-account workers. Earnings are reported in logarithm and are in 2010 Sri Lanka rupee values. A discrete variable with nine categories of skill and industry for each member of the household was used as a proxy of family income. Sri Lanka is reweighting Labour Force Survey aggregates and microdata using revised Sri Lanka and subnational population estimates consistent with the 2012 census; however, the data are not available for us for 2011. Therefore, we used a simple linear population projection to adjust the 2011 population indicators.

Note: Standard errors in parentheses. OLS = ordinary least squares.

*** $p < 0.01$, ** $p < 0.05$, * $p < 0.1$.

Table C.9 Mincer Earnings Regression, 2009, Excluding Northern Province: OLS and Heckman Selection Maximum Likelihood Estimates

	All			Female			Male		
	OLS	Heckman		OLS	Heckman		OLS	Heckman	
Variables	Log of earnings	Log of earnings	Be a paid employee	Log of earnings	Log of earnings	Be a paid employee	Log of earnings	Log of earnings	Be a paid employee
	(1)	(2)	(3)	(1)	(2)	(3)	(1)	(2)	(3)
Household characteristics									
Children under age 5 living in the household	0.0144	0.0140	-0.0218	0.0205	0.0201	-0.0513*	-0.00879	-0.00920	-0.0233
	(0.0173)	(0.0173)	(0.0173)	(0.0252)	(0.0252)	(0.0292)	(0.0233)	(0.0233)	(0.0199)
People over age 64 living in the household	0.0277	0.0291	0.0904***	0.0108	0.0119	0.128***	0.0406*	0.0413*	0.0525**
	(0.0178)	(0.0178)	(0.0184)	(0.0257)	(0.0256)	(0.0285)	(0.0246)	(0.0246)	(0.0225)
Member of female-headed household	0.0294	0.0272	-0.137***	0.0526	0.0511	-0.178***	0.0167	0.0158	-0.0655*
	(0.0370)	(0.0370)	(0.0306)	(0.0543)	(0.0545)	(0.0493)	(0.0514)	(0.0514)	(0.0385)
Individual characteristics									
Female	-0.317***	-0.317***	0.00107						
	(0.0313)	(0.0313)	(0.0253)						
Head of household	0.136***	0.137***	0.0819***	0.0179	0.0181	0.00665	0.153***	0.153***	-0.0192
	(0.0311)	(0.0312)	(0.0287)	(0.0687)	(0.0687)	(0.0622)	(0.0397)	(0.0397)	(0.0367)
Female head of household	-0.104	-0.104	-0.0156						
	(0.0690)	(0.0690)	(0.0591)						
Married	0.0879***	0.0873***	-0.0336	-0.0501	-0.0519	-0.184***	0.190***	0.191***	0.115***
	(0.0315)	(0.0315)	(0.0265)	(0.0446)	(0.0445)	(0.0387)	(0.0467)	(0.0468)	(0.0362)
Potential experience	0.0252***	0.0255***	0.0162***	0.0261***	0.0263***	0.0215***	0.0214***	0.0217***	0.0137***
	(0.00363)	(0.00363)	(0.00280)	(0.00559)	(0.00559)	(0.00424)	(0.00483)	(0.00484)	(0.00371)
Potential experience squared	-0.000450***	-0.000461***	-0.000504***	-0.000378***	-0.000385***	-0.000607***	-0.000437***	-0.000446***	-0.000455***
	(5.95e-05)	(5.97e-05)	(4.59e-05)	(9.72e-05)	(9.76e-05)	(7.39e-05)	(7.63e-05)	(7.68e-05)	(5.82e-05)

table continues next page

Table C.9 Mincer Earnings Regression, 2009, Excluding Northern Province: OLS and Heckman Selection Maximum Likelihood Estimates *(continued)*

Variables	All			Female			Male		
	OLS	Heckman		OLS	Heckman		OLS	Heckman	
	Log of earnings	Log of earnings	Be a paid employee	Log of earnings	Log of earnings	Be a paid employee	Log of earnings	Log of earnings	Be a paid employee
	(1)	(2)	(3)	(1)	(2)	(3)	(1)	(2)	(3)
Education									
Below grade 6	-0.0994*	-0.102*	-0.116**	0.00193	0.000659	-0.0968	-0.142***	-0.143***	-0.0418
	(0.0566)	(0.0566)	(0.0586)	(0.0885)	(0.0883)	(0.0825)	(0.0545)	(0.0546)	(0.0821)
Grades 7 to 9	-0.0539	-0.0576	-0.185***	0.0338	0.0312	-0.238***	-0.0892*	-0.0903*	-0.0720
	(0.0568)	(0.0569)	(0.0599)	(0.101)	(0.101)	(0.0886)	(0.0539)	(0.0540)	(0.0824)
O-levels completed	0.0891	0.0854	-0.188***	0.126	0.123	-0.352***	0.0665	0.0660	-0.0311
	(0.0589)	(0.0590)	(0.0595)	(0.103)	(0.103)	(0.0868)	(0.0539)	(0.0540)	(0.0821)
A-levels completed	0.317***	0.320***	0.184***	0.407***	0.407***	0.0760	0.254***	0.259***	0.319***
	(0.0641)	(0.0641)	(0.0632)	(0.114)	(0.114)	(0.0921)	(0.0640)	(0.0640)	(0.0867)
University	0.632***	0.645***	0.872***	0.729***	0.735***	0.765***	0.560***	0.574***	0.995***
	(0.0725)	(0.0723)	(0.0800)	(0.119)	(0.119)	(0.115)	(0.0863)	(0.0862)	(0.110)
Ethnicity									
Sri Lankan Tamil	-0.113**	-0.107**	0.356***	-0.0515	-0.0470	0.484***	-0.148**	-0.143**	0.290***
	(0.0464)	(0.0463)	(0.0487)	(0.0634)	(0.0631)	(0.0820)	(0.0624)	(0.0622)	(0.0540)
Indian Tamil	-0.198***	-0.187***	0.676***	-0.128*	-0.119	1.019***	-0.258**	-0.250**	0.485***
	(0.0691)	(0.0687)	(0.0843)	(0.0758)	(0.0746)	(0.128)	(0.105)	(0.105)	(0.0953)
Sri Lankan Moor	0.0198	0.0186	-0.0641	-0.0564	-0.0591	-0.270***	0.00606	0.00556	-0.0316
	(0.0508)	(0.0508)	(0.0431)	(0.0698)	(0.0697)	(0.0879)	(0.0584)	(0.0584)	(0.0468)
Malay	0.0835	0.0870	0.189	0.146	0.149	0.320	0.0682	0.0702	0.115
	(0.0971)	(0.0968)	(0.203)	(0.111)	(0.112)	(0.372)	(0.112)	(0.111)	(0.238)

table continues next page

Table C.9 Mincer Earnings Regression, 2009, Excluding Northern Province: OLS and Heckman Selection Maximum Likelihood Estimates (continued)

	All			Female			Male		
	OLS	Heckman		OLS	Heckman		OLS	Heckman	
	Log of earnings	Log of earnings	Be a paid employee	Log of earnings	Log of earnings	Be a paid employee	Log of earnings	Log of earnings	Be a paid employee
Variables	(1)	(2)	(3)	(1)	(2)	(3)	(1)	(2)	(3)
Burgher	0.414***	0.416***	0.105	0.914***	0.917***	0.326	0.0964	0.0958	−0.0536
	(0.155)	(0.155)	(0.239)	(0.246)	(0.245)	(0.337)	(0.112)	(0.112)	(0.290)
Industry type, sector and province									
Public sector	0.612***	0.612***		0.861***	0.862***		0.491***	0.492***	
	(0.0304)	(0.0304)		(0.0558)	(0.0559)		(0.0368)	(0.0368)	
Private formal	0.424***	0.425***		0.666***	0.667***		0.339***	0.339***	
	(0.0302)	(0.0302)		(0.0556)	(0.0557)		(0.0375)	(0.0375)	
Urban sector	0.214***	0.198***	−0.944***	0.290***	0.280***	−1.101***	0.190*	0.177*	−0.819***
	(0.0726)	(0.0724)	(0.0780)	(0.0811)	(0.0807)	(0.119)	(0.107)	(0.107)	(0.0892)
Rural sector	0.119*	0.102	−0.984***	0.153**	0.143**	−1.133***	0.108	0.0941	−0.872***
	(0.0652)	(0.0651)	(0.0737)	(0.0672)	(0.0665)	(0.109)	(0.0989)	(0.0991)	(0.0841)
Central Province	−0.192***	−0.199***	−0.375***	−0.203***	−0.207***	−0.387***	−0.190***	−0.196***	−0.364***
	(0.0423)	(0.0421)	(0.0338)	(0.0578)	(0.0575)	(0.0561)	(0.0572)	(0.0569)	(0.0397)
Southern Province	−0.0638**	−0.0732**	−0.521***	−0.131***	−0.136***	−0.564***	−0.0451	−0.0531	−0.502***
	(0.0291)	(0.0287)	(0.0306)	(0.0470)	(0.0464)	(0.0495)	(0.0357)	(0.0351)	(0.0366)
Northern Province	—	—	—	—	—	—	—	—	—
Eastern Province	0.0394	0.0312	−0.465***	−0.0474	−0.0549	−0.756***	0.0753	0.0699	−0.348***
	(0.0445)	(0.0444)	(0.0444)	(0.0844)	(0.0845)	(0.0836)	(0.0519)	(0.0517)	(0.0492)
North Western Province	−0.0831**	−0.0885**	−0.311***	−0.164***	−0.169***	−0.501***	−0.0478	−0.0510	−0.212***
	(0.0366)	(0.0364)	(0.0334)	(0.0596)	(0.0591)	(0.0547)	(0.0436)	(0.0435)	(0.0389)

table continues next page

Table C.9 Mincer Earnings Regression, 2009, Excluding Northern Province: OLS and Heckman Selection Maximum Likelihood Estimates (continued)

	All			Female			Male		
	OLS	Heckman		OLS	Heckman		OLS	Heckman	
	Log of earnings	Log of earnings	Be a paid employee	Log of earnings	Log of earnings	Be a paid employee	Log of earnings	Log of earnings	Be a paid employee
Variables	(1)	(2)	(3)	(1)	(2)	(3)	(1)	(2)	(3)
North Central Province	−0.0704	−0.0823*	−0.653***	−0.233**	−0.242**	−0.806***	0.0200	0.0111	−0.562***
	(0.0504)	(0.0496)	(0.0365)	(0.112)	(0.111)	(0.0607)	(0.0461)	(0.0453)	(0.0441)
Uva Province	−0.193***	−0.204***	−0.590***	−0.228***	−0.235***	−0.751***	−0.184***	−0.192***	−0.481***
	(0.0479)	(0.0475)	(0.0404)	(0.0829)	(0.0807)	(0.0627)	(0.0561)	(0.0559)	(0.0488)
Sabaragamuwa Province	−0.139***	−0.145***	−0.340***	−0.0913*	−0.0946*	−0.325***	−0.168***	−0.174***	−0.345***
	(0.0367)	(0.0365)	(0.0346)	(0.0541)	(0.0539)	(0.0543)	(0.0475)	(0.0473)	(0.0415)
Constant	8.193***	8.177***	0.559***	7.637***	7.630***	0.809***	8.275***	8.256***	0.270**
	(0.101)	(0.101)	(0.102)	(0.134)	(0.136)	(0.146)	(0.140)	(0.140)	(0.130)
Controls for income	Yes	Yes	Yes	Yes	Yes	Yes	Yes	Yes	Yes
Observations	12,877	28,927	28,927	4,701	10,339	10,339	8,176	18,588	18,588
R^2	0.216			0.277			0.176		
Rho		0.0283	0.0283		0.0167	0.0167		0.0247	0.0247
F-test		114.5	114.5		66.40	66.40		67.70	67.70
P-value		0	0		0	0		0	0

Source: Labour Force Survey 2009. The samples include population age 15 and older in all districts of all provinces except the Northern province, which has been excluded for comparability across years. Earnings are defined as all earnings (including other benefits) reported by employees and own-account workers. Earnings are reported in logarithm and are in 2010 Sri Lanka rupee values. A discrete variable with nine categories of skill and industry for each member of the household was used as a proxy of family income

Note: Standard errors in parentheses. OLS = ordinary least squares.

*** $p < 0.01$, ** $p < 0.05$, * $p < 0.1$.

Table C.10 Mincer Earnings Regression, 2006, Excluding Northern and Eastern Provinces: OLS and Heckman Selection Maximum Likelihood Estimates

	All			Female			Male		
	OLS	Heckman		OLS	Heckman		OLS	Heckman	
	Log of earnings	Log of earnings	Be a paid employee	Log of earnings	Log of earnings	Be a paid employee	Log of earnings	Log of earnings	Be a paid employee
Variables	(1)	(2)	(3)	(1)	(2)	(3)	(1)	(2)	(3)
Household characteristics									
Children under age 5 living in the household	-0.00584	0.0135	-0.0206	-0.00191	0.0216	-0.0159	-0.0231	0.0138	-0.0329*
	(0.0195)	(0.0232)	(0.0160)	(0.0340)	(0.0363)	(0.0265)	(0.0226)	(0.0275)	(0.0192)
People over age 64 living in the household	0.0105	-0.0431*	0.0520***	-0.0256	-0.104***	0.0857***	0.0348	0.00725	0.0190
	(0.0244)	(0.0249)	(0.0169)	(0.0361)	(0.0366)	(0.0252)	(0.0322)	(0.0325)	(0.0221)
Member of female-headed household	-0.0316	0.0672*	-0.0810***	-0.0279	0.129**	-0.104***	-0.0326	-0.0101	-0.0309
	(0.0345)	(0.0371)	(0.0261)	(0.0536)	(0.0567)	(0.0402)	(0.0467)	(0.0487)	(0.0348)
Individual characteristics									
Female	-0.309***	-0.371***	0.0557**						
	(0.0336)	(0.0344)	(0.0232)						
Head of household	0.146***	0.0176	0.113***	-0.0682	0.0654	-0.0616	0.176***	0.139***	0.0265
	(0.0344)	(0.0377)	(0.0262)	(0.0747)	(0.0773)	(0.0537)	(0.0435)	(0.0472)	(0.0334)
Female head of household	-0.169**	-0.0133	-0.121**						
	(0.0808)	(0.0817)	(0.0554)						
Married	0.0767**	0.204***	-0.0751***	-0.0348	0.251***	-0.182***	0.162***	0.108**	0.0432
	(0.0332)	(0.0350)	(0.0240)	(0.0462)	(0.0488)	(0.0336)	(0.0475)	(0.0491)	(0.0336)
Potential experience	0.0303***	0.00939**	0.00753***	0.0314***	0.00876	0.00948**	0.0273***	0.00964**	0.00705**

table continues next page

Table C.10 Mincer Earnings Regression, 2006, Excluding Northern and Eastern Provinces: OLS and Heckman Selection Maximum Likelihood Estimates *(continued)*

	All			Female			Male		
	OLS	Heckman		OLS	Heckman		OLS	Heckman	
	Log of earnings	Log of earnings	Be a paid employee	Log of earnings	Log of earnings	Be a paid employee	Log of earnings	Log of earnings	Be a paid employee
Variables	(1)	(2)	(3)	(1)	(2)	(3)	(1)	(2)	(3)
	(0.00383)	(0.00373)	(0.00246)	(0.00579)	(0.00586)	(0.00379)	(0.00508)	(0.00480)	(0.00326)
Potential experience squared	−0.000517***	6.97e−05	−0.000337***	−0.000436***	0.000180*	−0.000402***	−0.000525***	1.27e−05	−0.000317***
	(6.25e−05)	(6.24e−05)	(3.98e−05)	(9.18e−05)	(0.000104)	(6.60e−05)	(8.21e−05)	(7.65e−05)	(5.02e−05)
Education									
Below grade 6	−0.0809*	0.286***	−0.276***	−0.0683	0.268***	−0.321***	−0.0481	0.226**	−0.151**
	(0.0416)	(0.0663)	(0.0495)	(0.0578)	(0.0898)	(0.0702)	(0.0555)	(0.0924)	(0.0679)
Grades 7 to 9	0.0206	0.546***	−0.421***	0.0399	0.650***	−0.561***	0.0407	0.414***	−0.252***
	(0.0457)	(0.0713)	(0.0516)	(0.0751)	(0.107)	(0.0780)	(0.0579)	(0.0947)	(0.0687)
O-levels completed	0.152***	0.645***	−0.358***	0.239***	0.910***	−0.593***	0.137**	0.445***	−0.154**
	(0.0471)	(0.0705)	(0.0514)	(0.0723)	(0.103)	(0.0750)	(0.0608)	(0.0950)	(0.0689)
A-levels completed	0.412***	0.620***	−0.0746	0.474***	0.845***	−0.326***	0.385***	0.410***	0.165**
	(0.0550)	(0.0752)	(0.0550)	(0.1000)	(0.114)	(0.0808)	(0.0673)	(0.101)	(0.0735)
University	0.762***	0.386***	0.483***	0.763***	0.559***	0.177*	0.772***	0.246**	0.767***
	(0.0812)	(0.0968)	(0.0707)	(0.155)	(0.149)	(0.101)	(0.0900)	(0.125)	(0.0947)
Ethnicity									
Sri Lankan Tamil	−0.0238	−0.303***	0.267***	−0.0297	−0.409***	0.427***	−0.00728	−0.219***	0.201***
	(0.0506)	(0.0687)	(0.0552)	(0.0911)	(0.109)	(0.102)	(0.0550)	(0.0782)	(0.0628)
Indian Tamil	0.101*	−0.285***	0.291***	0.223***	−0.183	0.447***	−0.00472	−0.343***	0.189**
	(0.0526)	(0.0840)	(0.0694)	(0.0827)	(0.116)	(0.113)	(0.0635)	(0.0985)	(0.0775)
Sri Lankan Moor	0.0600	0.151***	−0.190***	0.0972	0.550***	−0.447***	0.0238	0.0489	−0.123***

table continues next page

Table C.10 Mincer Earnings Regression, 2006, Excluding Northern and Eastern Provinces: OLS and Heckman Selection Maximum Likelihood Estimates (continued)

	All			Female			Male		
	OLS	Heckman		OLS	Heckman		OLS	Heckman	
	Log of earnings	Log of earnings	Be a paid employee	Log of earnings	Log of earnings	Be a paid employee	Log of earnings	Log of earnings	Be a paid employee
Variables	(1)	(2)	(3)	(1)	(2)	(3)	(1)	(2)	(3)
	(0.0390)	(0.0539)	(0.0383)	(0.0795)	(0.137)	(0.0925)	(0.0431)	(0.0571)	(0.0415)
Malay	−0.129	−0.136	0.207	0.257*	−0.320	0.260	−0.262	−0.108	0.256
	(0.277)	(0.223)	(0.248)	(0.148)	(0.260)	(0.209)	(0.349)	(0.285)	(0.340)
Burgher	0.546***	0.473**	0.193	0.485**	0.380	−0.0296	0.590***	0.591**	0.320
	(0.145)	(0.220)	(0.236)	(0.192)	(0.308)	(0.264)	(0.202)	(0.284)	(0.291)
Industry type, sector and province									
Public sector	0.548***	0.392***		0.871***	0.612***		0.394***	0.295***	
	(0.0399)	(0.0238)		(0.0862)	(0.0473)		(0.0438)	(0.0259)	
Private formal	0.409***	0.273***		0.627***	0.410***		0.330***	0.227***	
	(0.0318)	(0.0218)		(0.0627)	(0.0393)		(0.0354)	(0.0253)	
Urban sector	0.446***	1.290***	−0.834***	0.587***	1.339***	−0.744***	0.382***	1.235***	−0.821***
	(0.0651)	(0.0935)	(0.0717)	(0.0972)	(0.130)	(0.107)	(0.0757)	(0.109)	(0.0836)
Rural sector	0.327***	1.201***	−0.897***	0.419***	1.318***	−0.979***	0.288***	1.115***	−0.804***
	(0.0590)	(0.0922)	(0.0683)	(0.0881)	(0.126)	(0.0960)	(0.0680)	(0.105)	(0.0793)
Central Province	−0.0711**	0.102**	−0.206***	−0.0713	0.174**	−0.285***	−0.0745*	0.0532	−0.166***
	(0.0344)	(0.0424)	(0.0289)	(0.0512)	(0.0677)	(0.0457)	(0.0435)	(0.0498)	(0.0345)
Southern Province	−0.0229	0.309***	−0.349***	0.00124	0.390***	−0.397***	−0.0329	0.253***	−0.317***
	(0.0296)	(0.0414)	(0.0260)	(0.0476)	(0.0660)	(0.0401)	(0.0370)	(0.0491)	(0.0315)
Northern Province	—	—	—	—	—	—	—	—	—
Eastern Province	—	—	—	—	—	—	—	—	—

table continues next page

147

Table C.10 Mincer Earnings Regression, 2006, Excluding Northern and Eastern Provinces: OLS and Heckman Selection Maximum Likelihood Estimates *(continued)*

	All			Female			Male		
	OLS	Heckman		OLS	Heckman		OLS	Heckman	
	Log of earnings	Log of earnings	Be a paid employee	Log of earnings	Log of earnings	Be a paid employee	Log of earnings	Log of earnings	Be a paid employee
Variables	(1)	(2)	(3)	(1)	(2)	(3)	(1)	(2)	(3)
North Western Province	-0.164***	-0.00241	-0.120***	-0.227***	-0.0241	-0.146***	-0.128***	-0.00231	-0.106***
	(0.0420)	(0.0425)	(0.0284)	(0.0706)	(0.0678)	(0.0449)	(0.0491)	(0.0504)	(0.0345)
North Central Province	-0.180**	0.398***	-0.443***	-0.214*	0.459***	-0.502***	-0.148*	0.353***	-0.404***
	(0.0731)	(0.0630)	(0.0390)	(0.123)	(0.106)	(0.0635)	(0.0809)	(0.0735)	(0.0475)
Uva Province	-0.0617*	0.398***	-0.494***	-0.109	0.417***	-0.521***	-0.0302	0.381***	-0.471***
	(0.0370)	(0.0551)	(0.0348)	(0.0669)	(0.0844)	(0.0534)	(0.0383)	(0.0646)	(0.0420)
Sabaragamuwa Province	-0.281***	0.00225	-0.175***	-0.206***	0.159**	-0.185***	-0.327***	-0.105*	-0.156***
	(0.0465)	(0.0492)	(0.0320)	(0.0748)	(0.0771)	(0.0499)	(0.0581)	(0.0588)	(0.0390)
Constant	7.853***	8.560***	0.536***	7.290***	7.621***	0.888***	7.896***	8.901***	0.211*
	(0.0982)	(0.121)	(0.0924)	(0.166)	(0.176)	(0.134)	(0.115)	(0.153)	(0.115)
Controls for income	Yes	Yes	Yes	Yes	Yes	Yes	Yes	Yes	Yes
Observations	12,485	29,370	29,370	4,756	10,671	10,671	7,729	18,699	18,699
R^2	0.197			0.213			0.177		
Rho		-0.972			-0.975			-0.970	
F-test		59.08			37.01			37.55	
P-value		0			0			0	

Source: Labour Force Survey 2006. The samples include population age 15 and older in all districts of all provinces except the Northern and Eastern Provinces, which have been excluded for comparability across years. Earnings are defined as all earnings (including other benefits) reported by employees and own-account workers. Earnings are reported in logarithm and are in 2010 Sri Lanka rupee values. A discrete variable with nine categories of skill and industry for each member of the household was used as a proxy of family income

Note: Standard errors in parentheses. OLS = ordinary least squares.

*** $p < 0.01$, ** $p < 0.05$, * $p < 0.1$.

Table C.11 Unemployment Regressions, 2015, Selection Corrected

Variables	All	All males	All females	Urban, all	Urban, males	Urban, females	Estate and rural, all	Estate and rural, male	Estate and rural, female
	(1)	(2)	(3)	(4)	(5)	(6)	(7)	(8)	(9)
Household characteristics									
Children under age 5	-0.00882***	-0.00848***	-0.00895*	-0.0127*	-0.00837	-0.0228	-0.00835***	-0.00866***	-0.00720
	(0.00253)	(0.00275)	(0.00469)	(0.00711)	(0.00717)	(0.0165)	(0.00268)	(0.00295)	(0.00488)
Elderly over age 64	-0.000182	0.000537	-0.000866	-0.00769	-0.00377	-0.0157	0.00104	0.00117	0.00168
	(0.00218)	(0.00222)	(0.00429)	(0.00605)	(0.00586)	(0.0131)	(0.00233)	(0.00240)	(0.00447)
Member of female-headed household	-0.00408	-0.00703**	0.00201	-0.0142*	-0.0162*	-0.00925	-0.00136	-0.00487	0.00400
	(0.00333)	(0.00312)	(0.00721)	(0.00834)	(0.00837)	(0.0183)	(0.00361)	(0.00335)	(0.00781)
Individual characteristics									
Female	0.0341***			0.0123*			0.0386***		
	(0.00263)			(0.00706)			(0.00282)		
Head of household	-0.0140***	-0.00556	-0.00244	-0.0404***	-0.0265**	-0.0404	-0.00817*	2.35e-05	0.00408
	(0.00443)	(0.00396)	(0.0104)	(0.0117)	(0.0105)	(0.0293)	(0.00476)	(0.00437)	(0.0112)
Female head of household	0.00430			-0.00172			0.00462		
	(0.00731)			(0.0229)			(0.00773)		
Married	-0.0224***	-0.0264***	-0.0238***	-0.0147*	-0.0237**	-0.00414	-0.0240***	-0.0271***	-0.0270***
	(0.00299)	(0.00320)	(0.00600)	(0.00837)	(0.00956)	(0.0166)	(0.00316)	(0.00330)	(0.00637)
Potential experience	-0.00569***	-0.00381***	-0.00877***	-0.00444***	-0.00333***	-0.00688***	-0.00591***	-0.00397***	-0.00900***
	(0.000309)	(0.000306)	(0.000640)	(0.000867)	(0.000906)	(0.00174)	(0.000328)	(0.000323)	(0.000678)
Potential experience squared	5.56e-05***	4.10e-05***	7.71e-05***	4.66e-05***	3.86e-05***	6.53e-05**	5.72e-05***	4.21e-05***	7.83e-05***
	(4.98e-06)	(4.33e-06)	(1.12e-05)	(1.39e-05)	(1.41e-05)	(2.96e-05)	(5.30e-06)	(4.48e-06)	(1.19e-05)

table continues next page

Table C.11 **Unemployment Regressions, 2015, Selection Corrected** (continued)

Variables	All	All males	All females	Urban, all	Urban, males	Urban, females	Estate and rural, all	Estate and rural, male	Estate and rural, female
	(1)	(2)	(3)	(4)	(5)	(6)	(7)	(8)	(9)
Ethnicity									
Sri Lankan Tamil	0.00853	0.00107	0.0198*	0.0122	0.00792	0.0193	0.00724	−0.00177	0.0211*
	(0.00524)	(0.00549)	(0.0107)	(0.0102)	(0.0107)	(0.0209)	(0.00594)	(0.00649)	(0.0122)
Indian Tamil	−0.00844	0.00364	−0.0276*	0.00668	−0.0151	0.0286	−0.00935	0.00493	−0.0344**
	(0.00699)	(0.00662)	(0.0142)	(0.0235)	(0.0296)	(0.0429)	(0.00728)	(0.00669)	(0.0146)
Sri Lankan Moor	0.0247***	0.0159***	0.0435***	0.0118	0.0106	0.00735	0.0283***	0.0177***	0.0537***
	(0.00479)	(0.00419)	(0.0113)	(0.0109)	(0.0101)	(0.0302)	(0.00517)	(0.00443)	(0.0121)
Malay	0.0342	0.0188	0.0549	0.0420	0.0290	0.0667			
	(0.0263)	(0.0217)	(0.0684)	(0.0280)	(0.0267)	(0.0675)			
Burgher	0.0331		0.139*	0.0151		0.0689	0.0495		0.191*
	(0.0348)		(0.0776)	(0.0380)		(0.0663)	(0.0475)		(0.112)
Sector and province									
Urban sector	−0.00482	0.00209	−0.0194**						
	(0.00406)	(0.00368)	(0.00874)						
Central Province	0.00840*	0.00632	0.0129	0.0204	0.0150	0.0340	0.00610	0.00487	0.0102
	(0.00472)	(0.00466)	(0.00960)	(0.0148)	(0.0160)	(0.0274)	(0.00497)	(0.00478)	(0.0103)
Southern Province	0.0173***	0.00597	0.0395***	0.0359**	0.0217	0.0625**	0.0145***	0.00385	0.0358***
	(0.00436)	(0.00396)	(0.00899)	(0.0161)	(0.0133)	(0.0288)	(0.00442)	(0.00414)	(0.00930)
Northern Province	−0.00867	−0.0174**	0.0127	−0.0101	−0.0323*	0.0305	−0.00859	−0.0142*	0.00780
	(0.00694)	(0.00723)	(0.0143)	(0.0165)	(0.0171)	(0.0326)	(0.00776)	(0.00821)	(0.0162)
Eastern Province	0.00308	−0.0101*	0.0337***	−0.00742	−0.0200	0.0246	0.00487	−0.00841	0.0352**
	(0.00572)	(0.00564)	(0.0122)	(0.0135)	(0.0137)	(0.0278)	(0.00646)	(0.00634)	(0.0139)

table continues next page

Table C.11 Unemployment Regressions, 2015, Selection Corrected (continued)

Variables	All	All males	All females	Urban, all	Urban, males	Urban, females	Estate and rural, all	Estate and rural, male	Estate and rural, female
	(1)	(2)	(3)	(4)	(5)	(6)	(7)	(8)	(9)
North Western Province	-4.99e-05	-0.00675	0.0132	0.0359	0.00145	0.0850**	-0.00216	-0.00756	0.00963
	(0.00481)	(0.00474)	(0.00978)	(0.0219)	(0.0300)	(0.0414)	(0.00499)	(0.00479)	(0.0102)
North Central Province	-0.0104*	-0.0177***	-0.00186	0.0524**	0.0583***		-0.0140**	-0.0224***	-0.00403
	(0.00633)	(0.00674)	(0.0121)	(0.0248)	(0.0208)		(0.00654)	(0.00701)	(0.0125)
Uva Province	0.00838	-0.00590	0.0308***	-0.00985	-0.0286	0.0119	0.00722	-0.00659	0.0299***
	(0.00557)	(0.00623)	(0.0108)	(0.0226)	(0.0285)	(0.0401)	(0.00581)	(0.00629)	(0.0114)
Sabaragamuwa Province	0.0169***	0.00818**	0.0329***	0.0253*	-0.000832	0.0660**	0.0154***	0.00783*	0.0293***
	(0.00417)	(0.00399)	(0.00864)	(0.0133)	(0.0174)	(0.0260)	(0.00444)	(0.00413)	(0.00925)
Unemployment rate in the district in 2012	0.152*	0.132	0.175	0.132	0.289	-0.179	0.144	0.111	0.188
	(0.0890)	(0.0888)	(0.175)	(0.344)	(0.334)	(0.636)	(0.0908)	(0.0896)	(0.183)
Control for income	Yes	Yes	Yes	Yes	Yes	Yes	Yes	Yes	Yes
Observations	32,894	21,151	11,720	4,739	3,161	1,547	28,132	17,971	10,149

Source: Labour Force Survey 2015. The samples include population age 15 and older in all districts. The labor force was defined as those identified as employed and unemployed. Unemployment includes those who were not employed in the reference period but they had found a job or enterprise or expected to do a paid job or had looked for a job in the past four weeks.

Note: Standard errors in parentheses.

*** $p < 0.01$, ** $p < 0.05$, * $p < 0.1$.

Table C.12 Unemployment Regressions, 2009, Excluding Northern Province, Selection Corrected

Variables	All	All males	All females	Urban, all	Urban, males	Urban, females	Estate and rural, all	Estate and rural, male	Estate and rural, female
	(1)	(2)	(3)	(4)	(5)	(6)	(7)	(8)	(9)
Household Characteristics									
Children under age 5	−0.00181	−0.00115	−0.00469	0.00541	−0.000192	0.0164	−0.00232	−0.00119	−0.00634
	(0.00256)	(0.00274)	(0.00486)	(0.00770)	(0.00995)	(0.0118)	(0.00271)	(0.00283)	(0.00512)
Elderly over age 64	−0.00276	−0.00605**	0.00148	−0.00835	−0.0151*	0.00443	−0.00214	−0.00478*	0.00118
	(0.00232)	(0.00255)	(0.00455)	(0.00668)	(0.00848)	(0.0103)	(0.00245)	(0.00265)	(0.00488)
Member of female-headed household	0.00718**	0.00902***	0.00905	0.0166*	0.0161	0.0112	0.00563	0.00774**	0.00757
	(0.00340)	(0.00346)	(0.00685)	(0.00914)	(0.0104)	(0.0155)	(0.00363)	(0.00368)	(0.00736)
Individual characteristics									
Female	0.0294***			0.00318			0.0326***		
	(0.00279)			(0.00759)			(0.00300)		
Head of household	−0.0253***	−0.0299***	−0.0363***	−0.0467***	−0.0522***	−0.0220	−0.0219***	−0.0269***	−0.0393***
	(0.00492)	(0.00442)	(0.0132)	(0.0139)	(0.0140)	(0.0279)	(0.00523)	(0.00467)	(0.0143)
Female head of household	−0.0102			0.00799			−0.0141		
	(0.0102)			(0.0279)			(0.0109)		
Married	−0.0281***	−0.0248***	−0.0377***	−0.0448***	−0.0442***	−0.0493***	−0.0267***	−0.0228***	−0.0365***
	(0.00319)	(0.00340)	(0.00609)	(0.0101)	(0.0126)	(0.0185)	(0.00337)	(0.00353)	(0.00643)
Potential experience	−0.00610***	−0.00396***	−0.00864***	−0.00493***	−0.00420***	−0.00452*	−0.00624***	−0.00397***	−0.00893***
	(0.000308)	(0.000326)	(0.000679)	(0.000941)	(0.00111)	(0.00244)	(0.000326)	(0.000346)	(0.000712)
Potential experience squared	6.63e−05***	5.00e−05***	7.61e−05***	5.57e−05***	5.83e−05***	6.46e−06	6.77e−05***	4.94e−05***	8.05e−05***
	(4.91e−06)	(4.54e−06)	(1.34e−05)	(1.62e−05)	(1.79e−05)	(5.42e−05)	(5.14e−06)	(4.70e−06)	(1.39e−05)
Ethnicity									
Sri Lankan Tamil	−0.00464	0.00222	−0.0184	−0.0170	−0.0234	−0.0244	−0.00115	0.00882	−0.0187
	(0.00588)	(0.00597)	(0.0119)	(0.0131)	(0.0165)	(0.0212)	(0.00643)	(0.00628)	(0.0135)
Indian Tamil	−0.0306***	−0.00694	−0.0761***	0.00788	−0.0103	0.0143	−0.0341***	−0.00653	−0.0861***
	(0.00941)	(0.00923)	(0.0202)	(0.0216)	(0.0250)	(0.0300)	(0.0101)	(0.00960)	(0.0218)

table continues next page

Table C.12 Unemployment Regressions, 2009, Excluding Northern Province, Selection Corrected *(continued)*

Variables	All	All males	All females	Urban, all	Urban, males	Urban, females	Estate and rural, all	Estate and rural, male	Estate and rural, female
	(1)	(2)	(3)	(4)	(5)	(6)	(7)	(8)	(9)
Sri Lankan Moor	0.00660	0.00850	−0.00446	0.0186*	0.0178	0.0135	0.00117	0.00502	−0.00968
	(0.00578)	(0.00522)	(0.0134)	(0.0108)	(0.0124)	(0.0206)	(0.00701)	(0.00625)	(0.0158)
Malay	0.0508*	0.0565***		0.0519	0.0567*		0.0498	0.0623**	
	(0.0260)	(0.0208)		(0.0335)	(0.0292)		(0.0364)	(0.0301)	
Burgher	0.0170	0.0137	0.0220	0.0269	0.0218	0.0573			
	(0.0310)	(0.0329)	(0.0291)	(0.0379)	(0.0477)	(0.0358)			
Sector and province									
Urban sector	0.00705	0.00950**	−0.00514						
	(0.00439)	(0.00439)	(0.00898)						
Central Province	0.0262***	0.00938*	0.0591***	0.0250*	0.0206	0.0307	0.0250***	0.00761	0.0575***
	(0.00477)	(0.00493)	(0.00967)	(0.0129)	(0.0147)	(0.0279)	(0.00522)	(0.00539)	(0.0104)
Southern Province	0.0220***	0.00753	0.0523***	−0.000601	0.00520	−0.0118	0.0236***	0.00813*	0.0553***
	(0.00479)	(0.00474)	(0.00997)	(0.0157)	(0.0196)	(0.0244)	(0.00501)	(0.00482)	(0.0105)
Northern Province	—	—	—	—	—	—	—	—	—
Eastern Province	0.0217***	−0.00410	0.0828***	0.0211*	−0.00124	0.0814***	0.0210***	−0.00564	0.0790***
	(0.00598)	(0.00627)	(0.0118)	(0.0119)	(0.0145)	(0.0217)	(0.00693)	(0.00725)	(0.0136)
North Western Province	0.0287***	0.0111*	0.0604***	0.0417**	0.0196	0.0962***	0.0250***	0.00901	0.0529***
	(0.00606)	(0.00668)	(0.0116)	(0.0193)	(0.0301)	(0.0250)	(0.00658)	(0.00713)	(0.0126)
North Central Province	0.0119*	1.51e−05	0.0357***	0.0598***	0.0301	0.118***	0.00843	−0.00207	0.0291**
	(0.00633)	(0.00699)	(0.0117)	(0.0193)	(0.0236)	(0.0358)	(0.00675)	(0.00727)	(0.0126)
Uva Province	0.0174***	0.00397	0.0453***	0.0578***	0.0598***	0.0648**	0.0136**	0.000249	0.0403***

table continues next page

Table C.12 Unemployment Regressions, 2009, Excluding Northern Province, Selection Corrected (continued)

Variables	All	All males	All females	Urban, all	Urban, males	Urban, females	Estate and rural, all	Estate and rural, male	Estate and rural, female
	(1)	(2)	(3)	(4)	(5)	(6)	(7)	(8)	(9)
Sabaragamuwa Province	0.0116**	0.00476	0.0260***	0.0219	−0.00740	0.0460*	0.0112**	0.00442	0.0248**
	(0.00627)	(0.00705)	(0.0121)	(0.0158)	(0.0201)	(0.0318)	(0.00677)	(0.00750)	(0.0131)
Unemployment rate in the district in 1996	0.647***	0.530***	0.825***	1.332***	0.587	2.709***	0.539***	0.462***	0.611**
	(0.144)	(0.147)	(0.292)	(0.423)	(0.508)	(0.722)	(0.155)	(0.158)	(0.311)
Control for income	Yes	Yes	Yes	Yes	Yes	Yes	Yes	Yes	Yes
Observations	28,927	18,588	10,327	3,419	2,278	1,093	25,479	16,247	9,224

Source: Labour Force Survey 2009. The samples include population age 15 and older in all districts except the Northern Province, which has been excluded for comparability across years. The labor force was defined as those identified as employed and unemployed. Unemployment includes those who were not employed in the reference period but had found a job or enterprise or expected to do a paid job or had looked for a job in the past four weeks.

Note: Standard errors in parentheses.

*** $p < 0.01$, ** $p < 0.05$, * $p < 0.1$.

Table C.13 Oaxaca-Blinder Decomposition of Labor Force Participation

	2011			2013			2015		
	Overall	Explained	Unexplained	Overall	Explained	Unexplained	Overall	Explained	Unexplained
Male	0.744***			0.752***			0.750***		
	(0.00313)			(0.00245)			(0.00248)		
Female	0.345***			0.346***			0.360***		
	(0.00364)			(0.00274)			(0.00292)		
Gap	0.399***			0.406***			0.390***		
	(0.00466)			(0.00367)			(0.00373)		
Explained	0.0297***			0.0314***			0.0267***		
	(0.00295)			(0.00248)			(0.00236)		
Unexplained	0.369***			0.374***			0.363***		
	(0.00508)			(0.00387)			(0.00403)		
Family		0.0295***	0.00175		0.0331***	-0.00458		0.0267***	0.00401
		(0.00230)	(0.00491)		(0.00185)	(0.00358)		(0.00188)	(0.00371)
Children		0.000323***	0.0213***		0.000328***	0.0270***		0.000258***	0.0256***
		(8.41e-05)	(0.00316)		(8.89e-05)	(0.00243)		(5.74e-05)	(0.00254)
Elderly		-0.000488***	0.00851**		-0.000632***	0.00836***		-0.000379***	0.00934***
		(0.000129)	(0.00362)		(0.000132)	(0.00288)		(8.19e-05)	(0.00305)
Education		3.64e-05	0.0670***		-0.000975***	0.0702***		-0.000823**	0.0724***
		(0.000417)	(0.00767)		(0.000347)	(0.00600)		(0.000335)	(0.00726)
Age x Experience		0.000589	0.210**		-0.000102	0.293***		0.0163	0.305***
		(0.00144)	(0.0983)		(0.00135)	(0.0762)		(0.00112)	(0.0816)
Ethnicity		-0.000272*	-0.115**		-1.95e-05	-0.0210		-0.000439***	-0.0538*
		(0.000162)	(0.0487)		(0.000204)	(0.0297)		(0.000150)	(0.0285)
Location		1.03e-06	0.00284		-0.000332	-0.0117**		-0.000271**	0.00132
		(0.000184)	(0.00741)		(0.000217)	(0.00535)		(0.000117)	(0.00533)
Constant			0.173			0.0131			-0.000322
			(0.109)			(0.0805)			(0.0835)
Observations	58,829	58,829	58,829	42,271	42,271	42,271	61,598	61,598	61,598

Sources: Labour Force Surveys 2011, 2013, 2015. The samples include population age 15 and older in all districts. The labor force was defined as those identified as employed and unemployed. Unemployment includes those who were not employed in the reference period but had found a job or enterprise or expected to do a paid job or had looked for a job in the past four weeks. Sri Lanka is reweighting Labour Force Survey aggregates and microdata using revised Sri Lanka and subnational population estimates consistent with the 2012 Census; however, the data are not available for 2011 and 2013. Therefore, we used a simple linear population projection to adjust the 2011 and 2013 population indicators by Census 2012.

Note: Standard errors in parentheses.

*** $p < 0.01$, ** $p < 0.05$, * $p < 0.1$.

Table C.14 Oaxaca-Blinder Decomposition of Labor Force Participation, Excluding Northern and Eastern Provinces

	2009			2006		
	Overall	*Explained*	*Unexplained*	*Overall*	*Explained*	*Unexplained*
Male	0.749***			0.771***		
	(0.00270)			(0.00263)		
Female	0.374***			0.396***		
	(0.00309)			(0.00330)		
Gap	0.375***			0.375***		
	(0.00410)			(0.00410)		
Explained	0.0294***			0.0336***		
	(0.00261)			(0.00233)		
Unexplained	0.346***			0.341***		
	(0.00416)			(0.00442)		
Family		0.0270***	0.00685*		0.0336***	−0.00382
		(0.00181)	(0.00394)		(0.00181)	(0.00393)
Children		0.000537***	0.0222***		0.000339***	0.0227***
		(0.000116)	(0.00250)		(6.99e−05)	(0.00262)
Elderly		−0.000460***	0.0126***		−0.000367***	0.0153***
		(0.000118)	(0.00293)		(9.09e−05)	(0.00282)
Education		−0.000265	0.0673***		−0.000447	0.0702***
		(0.000454)	(0.00566)		(0.000402)	(0.00563)
Age x Experience		0.00245	0.180**		0.000232	0.261***
		(0.00160)	(0.0812)		(0.00119)	(0.0772)
Ethnicity		9.48e−05	−0.00934		2.86e−05	0.00499
		(0.000201)	(0.0244)		(0.000159)	(0.0364)
Location		4.12e−05	−0.00653		0.000239*	−0.0256***
		(0.000207)	(0.00633)		(0.000139)	(0.00634)
Constant			0.0725			−0.00338
			(0.0845)			(0.0859)
Observations	49,636	49,636	49,636	51,766	51,766	51,766

Sources: Labour Force Surveys 2006, 2009. The samples include population age 15 and older in all districts except the Northern and Eastern Provinces, which have been excluded for comparability across years. The labor force was defined as those identified as employed and unemployed. Unemployment includes those who were not employed in the reference period but had found a job or enterprise or expected to do a paid job or had looked for a job in the past four weeks.

Note: Standard errors in parentheses.

*** $p < 0.01$, ** $p < 0.05$, * $p < 0.1$.

Table C.15 Oaxaca-Blinder Decomposition of Log Earnings

	2011			2013			2015		
	Overall	Explained	Unexplained	Overall	Explained	Unexplained	Overall	Explained	Unexplained
Male	9.520***			9.592***			9.762***		
	(0.00933)			(0.00767)			(0.00725)		
Female	9.249***			9.324***			9.506***		
	(0.0150)			(0.0114)			(0.0114)		
Gap	0.271***			0.269***			0.256***		
	(0.0161)			(0.0123)			(0.0121)		
Explained	-0.0109			-0.0212**			-0.0462***		
	(0.0127)			(0.0101)			(0.00993)		
Unexplained	0.282***			0.290***			0.302***		
	(0.0147)			(0.0124)			(0.0115)		
Family		0.0291***	-0.0220*		0.0359***	-0.00767		0.0347***	-0.00555
		(0.00676)	(0.0132)		(0.00613)	(0.0106)		(0.00546)	(0.00998)
Children		-0.00121	-0.00864		0.000288	0.00348		0.000286	0.00873
		(0.000988)	(0.00669)		(0.000668)	(0.00543)		(0.000612)	(0.00548)
Elderly		-0.000393	-0.00243		-0.000469	0.00369		0.000210	-0.00917*
		(0.000478)	(0.00681)		(0.000742)	(0.00574)		(0.000339)	(0.00540)
Education		-0.0137***	-0.0265		-0.0132***	-0.00226		-0.0326***	-0.0224
		(0.00378)	(0.0293)		(0.00478)	(0.0273)		(0.00504)	(0.0289)
Age x Experience		-0.0131***	0.305		-0.0307***	-0.0161		-0.0238***	0.422*
		(0.00469)	(0.288)		(0.00542)	(0.229)		(0.00498)	(0.225)
Structure		0.0322***	0.167***		0.0270***	0.112***		0.0244***	0.118***
		(0.00704)	(0.0461)		(0.00573)	(0.0376)		(0.00587)	(0.0360)
Employment		-0.0545***	-0.248***		-0.0488***	-0.205***		-0.0556***	-0.255***
		(0.00476)	(0.0257)		(0.00367)	(0.0194)		(0.00372)	(0.0180)
Ethnicity		0.00570***	0.0913		0.00154	-0.132**		0.00281*	-0.0758
		(0.00216)	(0.0669)		(0.00142)	(0.0517)		(0.00152)	(0.0507)

table continues next page

Table C.15 Oaxaca-Blinder Decomposition of Log Earnings (continued)

	2011			2013			2015		
	Overall	Explained	Unexplained	Overall	Explained	Unexplained	Overall	Explained	Unexplained
Location		0.00500***	0.0207		0.00726***	0.0349***		0.00356**	0.0124
		(0.00192)	(0.0162)		(0.00184)	(0.0118)		(0.00139)	(0.0105)
Constant			0.00473			0.499**			0.110
			(0.269)			(0.213)			(0.207)
Observations	9,319	9,319	9,319	13,595	13,595	13,595	14,639	14,639	14,639

Sources: Labour Force Surveys 2011, 2013, 2015. The samples include population age 15 and older in all districts of all provinces. Earnings are defined as all earnings (including other benefits) reported by employees and own-account workers. Earnings are reported in logarithm and are in 2010 Sri Lanka rupee values. Sri Lanka is reweighting Labour Force Survey aggregates and microdata using revised Sri Lanka and subnational population estimates consistent with the 2012 Census; however, the data are not available for 2011 and 2013. Therefore, we used a simple linear population projection to adjust the 2011 and 2013 population indicators by Census 2012.

Note: Standard errors in parentheses.

*** $p < 0.01$, ** $p < 0.05$, * $p < 0.1$

Table C.16 Oaxaca-Blinder Decomposition of Log Earnings, Excluding Northern and Eastern Provinces

	2009			2006		
	Overall	Explained	Unexplained	Overall	Explained	Unexplained
Male	9.354***			9.356***		
	(0.0149)			(0.0150)		
Female	9.053***			9.025***		
	(0.0195)			(0.0212)		
Gap	0.301***			0.330***		
	(0.0231)			(0.0244)		
Explained	−0.00571			0.0255		
	(0.0173)			(0.0186)		
Unexplained	0.307***			0.305***		

table continues next page

Table C.16 Oaxaca-Blinder Decomposition of Log Earnings, Excluding Northern and Eastern Provinces *(continued)*

	2009			2006		
	Overall	Explained	Unexplained	Overall	Explained	Unexplained
	(0.0270)			(0.0294)		
Family		0.0604***	-0.0113		0.0419***	-0.0316
		(0.0124)	(0.0245)		(0.0121)	(0.0234)
Children		0.00117	-0.0156		-0.000497	-0.00108
		(0.00123)	(0.0112)		(0.00136)	(0.0122)
Elderly		-0.00119	0.0104		0.000218	0.0187
		(0.00101)	(0.0114)		(0.000689)	(0.0135)
Education		-0.0217***	0.0360		-0.0199***	-0.0870***
		(0.00693)	(0.0440)		(0.00444)	(0.0310)
Age x Experience		-0.00694	-0.536		0.00789*	0.744*
		(0.00490)	(0.537)		(0.00450)	(0.437)
Structure		0.0197*	-0.0328		0.0466***	-0.0110
		(0.0115)	(0.0707)		(0.0114)	(0.0640)
Employment		-0.0706***	-0.177***		-0.0588***	-0.190***
		(0.00623)	(0.0441)		(0.00571)	(0.0484)
Ethnicity		0.00728**	0.222**		0.00547	-1.281***
		(0.00324)	(0.0908)		(0.00383)	(0.0799)
Location		0.00618***	0.0473		0.00256	0.0597**
		(0.00197)	(0.0312)		(0.00180)	(0.0279)
Constant			0.763			1.083**
			(0.507)			(0.422)
Observations	12,061	12,061	12,061	12,507	12,507	12,507

Sources: Labour Force Surveys 2006, 2009. The samples include population age 15 and older in all districts of all provinces except the Northern and Eastern Provinces, which have been excluded for comparability across years. Earnings are defined as all earnings (including other benefits) reported by employees and own-account workers. Earnings are reported in logarithm and are in 2010 Sri Lanka rupee values.

Note: Standard errors in parentheses.

*** $p < 0.01$, ** $p < 0.05$, * $p < 0.1$.

Table C.17 Oaxaca-Blinder Decomposition of Log Earnings by Employment Category, 2015

	Public			Private formal			Private informal		
	Overall	Explained	Unexplained	Overall	Explained	Unexplained	Overall	Explained	Unexplained
Male	10.06***			9.909***			9.473***		
	(0.0112)			(0.0138)			(0.00954)		
Female	9.989***			9.509***			8.866***		
	(0.0141)			(0.0162)			(0.0177)		
Gap	0.0692***			0.400***			0.608***		
	(0.0158)			(0.0194)			(0.0196)		
Explained	-0.0589***			0.163***			0.139***		
	(0.0148)			(0.0170)			(0.0137)		
Unexplained	0.128***			0.237***			0.469***		
	(0.0184)			(0.0179)			(0.0223)		
Family		0.0216**	0.0332*		0.0257***	-0.0309		0.0615***	-0.0391**
		(0.0108)	(0.0178)		(0.00887)	(0.0223)		(0.00859)	(0.0152)
Children		-4.08e-05	-0.0158**		0.000406	0.00538		0.00234	0.0248***
		(0.000160)	(0.00788)		(0.00185)	(0.0108)		(0.00162)	(0.00957)
Elderly		0.00161	-0.0272***		0.000125	-0.00376		1.16e-05	-0.00648
		(0.00110)	(0.00833)		(0.000251)	(0.00872)		(0.000414)	(0.0110)
Education		-0.0188	-0.213**		-0.00478	-0.0290		-0.0103***	0.0899***
		(0.0158)	(0.0870)		(0.00811)	(0.0477)		(0.00315)	(0.0330)
Age x Experience		-0.0491***	0.660		0.0404***	0.863***		0.00754*	0.560
		(0.0165)	(0.456)		(0.00887)	(0.333)		(0.00393)	(0.360)
Structure		-0.0208**	0.0577		0.0847***	0.0882		0.0858***	0.215***
		(0.0103)	(0.0838)		(0.00953)	(0.0542)		(0.00876)	(0.0496)
Ethnicity		0.00320**	0.0912***		-0.00198	-0.115**		0.000274	-0.0681
		(0.00163)	(0.0212)		(0.00365)	(0.0579)		(0.00249)	(0.0701)
Location		0.00356*	-0.0280		0.0183***	0.0373**		-0.00789**	0.0269
		(0.00208)	(0.0186)		(0.00346)	(0.0155)		(0.00309)	(0.0202)
Constant			-0.430			-0.578*			-0.335
			(0.392)			(0.310)			(0.366)
Observations	4,742	4,742	4,742	4,285	4,285	4,285	5,612	5,612	5,612

Source: Labour Force Survey 2015. The sample includes population age 15 and older in all districts of all provinces. Earnings are defined as all earnings (including other benefits) reported by employees and own-account workers. Earnings are reported in logarithm and are in 2010 Sri Lanka rupee values.

Note: Standard errors in parentheses.

*** $p < 0.01$, ** $p < 0.05$, * $p < 0.1$.

Table C.18 Oaxaca-Blinder Decomposition of Log Earnings by Employment Category, 2013

	Public			Private formal			Private informal		
	Overall	Explained	Unexplained	Overall	Explained	Unexplained	Overall	Explained	Unexplained
Male	9.830***			9.763***			9.321***		
	(0.0124)			(0.0143)			(0.0105)		
Female	9.679***			9.379***			8.765***		
	(0.0159)			(0.0163)			(0.0192)		
Gap	0.151***			0.384***			0.556***		
	(0.0172)			(0.0201)			(0.0210)		
Explained	−0.0329*			0.189***			0.137***		
	(0.0169)			(0.0166)			(0.0147)		
Unexplained	0.184***			0.195***			0.419***		
	(0.0208)			(0.0191)			(0.0231)		
Family		0.0205	−0.0181		0.0607***	−0.00710		0.0350***	−0.0375**
		(0.0127)	(0.0208)		(0.00947)	(0.0206)		(0.00885)	(0.0172)
Children		0.000194	0.0138		0.000704	0.00850		0.00230	−0.0105
		(0.000428)	(0.00899)		(0.000956)	(0.00865)		(0.00246)	(0.00938)
Elderly		0.00208	0.00125		−0.00171*	0.00199		−0.000402	0.00230
		(0.00153)	(0.00880)		(0.000976)	(0.00969)		(0.00128)	(0.0114)
Education		0.0177	−0.0126		−0.00222	0.0543		−0.0113***	−0.0152
		(0.0132)	(0.0746)		(0.00874)	(0.0525)		(0.00428)	(0.0401)
Age x Experience		−0.0614***	−0.663		0.0465***	0.312		0.0160***	0.472
		(0.0141)	(0.430)		(0.0106)	(0.412)		(0.00614)	(0.395)
Structure		−0.0167*	−0.00375		0.0656***	0.151**		0.0948***	0.170***
		(0.00946)	(0.103)		(0.00861)	(0.0610)		(0.00950)	(0.0483)
Ethnicity		0.00352	−0.296***		0.00166	−0.0386		−0.000155	−0.128***
		(0.00229)	(0.0234)		(0.00197)	(0.0611)		(0.00269)	(0.0411)
Location		0.00123	−0.0262		0.0181***	0.0203		0.000853	0.110***
		(0.00286)	(0.0194)		(0.00368)	(0.0162)		(0.00367)	(0.0240)
Constant			1.189***			−0.309			−0.144
			(0.387)			(0.373)			(0.390)
Observations	4,444	4,444	4,444	3,905	3,905	3,905	5,246	5,246	5,246

Sources: Labour Force Survey 2013. The sample includes population age 15 and older in all districts of all provinces. Earnings are defined as all earnings (including other benefits) reported by employees and own-account workers. Earnings are reported in logarithm and are in 2010 Sri Lanka rupee values.

Note: Standard errors in parentheses.

*** $p < 0.01$, ** $p < 0.05$, * $p < 0.1$.

Table C.19 Oaxaca-Blinder Decomposition of Log Earnings by Employment Category, 2011

	Public			Private formal			Private informal		
	Overall	Explained	Unexplained	Overall	Explained	Unexplained	Overall	Explained	Unexplained
Male	9.813*** (0.0125)			9.665*** (0.0181)			9.215*** (0.0125)		
Female	9.668*** (0.0213)			9.290*** (0.0212)			8.638*** (0.0234)		
Gap	0.145*** (0.0228)			0.375*** (0.0247)			0.578*** (0.0264)		
Explained	0.00415 (0.0202)			0.203*** (0.0208)			0.125*** (0.0165)		
Unexplained	0.141*** (0.0250)			0.172*** (0.0209)			0.453*** (0.0289)		
Family		0.00454 (0.0144)	-0.00799 (0.0232)		0.0418*** (0.0101)	-0.00302 (0.0229)		0.0413*** (0.00995)	-0.0274 (0.0243)
Children		-0.000425 (0.000611)	-0.0165 (0.0110)		0.00194 (0.00199)	-0.0177* (0.0107)		-0.00265 (0.00313)	0.0118 (0.0117)
Elderly		0.000235 (0.00153)	-0.0131 (0.0102)		-0.000251 (0.000819)	0.0174 (0.0124)		-0.00361* (0.00189)	-0.0205 (0.0138)
Education		-0.00607 (0.0106)	-0.0438 (0.0737)		-0.0256** (0.0106)	0.0281 (0.0553)		-0.00457 (0.00683)	-0.0147 (0.0548)
Age x Experience		-0.0267** (0.0118)	-0.0173 (0.507)		0.0696*** (0.0152)	0.368 (0.441)		0.0198** (0.00885)	0.794* (0.469)
Structure		0.0281* (0.0147)	-0.0387 (0.118)		0.0958*** (0.0122)	0.178*** (0.0639)		0.0695*** (0.0106)	0.281*** (0.0685)
Ethnicity		0.00237 (0.00406)	0.0210 (0.0128)		0.00676** (0.00344)	0.193*** (0.0510)		0.00533 (0.00365)	0.0263 (0.0428)
Location		0.00205 (0.00338)	-0.0197 (0.0287)		0.0126*** (0.00368)	0.0290 (0.0208)		-0.000342 (0.00369)	0.0276 (0.0296)
Constant			0.277 (0.474)			-0.621 (0.393)			-0.625 (0.479)
Observations	3,057	3,057	3,057	2,753	2,753	2,753	3,510	3,510	3,510

Source: Labour Force Survey 2011. The sample includes population age 15 and older in all districts of all provinces. Earnings are defined as all earnings (including other benefits) reported by employees and own-account workers. Earnings are reported in logarithm and are in 2010 Sri Lanka rupee values. Sri Lanka is reweighting Labour Force Survey aggregates and microdata using revised Sri Lanka and subnational population estimates consistent with the 2012 census; however, the data are not available for the year 2011. Therefore, we used a simple linear population projection to adjust the 2011 population indicators.

Note: Standard errors in parentheses.

*** $p < 0.01$, ** $p < 0.05$, * $p < 0.1$.

Table C.20 Oaxaca-Blinder Decomposition of Log Earnings by Employment Category, Excluding Northern Province, 2009

	Public			Private formal			Private informal		
	Overall	Explained	Unexplained	Overall	Explained	Unexplained	Overall	Explained	Unexplained
Male	9.757***			9.500***			9.000***		
	(0.0175)			(0.0240)			(0.0244)		
Female	9.586***			9.058***			8.380***		
	(0.0243)			(0.0264)			(0.0398)		
Gap	0.171***			0.443***			0.620***		
	(0.0267)			(0.0342)			(0.0465)		
Explained	0.0243			0.226***			0.165***		
	(0.0273)			(0.0278)			(0.0294)		
Unexplained	0.147***			0.216***			0.455***		
	(0.0368)			(0.0400)			(0.0585)		
Family		0.0550**	0.0456		0.0336**	−0.0938**		0.0735***	−0.0101
		(0.0232)	(0.0431)		(0.0165)	(0.0468)		(0.0199)	(0.0392)
Children		2.05e−06	0.000584		0.000547	−0.00340		0.00549	−0.0283
		(3.87e−05)	(0.0133)		(0.00363)	(0.0179)		(0.00406)	(0.0217)
Elderly		0.00118	−0.0186		−0.000283	0.00248		−0.00483*	0.0256
		(0.00228)	(0.0130)		(0.000627)	(0.0214)		(0.00260)	(0.0229)
Education		−0.0204	0.136		−0.00788	0.129		0.00256	0.149
		(0.0183)	(0.111)		(0.0193)	(0.0998)		(0.0122)	(0.132)
Age x Experience		−0.0377***	−1.275*		0.0744***	−0.390		0.00800	−0.403
		(0.0139)	(0.718)		(0.0254)	(0.959)		(0.00921)	(0.926)
Structure		0.0101	−0.113		0.108***	−0.0552		0.0699***	0.163*
		(0.0170)	(0.202)		(0.0168)	(0.120)		(0.0219)	(0.0902)
Ethnicity		0.0132***	−0.255***		0.00173	0.248**		0.00328	0.267**
		(0.00475)	(0.0437)		(0.00587)	(0.104)		(0.00558)	(0.122)
Location		0.00292	−0.0264		0.0161***	0.0663		0.00662	0.0589
		(0.00331)	(0.0342)		(0.00570)	(0.0408)		(0.00468)	(0.0673)
Constant			1.653**			0.313			0.233
			(0.657)			(0.898)			(0.938)
Observations	4,231	4,231	4,231	3,836	3,836	3,836	4,898	4,898	4,898

Source: Labour Force Survey 2009. The sample includes population age 15 and older in all districts of all provinces except the Northern Province, which has been excluded for comparability across years. Earnings are defined as all earnings (including other benefits) reported by employees and own-account workers. Earnings are reported in logarithm and are in 2010 Sri Lanka rupee values.

Note: Standard errors in parentheses.

*** $p < 0.01$, ** $p < 0.05$, * $p < 0.1$.

Table C.21 Oaxaca-Blinder Decomposition of Log Earnings by Employment Category, Excluding Northern and Eastern Provinces, 2006

	Public			Private formal			Private informal		
	Overall	Explained	Unexplained	Overall	Explained	Unexplained	Overall	Explained	Unexplained
Male	9.747***			9.478***			8.990***		
	(0.0250)			(0.0240)			(0.0247)		
Female	9.635***			8.973***			8.375***		
	(0.0277)			(0.0311)			(0.0448)		
Gap	0.112***			0.504***			0.615***		
	(0.0352)			(0.0369)			(0.0509)		
Explained	0.0808**			0.260***			0.120***		
	(0.0390)			(0.0248)			(0.0333)		
Unexplained	0.0310			0.245***			0.494***		
	(0.0543)			(0.0423)			(0.0617)		
Family		0.0728**	−0.0345		0.0374**	−0.0460		0.0357**	−0.0701*
		(0.0289)	(0.0604)		(0.0184)	(0.0369)		(0.0169)	(0.0396)
Children		−0.000201	0.0166		−0.000297	0.0133		−0.00173	−0.00394
		(0.000463)	(0.0207)		(0.00299)	(0.0178)		(0.00496)	(0.0281)
Elderly		−0.00113	−0.00215		−0.000219	0.0230		−0.000326	0.00757
		(0.00259)	(0.0222)		(0.000675)	(0.0255)		(0.000904)	(0.0223)
Education		−0.0120	−0.0570		−0.00884	−0.115**		−0.0252	0.0866
		(0.0225)	(0.103)		(0.0181)	(0.0553)		(0.0162)	(0.0889)
Age x Experience		−0.0166	0.942		0.0781***	0.890		0.0282*	0.942
		(0.0199)	(1.172)		(0.0188)	(0.641)		(0.0164)	(0.756)
Structure		0.0400*	−0.124		0.133***	0.0847		0.0741***	0.0913
		(0.0225)	(0.153)		(0.0183)	(0.101)		(0.0216)	(0.101)
Ethnicity		−0.000728	−0.0389		0.00288	−0.0281		0.0151	−0.965***
		(0.00330)	(0.0566)		(0.00435)	(0.0763)		(0.0165)	(0.256)
Location		−0.00124	−0.0233		0.0177***	0.0205		−0.00535	0.121**
		(0.00306)	(0.0553)		(0.00614)	(0.0388)		(0.00379)	(0.0573)
Constant			−0.648			−0.598			0.285
			(1.076)			(0.646)			(0.801)
Observations	3,723	3,723	3,723	4,401	4,401	4,401	4,383	4,383	4,383

Source: Labour Force Survey 2006. The sample includes population age 15 and older in all districts of all provinces except the Northern and Eastern Provinces, which have been excluded for comparability across years. Earnings are defined as all earnings (including other benefits) reported by employees and own-account workers. Earnings are reported in logarithm and are in 2010 Sri Lanka rupee values.

Note: Standard errors in parentheses.

*** $p < 0.01$, ** $p < 0.05$, * $p < 0.1$.

Descriptive Statistics from Primary Data Analysis

Table D.1 Characteristics of Workers (% of Workers)

	Tea	Commercial agriculture	Tourism	Garments	ICT	Total (n = 405)
Sex of worker						
Male	46.88	54.29	82.22	48.35	57.78	58.77
Female	53.13	45.71	17.78	51.65	42.22	41.23
Skill levels						
Managerial	6.25	12.86	33.33	14.29	24.44	19.26
Skilled	25	41.43	33.33	62.64	35.56	40.49
Unskilled	68.75	45.71	33.33	23.08	40	40.25
Educational attainment						
No education	4.69	0	3.33	0	1.11	1.73
Below grade 6	37.5	17.14	11.11	4.4	1.11	12.59
Below grade 9	26.56	14.29	17.78	4.4	1.11	11.85
O-levels completed	17.19	41.43	42.22	47.25	20	34.32
A-levels completed	10.94	22.86	17.78	34.07	61.11	30.86
University	3.13	4.29	7.78	9.89	15.56	8.64
Age categories						
Youth (15–29)	17.19	17.14	13.33	41.76	36.67	26.17
Adult (30–59)	82.81	77.14	60	58.24	58.89	65.93
Senior (60+)	0	5.71	26.67	0	4.44	7.9
Total last month's earnings (2012 rupees)	**14,432.56**	**15,379.49**	**19,286.67**	**19,044.04**	**23,854.28**	**18,804.79**

Source: Primary data.
Note: ICT = information and communication technology.

Table D.2 Characteristics of Worker Households (% of Households)

	Tea	Commercial agriculture	Tourism	Garments	ICT	Total (n = 405)
Education level of household head						
No education	7.81	4.29	2.22	0	0	2.47
Below grade 6	42.19	17.14	14.44	9.89	2.22	15.56
Below grade 9	23.44	14.29	21.11	18.68	0	15.06
O-levels completed	10.94	45.71	41.11	47.25	38.89	38.02
A-levels completed	12.5	12.86	13.33	19.78	50	22.72
University	3.13	5.71	7.78	4.4	8.89	6.17
Religion of head of household						
Buddhist	14.06	94.29	10	97.8	96.67	64.2
Hindu	78.13	5.71	66.67	0	0	28.15
Islam	1.56	0	14.44	0	1.11	3.7
Roman Catholic or Christian	6.25	0	8.89	2.2	2.22	3.95
Ethnicity of head of household						
Sinhala	14.06	94.29	11.11	100	98.89	65.43
Sri Lanka Tamil	84.38	5.71	67.78	0	0	29.38
Indian Tamil	0	0	1.11	0	0	0.25
Sri Lanka Moor	1.56	0	14.44	0	1.11	3.7
Burgher	0	0	5.56	0	0	1.23
5 quintiles of asset index						
1 (poorest)	51.56	37.14	20	1.1	2.22	19.75
2	23.44	24.29	23.33	10.99	1.11	15.8
3	9.38	15.71	18.89	41.76	7.78	19.51
4	7.81	14.29	20	29.67	27.78	20.99
5 (richest)	7.81	8.57	17.78	16.48	61.11	23.95
Annual household income (rupees)	**2,91,753**	**3,33,072**	**4,65,611**	**4,56,636**	**4,59,607**	**4,11,878**

Source: Primary data.
Note: ICT = information and communication technology.

Table D.3 Characteristics of All Individuals (Worker and Nonworker, %)

	Worker household			Nonworker household			All households		
	Man (n = 915)	Woman (n = 807)	All men and women in worker household (n = 1,722)	Man (n = 273)	Woman (n = 244)	Nonworker household (n = 517)	Man (n = 1,188)	Woman (n = 1,051)	Sample (n = 2,239)
Married									
No	51.91	43.87	48.14	56.04	49.59	53	52.86	45.2	49.26
Yes	48.09	56.13	51.86	43.96	50.41	47	47.14	54.8	50.74

table continues next page

Table D.3 Characteristics of All Individuals (Worker and Nonworker) *(continued)*

	Worker household			Nonworker household			All households		
	Man (n = 915)	Woman (n = 807)	All men and women in worker household (n = 1,722)	Man (n = 273)	Woman (n = 244)	Nonworker household (n = 517)	Man (n = 1,188)	Woman (n = 1,051)	Sample (n = 2,239)
Age categories									
Child (< 15)	17.05	14.5	15.85	16.85	18.03	17.41	17	15.32	16.21
Youth (15–29)	33.88	29.74	31.94	39.93	35.25	37.72	35.27	31.02	33.27
Adult (30–59)	40.66	48.95	44.54	40.29	42.62	41.39	40.57	47.48	43.81
Senior (60+)	8.42	6.82	7.67	2.93	4.1	3.48	7.15	6.18	6.7
Sex									
Male			53.14			52.8			53.06
Female			46.86			47.2			46.94
Education									
No education	1.2	3.1	2.09	1.83	2.46	2.13	1.35	2.95	2.1
Below grade 6	17.38	15.49	16.49	19.41	19.67	19.54	17.85	16.46	17.2
Below grade 9	13.22	12.64	12.95	11.72	13.11	12.38	12.88	12.75	12.82
O-levels completed	34.75	34.08	34.44	44.69	37.7	41.39	37.04	34.92	36.04
A-levels completed	24.37	27.01	25.61	16.85	21.72	19.15	22.64	25.78	24.12
University	5.14	4.71	4.94	0.73	0.41	0.58	4.12	3.71	3.93
No response	3.93	2.97	3.48	4.76	4.92	4.84	4.12	3.43	3.8
Computer skills									
None	58.69	59.73	59.18	59.71	57.79	58.8	58.92	59.28	59.09
Basic	14.64	13.14	13.94	12.45	15.57	13.93	14.14	13.7	13.93
Intermediate Word Excel	20.66	21.31	20.96	21.98	21.31	21.66	20.96	21.31	21.13
Advanced stat packages	0.98	1.36	1.16	0.37	0	0.19	0.84	1.05	0.94
Specialist	0.98	0.12	0.58	1.1	0	0.58	1.01	0.1	0.58
No response	4.04	4.34	4.18	4.4	5.33	4.84	4.12	4.57	4.33

Source: Primary data.

Table D.4 Characteristics of All Households (% of Households)

Head of household	Worker (n = 437)	Nonworker (n = 119)	All sample (n = 556)
Religion			
Buddhist	64.5	52.9	62.1
Hindu	28.1	35.3	29.7
Muslim	3.7	2.5	3.4
Roman Catholic or Christian	3.7	9.2	4.9

table continues next page

Table D.4 Characteristics of All Households (% of Households) *(continued)*

Head of household	Worker (n = 437)	Nonworker (n = 119)	All sample (n = 556)
Ethnicity			
Sinhala	65.7	52.9	62.9
Sri Lankan Tamil	15.8	18.5	16.4
Indian Tamil	13.7	24.4	16
Sri Lankan Moor	3.7	1.7	3.2
Burgher	1.1	2.5	1.4
Education level			
No education	2.7	4.2	3.1
Below grade 6	15.6	24.4	17.4
Below grade 9	16.2	16	16.2
O-levels completed	38.2	42.9	39.2
A-levels completed	21.3	10.9	19.1
University	5.9	1.7	5
Educational attainment			
Male-headed household			
No education	2.12	4.55	2.66
Below grade 6	15.87	23.64	17.62
Below grade 9	15.87	17.27	16.19
O-levels completed	37.04	42.73	38.32
A-levels completed	22.49	10	19.67
University	6.61	1.82	5.53
Female-headed household			
No education	6.78	0	5.88
Below grade 6	13.56	33.33	16.18
Below grade 9	18.64	0	16.18
O-levels completed	45.76	44.44	45.59
A-levels completed	13.56	22.22	14.71
University	1.69	0	1.47
5 quantiles of asset index			
1 (poorest)	19.5	22.7	20.1
2	18.1	26.9	20
3	18.8	24.4	20
4	21.5	14.3	20
5 (richest)	22.2	11.8	20
Household size	3.9	4.3	4
Annual household income (rupees)	4,02,633.80	2,74,694.10	3,75,251
Land with occupied housing	33.4	22.7	31.1
Asset index (mean value of the first factor)	0.1	-0.2	0

Source: Primary data.

Table D.5 Characteristics of Employers (% of Employers)

	Tea (n = 30)	Commercial agriculture (n = 32)	Tourism (n = 35)	Garments (n = 30)	ICT (n = 30)	Sample (n = 157)
Sex						
Male	90	81.3	88.6	76.7	73.3	82.2
Female	10	18.8	11.4	23.3	26.7	17.8
Education						
No education	0	3.1	0	6.7	0	1.9
Below grade 6	6.7	9.4	2.9	0	0	3.8
Below grade 9	6.7	15.6	14.3	20	0	11.5
O-levels completed	20	50	48.6	46.7	20	37.6
A-levels completed	56.7	18.8	11.4	10	56.7	29.9
Vocational training	3.3	0	2.9	3.3	3.3	2.5
University	6.7	3.1	20	13.3	20	12.7
Firm characteristics						
Among the owners of the firm, are there any females?	63.33	21.88	34.29	40	40	39.49
Is the top manager in this firm female?	3.33	15.63	25.71	30	10	17.2
English language						
Native speaker/read/ write	2.55	6.67	0	5.71	0	0
Speak/read/ write	50.32	63.33	25	60	23.33	80
Speak only	10.83	0	9.38	34.29	0	6.67
Read/write only	20.38	16.67	12.5	0	63.33	13.33
No language proficiency	15.92	13.33	53.13	0	13.33	0
Does your institution or enterprise maintain a system of formal written accounts?	48.41	70	15.63	68.57	26.67	60
To which sector does the firm belong?						
Semi-government	1.27	0	0	0	0	6.67
Private	98.73	100	100	100	100	93.33
Contract status of the majority of your workers?						
Permanent	61.15	63.33	25	77.14	83.33	56.67
Temporary	21.66	26.67	50	5.71	16.67	10
Casual	5.1	0	6.25	17.14	0	0
Other	12.1	10	18.75	0	0	33.33

Source: Primary data.
Note: ICT = information and communication technology.

APPENDIX E

Key Informant Interviews

This appendix provides details of key informant interviews conducted with select education practitioners, labor market experts, and industry leaders to gather recommendations for improving labor force participation and labor market outcomes for women in Sri Lanka's workforce.

Name	Designation	Institution	Interview location
Hasini Abeywickrama	PhD candidate, University of Melbourne	University of Technology, Sydney	Sydney, Australia
Kshanika Anthony	Director, Talent Management and Development	Medtronic Australasia Pty Ltd	Sydney, Australia
Kumari Amaradasa	Teacher	Visakha Vidyalaya Girls School	Colombo
Harsha Arturupane	Lead Economist and Program Leader for Human Development for Sri Lanka and the Maldives, South Asia	World Bank	Colombo
Samitha Athukorale	Teacher	Visakha Vidyalaya Girls School	Colombo
Sandamali Aviruppola	Principal	Visakha Vidyalaya Girls School	Colombo
Aldjia Begriche	Vice-President	Smart Textile OMsignal	Montreal, Canada
Susan Bosher	Professor	St. Catherine University	St. Paul, Minnesota
Bani Chandrasena	Head of Human Resources	London Stock Exchange Group	Colombo
Anurika de Silva	Teacher	Visakha Vidyalaya Girls School	Colombo
Preeni Dias	Teacher	Visakha Vidyalaya Girls School	Colombo
Vindhya V. Fernando	Head of Advisory Services	Chrysalis	Colombo
Seshika V. Fernando	Associate Director, Head of Financial Relations	WS02 (Web Service Oxygen)	Colombo
Vathsala Ganeshan	Pediatrician	Health Partners	St. Paul, Minnesota
Ashika Gunasena	CEO	Chrysalis	Colombo

table continues next page

Name	Designation	Institution	Interview location
Sylvia Heisel	Fashion Designer and Creative Technologist	Sylvia Heisel	St. Paul, Minnesota
Shamara Herat	Consultant	Sifani Jewellers and former Board Member, Regional Development Bank of Sri Lanka	Colombo
Nirmali Hettiarachchi	English Educator, Workforce Training Provider, Teacher Trainer	Independent Consultant Focusing on Inclusivity and Diversity in the Workplace	Colombo
Dilinika Peiris-Holsinger	Communications Associate	World Bank	Colombo
Laura Dudley Jenkins	Associate Professor of Political Science	University of Cincinnati	Cincinnati, Ohio
Kamani Madhya Jinadasa	Founding Executive Director i	Shanthi Maargam	Colombo
Janakie Karunaratne	Manager of Community Affairs	Microsoft, Sri Lanka Division	Colombo
Shiranee Mills	Executive Director	Women's Education and Research Centre	Colombo
Carmen Niethammer	Program Manager, Women in Work	International Finance Corporation	Colombo
Anupama Pasricha	Associate Professor and Department Chair, Apparel, Merchandising and Design	St. Catherine University	St. Paul, Minnesota
Hashika Perumbuli	Teacher	Microsoft Innovation School	Pitipana-Homagana
Yukari Shibuya	Social Development Specialist	World Bank	Washington, DC
Jennifer Solotaroff	Senior Social Development Specialist	World Bank	Washington, DC
Shalika Subasinghe	Education Global Practice	World Bank	Colombo
Isura Silva	General Manager	Sarvodaya-Fusion	Colombo
Chinthi Weerasinghe	President of the Diversity Collective	Sri Lanka London Stock Exchange Group	Colombo
Hiranthi Wijemanne	Public Health Physician, Expert Consultant	UN Committee on the Rights of the Child, UNICEF	Colombo

www.ingramcontent.com/pod-product-compliance
Lightning Source LLC
Chambersburg PA
CBHW080423270326
41929CB00018B/3134